HOPE FOR THE
HOPELESS
The Charles Mulli Mission

PAUL H. BOGE

CASTLE QUAY BOOKS

Hope for the Hopeless: The Charles Mulli Mission
Copyright ©2012 Paul H. Boge
All rights reserved
Printed in Canada
International Standard Book Number: **978-1-927355-03-9**

Electronic monograph in PDF format.
Issued also in print format.
ISBN 978-1-927355-04-6

Published by:
Castle Quay Books
1307 Wharf Street, Pickering, Ontario, L1W 1A5
Tel: (416) 573-3249
Email: info@castlequaybooks.com
www.castlequaybooks.com

Copy edited by Marina H. Hofman Willard
Cover design by **Burst Impressions**
Printed at Essence Publishing, Belleville, Ontario

Scripture taken from THE HOLY BIBLE, NEW INTERNATIONAL VERSION,
NIV Copyright © 1973, 1978, 1984, 2010 by Biblica, Inc.™ Used by permission.
All rights reserved worldwide.
Scripture taken from the *New American Standard Bible*, copyright © The Lockman
Foundation 1960, 1962, 1963, 1968, 1971, 1972, 1973. All rights reserved.
Scripture taken from the New King James Version. Copyright © 1979, 1980, 1982.
Thomas Nelson Inc., Publishers.

Library and Archives Canada Cataloguing in Publication
Boge, Paul H., 1973-
Hope for the hopeless : the Charles Mulli mission / Paul H. Boge, Marina H.
Hofman Willard.
Issued also in electronic format.
ISBN 978-1-927355-03-9

    1. Mulli, Charles. 2. Mully Children's Family. 3. Orphans—Services
for—Kenya. 4. Street children—Services for—Kenya. 5. Abandoned
children—Services for—Kenya. 6. Children of AIDS patients—Services for—
Kenya. 7. Christian biography—Kenya. 8. Kenya—Biography. I. Hofman
Willard, Marina H. II. Title.

HV28.M84B64 2012   362.73'2096762   C2012-
903717-6

ENDORSEMENTS

I am always amazed how a writer can communicate the essence of his story. In his latest book, Paul Boge has captured why and how MCF has been successful in its mission of rescuing children and providing a meaningful future for them. Charles Mulli, the founder, has a heart for abandoned children because he himself was left alone by his family to fend for himself on the streets of Eldoret. Paul makes it clear that Mulli is 100 percent dependent on God to fulfill his dream to care for the homeless. Mulli says, "It came down to doing three simple things consistently: praying, reading the Bible and serving."

Your heart will be moved as you read the incredible true stories of those rescued, and you will be amazed at how Mulli steps over the edge, knowing that only God can provide. Your faith will be strengthened and surely you will realize that God hears the cry of the helpless but it needs people like Mulli, who are fully convicted and convinced that they can make a difference in peoples' lives.

I recommend this book, and I know you will see poverty from a completely different perspective and you will be thankful for men like Mulli and his family and the people that support this wonderful ministry.

HERB BULLER
Chairman, Norcraft Group of Companies, Canada

This is a treasure of truth and a testimony that is invaluable to all who desire to touch the young and helpless living on the streets. Dr. Mulli's dedication and passion for Christ, as well as his vision to bring hope to the suffering, is a beacon in a world that is increasingly centred on itself. The book reveals a very humble and selfless man, whose God is big and able to touch even the untouchables. May God cause each one who reads this book to hear the painful cry of the suffering in our communities.

PROFESSOR DANKIT NASSIUMA
Vice Chancellor, Kabarak University, Kenya

Hope for the Hopeless is a compelling and inspirational story. It will touch the hearts of those who read it and open the eyes of those who doubt that survivors of horrendous crimes can be renewed and grow to love life again. It's a story of the courageous Charles Mulli and the impact of his faith on countless orphans in Kenya. Paul Boge's immense talent is reflected in its pages.

JOY SMITH, B.ED, M.ED.
Member of Parliament, Kildonan-St. Paul, Canada
Chair, National Standing Committee on Health

Mulli is the George Muller of Africa, called by God to give up his wealth, prosperity and success and invest into the lives of orphans. It is a journey of faith, hope and surrender, as Mulli trusts in God for direction, strength and providence. And God does not disappoint. He miraculously supplies for this work and countless times stretches His hand of healing upon Mulli and his big family. God shows up right on time, not one minute early or one minute late. He keeps right on schedule. What faithfulness!

Pure religion, the Bible says, is visiting the widows and feeding the orphans. Mulli has exemplified pure religion by ministering hope to the hopeless and being a father to the fatherless. I have no doubt that this book will not only inspire you but also challenge you to share the love of Christ even to the least of this world. Mulli not only facilitates the provision of food, clothing, shelter and education for the children, but also ministers to their spiritual lives through the life-changing power of the Gospel message and in some cases, even to the children's families, like the case of Anika. For sure, there is more to life than a bag of riches, a big mansion and a fleet of cars. Only one thing counts, making a difference, and Mulli has made his. Will you?

BISHOP DR. HENRY Z. MULANDI
Founder and International Director
African Christian Missions International
Founder, Christian Church International, Kenya

A remarkable story of determination, passion and faith, *Hope for the Hopeless* is an enduring tribute to the continuing journey of Charles Mulli and his life's work of rescuing African children from the darkest depths of poverty and neglect. Mulli uses his enduring faith to provide the dignity of food, education and love to thousands of abandoned children and provide them with a future filled with hope. He is an inspiration to those who might be searching for a way to make the world a better place but question whether one person can make a difference.

KEVIN DANIEL FLYNN, M.B.A.
Member of Ontario Legislative Assembly, Canada

The love of Christ compels us to do what we never thought we could do, and go to the heights we never thought we could reach. Precious is the name of Jesus. This is a powerful testimony. May God grant you grace and favour.

KEN KIMIYWE
Senior Pastor, Nairobi Pentecostal Church Valley Road, Kenya

A remarkable leader within a remarkable ministry with a remarkable story. *Hope for the Hopeless* produces humility of the heart and yet great encouragement for the soul. It powerfully shines the hope of Christ within an otherwise dark and painful world. I have been personally challenged and admonished by the life of Charles Mulli and MCF and that has only been strengthened by the reading of this book. If you desire a wake-up call to the reality of life, sacrifice and love, then this book is for you. Truly inspiring, heartbreaking and yet hope filling.

ROBBIE SYMONS
Senior Pastor, Harvest Bible Chapel, Oakville, Canada

My life is committed to educating students and encouraging them to think beyond themselves. *Hope for the Hopeless* is proof that one person can make a difference in the world, and Mr. Mulli is a real example of someone not just fighting against injustice, but caring for the very children he is fighting for. My hope is that we can all be that courageous and make a difference in the world around us.

LEWIS LU
Chief Librarian, Changhua Senior High School
Founder, International Student Leadership Conference Taiwan

I found *Hope for the Hopeless* to be an eye-opening revelation of the dreadful effects that poverty, alcohol abuse, HIV/AIDS and drugs have on so many children in Africa. This poverty and suffering is so widespread, to a degree not seen in Europe. This book reveals the profound spiritual and practical transformation that the love of God has brought to so many thousands of children through the devotion of Charles Mulli and his family. *Hope for the Hopeless* is a compelling read!

DAVID HOWES
Former East Africa Representative, Hilfe für Brüder (Help for Brethren)

Hope for the Hopeless is a sobering reminder of the street children's daily plight in Kenya and unfortunately so many other parts of the world. What makes this story so intriguing is how Charles Mulli has turned his remarkable leadership skills into the services of God, with the purpose of addressing poverty, violence negligence, abuse and injustice among the most vulnerable segment of the children's population, namely the thousands of children that have been left to their own devices on the streets and slums of Kenya. The Charles Mulli story is first and foremost a story of hope, devotion and faith in God with the firm conviction that no child should be left to poverty, cruelty and self-destruction, but instead be put on a path to self-realization and development of their full potential in an environment free of prejudice, violence and discrimination. May Mulli's publication *Hope for the Hopeless* inspire, but also provide impulses and ideas to others as to how we can lift all children of the world out of destitution and misery.

KIRSTEN ENGEBAK
Head of Division for Eastern Africa, Norwegian Church Aid

Hope for the Hopeless is that rare sequel that is even more powerful and inspirational than its predecessor, *Father to the Fatherless*. I have known Charles Mulli personally since 2009 and my wife and I have been to MCF numerous times. The book is a true representation of what one finds there, except that the actual horror of life on the streets is worse than words can tell. The astounding restoration in the lives of children at MCF must be seen to be fully appreciated, and the depth of Charles and Esther's relationship with God cannot be fully comprehended by just reading about it. Charles Mulli is comparable, in my mind, to the biblical patriarch Abraham (whose name means father of a multitude), in that they are both clearly seen to be "a friend of God," and for the same reason—their full and complete level of trust in him (James 2:13). *Hope for the Hopeless* will stir up your own faith in God, in authentic men and women of God, and in the miracles that can happen when God and his people work together for good.

B. WAYNE CLARK
Vice President, Corporate Outreach, MedAssets, Inc., Georgia, USA

ACKNOWLEDGEMENTS

My heartfelt thank you to each of you for making this book possible.

God—for the incredible opportunity you gave me to write this story, for your love that reaches to the slums of Africa and all around the world, and that your love can truly change us completely.

Charles Mulli—for entrusting me with the task of writing this sequel, for your love and friendship, and for allowing me to see first-hand how God is using you to bless people around the world.

Charles Mulli's family, Mrs. Esther Mulli, Jane, Miriam, Grace, Ndondo, Kaleli, Mueni, Isaac and Dickson—for the joy of knowing you, for your friendship, for your invaluable help in all the research and in going over the drafts.

To all the MCF children—for showing me what it means to trust Christ, for your willingness to share your stories, and for your incredible love for the Lord.

The MCF translators and research team—for your thoughtfulness, time, and compassion in helping me to understand the issues. You have helped tremendously.

MCF supporters around the world—you have given tirelessly to this ministry. Your ongoing support makes this rescue ministry possible.

Larry Willard, my publisher, for taking on this second project and for your support and passion in getting this story told. And to the entire publishing team for your invaluable help.

Endorsers—for reading the draft and for your encouraging comments.

My family: Hans, Lorna, Hans, Tanya, Maya, Arianna, Hans Lukas, Elora, Adalia, Randy, Heidi, Olivia, Mark, Omi Boge and Oma Baerg—for your constant support and for sharing the vision of MCF.

For my friends, both old and new—who have so faithfully prayed and encouraged me in this book and with MCF.

To you, the reader—for caring about MCF and supporting the ministry through this book.

FOREWORD

It is a great honour to write the foreword of *Hope for the Hopeless*. How do I describe my friend, brother and hero in a few pages?

A man full of life, unwavering faith, and amazing vision, courage and determination. A man who has a close relationship with and trust in God, who demonstrates the fear of the Lord and puts God in first place. A compassionate and humble man, yet powerful in God. A man of excellent character, known for his honesty, truth and integrity. A man who has the ability to look past the impossible and come up with a successful plan of action. A man who sees the gold in everyone and has a unique way of drawing it out, a moulder of dreams.

I first met Charles and Esther 13 years ago at a business meeting in Australia. They were given five minutes to speak, during. During that time, they told a story of street children's lives changed forever, children that now have a hope and a future. Something drew me to them; they were different. I felt that I should visit MCF Kenya. Surely it couldn't be as life-changing as they had said? There must be some kind of catch! During the trip to MCF, I found that it was far better than they had said, and the experience changed my life forever. I wrote in the visitor's book in Eldoret:

"Now I have seen the Kingdom of God on earth as it is in heaven."

This book gives insight into the lives of the Kenyan people and the hope that God can bring through people who love him. Through those who are obedient to his call to lay down their lives for a bigger cause, bringing transformation to thousands of lives forever.

As with *Father to the Fatherless*, it is a book that draws you into the touching stories of precious lives, a journey of wanting to know how the chapter will end and what challenges the next chapter will bring.

Charles brings out the battles of the mind, the different voices we hear and the devastating effect they can have. He demonstrates how the battles can be won as a result of a close, intimate relationship with God. By depositing God's Word and his promises into our hearts, we can override the accusing, condemning and enticing words of the enemy and have victory over circumstances.

He tells of the horrors experienced by innocent children that cause them to grow up before their time. The horrors experienced by children and their families when law and order break down and man resorts to committing unimaginable acts of violence. All children in this world should have the right to be loved and nurtured in a family where food, shelter, safety and protection are the norm.

Money alone is not enough to transform lives. Charles is complemented by an amazing team. His wife, Esther, is a rock of support in all areas of the ministry, and his eight biological children, Miriam, Janey, Grace, Ndondo, Kaleli, Mueni, Isaac and Dickson, are key leaders. Added to this are the pastors, principals, teachers, farm managers, administration, accounting and many other staff members. Their compassion, dedication, selflessness, long hours, and love given to the children are appreciated and life-changing. In addition, there are the countless number of supporters from around the world who pray and give financially. All together they make an awesome team!

Mully Children's Family is a testimony to the transforming power of the gospel, where children's lives are changed forever, where children are made whole, healed and transformed into valuable members of society. Many, now with their own families, are filled with hope for the future and are achieving incredible exploits.

How does an abandoned six-year-old boy become a successful entrepreneur, then give it all up with no thought of self to take in and transform thousands of street children, rehabilitate over 7,000 children, have the wisdom and understanding to establish cutting edge, self-sustainable programs, assist local and international communities with food, clean water, environmental expertise and health care?

By submitting himself to a supernatural God, who loves his people and who is seeking faithful men and women who will bring salvation to the lost and hurting.

Charles, you are truly an amazing man. We know that you have many more dreams and visions inside you, and that you believe with God all things are possible. We look forward to hearing and reading about them in the years to come.

As you read the pages of this book be encouraged, inspired and challenged as to how a life surrendered to God can bring love to the unlovable, acceptance to the rejected, wholeness to the broken and hope to the hopeless.

David Rowlands
President & CEO
Rainbow Shade Products Australia

INTRODUCTION

In a world that has increasingly become hostile and violent to the young and vulnerable, few people are willing to step out selflessly and share their resources for the sake of giving others a future. This book brings to light the horrifying plight of many children living on the streets. The future of many young people is in danger from inhuman adults, but God still has a remnant among his people who have the courage to take his hand and make a difference. This is a book that everyone who cares about the intense suffering of others must read. It is a challenge and a profound lesson to each one of us to do something about the destitute in society.

H.E. Hon. Daniel Arap Moi
Second President of the Republic of Kenya

PAUL'S PREFACE

It was daytime. The sun was shining. The children came one by one and sat down across from me on a plain chair, at a plain table, under a plain covering at the Mully Children's Family homes in Ndalani and Yatta. It would normally have been a time to play a game with them, or for them to teach me words in Swahili. Instead, they spoke in a quiet voice, sometimes crying, as they felt the anguish of recalling events that had shaped them so deeply. They shared with me in detail about what it took to survive on the street, about the trials they had to endure in the slums of Kenya, and about the hope they found in the man they refer to as Daddy Mulli.

I am in awe of what God has done in the lives of the children at MCF. It's one thing to see a picture of an MCF child. It's something entirely different to get a glimpse into who they are and what they have gone through to forgive and become the people they are today. And so when Charles Mulli asked me to write this sequel, we desired that his stories and those of his children would give you a better understanding of how people are changed through MCF.

I had the privilege of speaking numerous times in person with Charles Mulli. His attention to detail, his compassion for all people and his uncanny ability to come to the right solution in every problem is truly something to behold. In the end, Mulli leads a simple and profound life because he loves God and he knows in his mind and in his heart that God loves him.

Another reason I hold Charles Mulli in such high respect is because he came to the end of himself. MCF is not about him. Even his own life is not about him. His life is about following Christ regardless of what that means for him. There is something truly inspiring about people who leave it all behind, including their sense of security, to follow Jesus. In Charles Mulli's own words: "We have no mandate to control our lives." There are two kinds of people in this world: those who say yes to Jesus Christ, and those who say no. And for people like Charles Mulli who say yes, they experience what they have been designed for.

I wrote this book to encourage even one person who is faced with the difficult task of forgiving someone who has hurt them. Maybe that's you. Whether you are a young girl or boy from a slum who has suffered abuse, or perhaps you are living in a relatively affluent part of the world and are struggling with the challenge of releasing someone, I hope their stories will inspire you to know that there is freedom in forgiveness.

If there is one person who reads this book who is able to see through the endless haze of thunderstorm clouds to a glimmer of light in the distance and has their life transformed by Christ, then I consider all of our efforts in this book to be worthwhile.

I hope this book will encourage us to realize that it's okay to forgive, that it's okay to let go, and that it's okay to carry out the calling God has placed on our lives. You never know the impact that following Christ can have, especially on children.

In a few instances I have compressed stories for the sake of space. I have kept the facts as they were presented to me.

And so I listened, at that plain table, under the plain covering, taking notes of the children's lives, hearing first-hand of their accounts. They have gone through things I couldn't even imagine. Their stories are not easy. I've made no attempt to soften what I have heard from them. They sat and patiently relayed the accounts of their lives from the beginning to where they are today.

This is what they told me.

Paul H. Boge
Holland and Canada, 2012

BRIEF WORD BY DR. CHARLES MULLI

In the world today, there never seems to be a fair deal, as everyone is for himself, but God remains for us all. I am one among many who have undergone immense suffering and could not attend school in childhood. It remained a dream. I never lost hope and aimed to touch the lives of others from poverty-stricken families. My ministry has seen over 7,000 young people successfully graduate with 2,800 currently under rehabilitation and care, and another 2,500 community children receiving support through provision of food, medical care and education. I give gratitude to God for his favour, grace and guidance in this otherwise challenging work.

Over the years, I have been enlightened and convinced that a whole person needs physical and spiritual nourishment—and this cannot be completed unless there is transformation of our environment, which needs to be considered a key factor in human development. It is therefore necessary to understand fully that while we care for our people and the present generation, which is getting depleted through the vices of this world, human beings will always need a good and conducive environment to work in.

My biography, *Father to the Fatherless,* was written and printed a few years ago, after which it was then translated into German and Mandarin. This book, which is a source of inspiration to many people across the globe, has won several awards in the "General Readership Book Category" in Canada. Many have been waiting to read this sequel.

It is my hope and prayer that as you read this book it will talk to you and make your heart yield for the poorest of the poor, who need our guidance, mentoring, prayers and help. This book highlights some of the things that I have been facing over the last 23 years in service to the most disadvantaged and vulnerable children as well as to communities in Africa. I hope that this book will shed more light on the lives of millions of children who are suffering all around us.

It is indeed a privilege to have you as a friend and someone who will walk with me for many miles to accomplish my dream and the vision that God gave me for the transformation of the present generation through giving the most marginalized children access to care and social justice as they get an opportunity to live a dignified life.

I wish to take this opportunity to thank my friend Paul Boge for taking his time, energy, resources, love and commitment in seeing this project come to completion. Paul, who has visited me in Kenya and has shared with me on several occasions during my visits to Canada, is a unique individual who has the Spirit of the Lord working in him. His great writing skills and talent are displayed once again through this book. Thank you, Paul, for sharing the story of my life and making it real in the eyes of all readers.

Dr. Charles Mulli
Kenya, 2012

CHAPTER 1

It was supposed to be a day like any other.

Six-year-old Mara opened her eyes. The Kenyan sun shone through the window, illuminating her entire room and making it as bright as her eyes.

She breathed in and then listened. Quiet. She heard the sound of footsteps approaching. Closer and closer they came down the hallway. She pulled the blanket over her. A knock at her bedroom door.

"No one is here," Mara said.

The door opened. Mara peeked out from behind the blanket and saw her father about to enter. She hid under her blanket and tried as best as she could to contain herself.

"If no one is here, then why am I hearing laughter?" Kiriro said.

At 30, Kiriro looked more like he was 20. Blessed with an incredible smile and piercing eyes that he had passed directly down to his daughter, Kiriro sat down on the side of the mattress that lay on the concrete floor in their simple rented metal-wall home. He pretended to lean against her.

"Are you sure there is no one here?" he asked. Mara giggled. He turned and started tickling her. Mara let out a loud laugh that was a perfect indication of a child who has the luxury of having no cares in the world simply because the father they admire is present.

"Daddy!"

She pushed away the covers and hugged him. Then, noticing her father's uniform, she pulled away.

"You're not working today, are you? Daddy, don't. Please. Just stay home and play here with me."

"Your breakfast is on the table."

"No, wait. I can make you a deal."

"The deal is, I work so that we can eat."

Kiriro stood up. Mara jumped out after him and clutched her hands and feet around his leg. He pulled her along as he walked to the front door of their home. "My leg has suddenly become much heavier from something. I don't know what it could be." The metal roof had let rain in last night, leaving a small puddle on the floor. Kiriro steered her around it. He grabbed a towel off the shelf and dropped it on the ground. He cleaned up the water and made a mental note to fix the roof.

Kiriro sat down so he could be at her level. She looked into her father's face and smiled. There was something so kind, so reassuring, so affirming in his eyes. It felt as if she were staring at a picture of herself.

"I love you and I will see you soon," he whispered as he kissed her.

Mara watched as he headed out the door. She followed after him to the end of their small yard to see him walk down the pathway. He stopped, which was uncharacteristic of him. Normally he would have continued on and disappeared into the distance down the street as he blended in with the others. But today was different. He turned back to look at Mara. He didn't say anything. Gave no big wave. Just father and daughter looking at one another, feeling that genuine connection people have when they can communicate everything just by seeing into each other's eyes. He smiled and turned to leave. Mara watched him walk down the street, trying to stay focused on him until it was impossible to distinguish him from the streams of people heading off to work.

I love you and I will see you soon.

Mara was about to go back inside when she heard a voice behind her.

"Mara?"

She was sure she recognized the voice, but somehow she couldn't quite place who it was. Her mind raced through all the connections she could recall from her brief time on this earth. And as she turned around her heart gave the answer before her eyes saw it.

Her mouth dropped open. Is it her? Is it really her?

Mara saw her coming from the opposite direction her father had gone.

"Mother?"

Jedidah was slender and short, attractive by any definition. She was flawless, if you counted out the part of her taking off on her husband, daughter and two other children.

Mara smiled and ran up to her. Jedidah crouched down and held out her arms. She hugged Mara and lifted her up against the bright sun.

"I haven't seen you in such a long time. I was wondering what you looked like," Jedidah said. "And look how pretty you are. How would you like to go shopping?"

"Yes, I would love to!"Mara said. "Did you see Daddy? He just left."

"He did?" Jedidah looked in the direction that Kiriro had gone. "I thought he started work earlier in the morning."

"He used to. But now he starts later and works until suppertime."

"Well, we won't be long. Are you ready?"

"I haven't eaten breakfast yet. Would you like to come inside?"

"Why don't I buy you a special treat for breakfast? How does that sound?"

Mara squeezed Jedidah's hand in anticipation. Her mother led her down the street away from where her father had gone. As they walked together Mara asked about her brother and sister, who were living with a relative because of financial constraints. Mara shared about her friends, about the games they played together, about her father. She was so engrossed in telling everything that had happened in her life in the year since she last saw her mother that she barely noticed that they had just passed the shopping centre.

"There it is," Mara exclaimed, wondering what her mother was going to buy her.

"Oh, we're going to go this way," Jedidah said, smiling. "We're going to another mall."

Jedidah turned and led them down a different street. That was fine with Mara. *Mom is taking me to a new shopping centre where I have never been before. I wonder what she will buy me. I wonder what I'm going to get.*

They walked farther and farther, and the area became stranger and stranger. Mara had never been this far before. They crossed the street into a market area and walked through a crowd of people where store owners sold everything imaginable. Shoes. Bananas. Mangoes. Clothing. Sports jerseys. They passed row after row of huts selling still more merchandise and came to an area filled with people and dozens of *matatus*—taxis, made up mostly of passenger vans that were often filled to double capacity.

As they walked through the maze of people, Jedidah shooed away the constant pressure from merchandisers desperate to sell anything that would help make ends meet. They reached a matatu and Jedidah paid the fare.

"I have an idea," Jedidah said, taking Mara to a seat at the back. They sat down. Mara's eyes were wide with amazement. There was so much activity. So much she was seeing for the first time. "What if we did something different today?"

"Like what?" Mara asked.

"How would you like to see Grandmother?"

"Really? That would be great! I haven't seen her in such a long time," Mara replied. But then a puzzled expression came over her face. "But what about Father? We won't be back in time before it gets dark."

"There will be plenty of time. Everything will be just fine."

The matatu took off, and they headed down a highway. Mara continued to ask questions. How is Grandma doing? What does it look like there? What games can we play? But Jedidah became increasingly quiet, giving only short, cursory answers, preferring instead to look outside at the passing cars.

They travelled for hours, and for Mara it felt like days. Finally, the matatu stopped. Jedidah and Mara pushed through the crowd and stepped off.

"Can Grandmother get me something to eat?"

"Grandmother is close by," Jedidah said. "We will see her very soon."

They walked off the street into a dusty, dry area. A few minutes later they had left all signs of civilization behind. They walked alone down a narrow path with only the setting sun behind to guide them.

They reached what looked to be like a dwelling. It was difficult to tell, and Mara felt awkward for wondering if that was where her mother lived or if it was the remains of a previous hut that had been abandoned because of its condition. The front door had half fallen off. The faded grey metal walls and roof sagged to the side, giving the impression the entire mess was about to fall over.

Jedidah opened what was left of the door. Inside was even worse.

Cracked concrete floor. A worn mattress off to the side. A beat-up wooden table. Dust everywhere. A group of bugs crawled away to the corner, afraid of the light. And the stench was the nastiest that Mara had ever taken in. What was that? Mara breathed in short bursts through her mouth.

"Is this where Grandmother is?" Mara asked, pointing to a bedroom door at the back.

Jedidah opened a cupboard and pulled out a metal tin.

"You wait here, and I will come right back."

Jedidah chugged half the contents of the tin. The sickening smell that Mara had been fighting off suddenly grew worse. The pungent odour of *chang'aa*, an illicit alcoholic brew, filled her nostrils.

Her mother shook her head to get it down, feeling the incredible sting of alcohol rush through her body. She left with the tin firmly in hand, walking down the path and out of sight.

The African sun set so quickly that it went from daylight to darkness in a matter of minutes. Mara sat on the floor waiting, wondering what would happen next. *Where is Grandmother? Why isn't she here? Why is Mother gone so long? Is Father home? I want to see him again. It's been so long. He's worried. How do I get home? We're so far away. I don't know the way back. What do I—*

It was the sound of someone shouting in the distance that startled Mara. She bit down on her lip. Her fingers suddenly felt cold. She swallowed. Waited. She heard it again. Mara breathed faster. The shouting grew closer. She pushed her way to the back of the hut. She pulled her knees up under her chin and wrapped her arms around her legs. Her eyes focused on the door. Her entire body felt like ice.

Close your eyes. It will all go away. You'll wake up. You'll be at home again. Everything will be fine. Just close your eyes.

She shut her eyes.

But the dread remained.

There were two voices. A man and a woman. Was that her mother? It didn't sound like her. Was she sick?

"Mara?" a voice called from outside.

It was her mother. At least it sounded like her. Or did it? Mara stayed frozen in the corner, under the protection of darkness.

The door opened. Jedidah looked in. Her eyes darted around the hut, trying to find Mara. She reached for the door frame but missed it altogether and crashed against the wall. She stumbled back but managed to recover her balance. She let out a hysterical laugh.

Jedidah dropped the tin. It was empty now. She saw Mara on the floor. If Jedidah noticed she was cold and afraid she gave no indication that she cared.

"Are you all right?" Mara asked.

"I want you to go to the room."

"Are you sick, Mother?"

"I am making a fire. A big burning fire for some hot water. But you. You, I would like you now to go into the room."

Mara looked beside her at the door that led to the only other room in the dwelling.

She stood up and went to the door. She glanced back at her mother, then put her hand on the handle. She pulled it down and opened the door. She peeked inside. A beaten mattress on the ground to the right. A cracked table to the left that needed the wall to help keep it up. A hole at the top of the wall with a flimsy screen over it acted as a window. She stepped in and looked up through the window. She was noticing the stars in the distance when she heard the sound of breathing behind her.

It startled her. How had she not heard her mother approaching? As she turned she heard the door close shut behind her.

And that's when she saw him.

He towered over her. His shifty eyes had a disgusting yellow tinge to them. That familiar stench of alcohol filled the room. Mara stepped back. Her heart beat so fast that she felt it pulsing in her ears. She felt like throwing up. She tried to scream for her mother. But her fear was so intense that it paralyzed her, forcing her to stand there like a statue.

Just close your eyes and it will all go away.

The man began to unbutton his shirt.

Scream. Scream for your mother.

I'm trying but I can't.

Scream for her. She will help you.

I'm trying. I just can't get the words out.

Scream! Scream!

The man took off his shirt and dropped it on the ground.

"You…" A smile came to his face, revealing his rotting teeth. "You are a very pretty young girl."

Mara opened her mouth to shout but nothing came out. She tried to exhale; it was all she could manage to let out a faint whimper. She took another step back and hit the wall.

"A pretty, pretty young girl."

Do it. Do it now. Scream! Scream!

The throbbing in her ears was so intense that she could hear nothing else. Not the man going on about her beauty, not her mother's drunken singing in the distance, not even the sound of her back scraping against the wall as she slid down to the ground. But then, finally, it happened.

Mara screamed.

It was a high-pitched shrill that scared the man so terribly it woke him out of his drunken daze. As if suddenly reminded of a long forgotten code of morality, he reached down to pick up his shirt and fastened the buttons as quickly as he could.

The door burst open. Jedidah's eyes were full of fury.

"What's going on?"

"The child," the man stuttered. "She…she does not want to."

"Of course she does! She's just new."

"No. She is terrified. I will not do this if she is scared of me."

Jedidah's expression suddenly changed. It was creepy how those eyes of hers went from rage to an apparent kindness in an instant.

"You have the money, don't you?"

"Of course."

"Just wait here with her. Give it some time. Let her get used to you. And then she will be yours."

But he continued getting his shirt back on. He tucked it in as best he could and hurried out of the hut.

"Wait! Wait!" Jedidah called out after him. But it was no use. He was out the door and gone.

Jedidah turned to Mara. Her eyes of rage were back again. And this time they were worse than before.

"What have you done?" she said in a slow, cold tone to emphasize each word.

"I was scared," Mara pleaded. "What was the man going to do to me?"

"What have you done, you worthless, rotten child?!"

In a moment of fury, Jedidah grabbed Mara by the arms and lifted her up. She shook her back and forth as hard as she could, smashing her against the wall. "How are we going to pay for our food now?! How will we get money?! We have nothing! Nothing! And this is all your fault!"

She threw Mara across the room. Her head smashed against the door frame, causing her to black out momentarily. Unfortunately, it was not enough to knock her out.

Which made her completely awake for what was to follow.

Mara struggled to her feet and stumbled out of the bedroom and into the main area. Jedidah followed after her.

"I want to go home," Mara said in a combination of sadness and fear. "I want to be with my father."

With an incredible show of strength from her frail body, Jedidah grabbed Mara by the throat, lifted her up and smashed her against the wall, pinning her there like an animal. Mara gasped for breath and kicked her legs as she struggled to try to break herself free from her mother's grip.

Jedidah clenched her teeth.

"You will never go back to your father, do you hear me? You are never going back!"

Jedidah slapped her in the face, sending her crashing to the ground. Mara crawled to the corner as if doing so could somehow protect her from the monster her mother had become.

Just close your eyes and it will—

But it didn't go away.

It just grew worse.

Tears flowed from Mara's face as she touched her jaw, which felt like it was broken.

In a slow, evil, calculating tone, Jedidah said, pointing a finger at Mara, "You are going to learn to do what I tell you to do."

She pulled Mara by the leg and dragged her to the centre of the room. Jedidah reached into a cupboard and pulled out a collection of tattered ropes that she used when she still kept animals.

"No! No, Mother. Please. Please don't."

"Shut up, you worthless whore!"

Jedidah leaned down on her, pushing her against the ground. Mara screamed and tried to twist herself free as Jedidah tied each of her hands and feet with a separate piece of rope. Then she tied each of the four ropes and secured them to a table or a bedpost. Mara lay there, spread-eagled, living in a state past fear and trembling.

Mara watched as Jedidah left the room. She pulled against the ropes, which proved impossible to move. The door opened, and Jedidah came back with the teakettle in her hand. Steam from the boiling water rose out of the spout, creating a mist around her. Some of it spilled out onto the ground as she came closer. Jedidah stood above her, glaring down at her.

"I hate you. I hate you. I hate you."

Jedidah tilted the kettle. The first drops of scalding water burned onto Mara. She screamed in terror and yanked with all her might on the ropes. Jedidah poured out more as the unbearable pain of the hot water ripped over Mara's entire body and up to her face. She pulled in vain against the impossible cords that kept her bound. The water that fell off her body went onto the concrete and burned against her back. It was eternity waiting for the kettle to finally empty.

And when it did, the agony of the scarring started forcing Mara to shake uncontrollably to deal with the pain.

Her mother looked down at her and laughed. She stumbled backwards against the wall.

Mara had screamed so hard and so long that her voice was completely gone. She lay in unbearable anguish, unsure whether what was happening was reality or part of a dream. *Am I really here? Is that really Mother?* She looked down at her body.

Why is my skin bubbling like that? Why can't I feel my hands or my feet?

She twisted her right wrist, and her hand slipped free. She turned on her blistering side and used her teeth to undo the cord on her left hand. She pulled her left foot and knocked over the chair. She stood up and was about to untie her foot when she looked back at her mother.

Her eyes were completely devoid of any semblance of humanity. Cold. Dark. Lifeless. It was as if she was a dead person that suddenly came to life. Her face was full of sweat from the steam that had risen off of Mara's body. But it was a flashed reflection that caught Mara's attention. The moonlight glistened off of something shiny that Jedidah was holding in her hand. Mara looked down.

She saw a machete.

Mara stepped back, dragging the chair her leg was tied to. Jedidah moved forward and raised her weapon. Mara tried to back up farther and make a run for the door, but the rope stayed tight around her ankle, and Jedidah put her foot through the legs of the chair to keep her daughter from leaving.

Jedidah directed the first slash at her head, but Mara brought up her left hand and took the blow to her arm, leaving an incredible gash. The second slash missed her head entirely and caught her in the rib cage. The blow was so forceful that it knocked her to the ground. Her head smashed against the concrete floor, creating a gash on her scalp.

Mara crossed her arms in front of her face, creating an X in the hope of shielding herself from the attack. Her mother stood above her, hurling insults and curses at her. She swung down at her daughter's head. The machete cut into Mara forearms. Blood poured out from the gashes, dripping over her and onto the ground. Jedidah swung again and again. The blows cut into Mara's arms, rendering them useless. Mara tried to force them back up to protect her head, but they would no longer respond. She had put up an incredible fight. She had done her best. But this was it. There was nothing left to do except to look her mother in the eye, see her own blood from the blade of the machete drip down on her, and wait for the inevitable.

The final blow from her mother's machete crashed down on her forehead with such force that it split through her skin and chipped her skull bone. The unspeakable pain from the migraine that instantly followed was accompanied by a ringing in her ears so intense that it shut down her system altogether. Her last image was that of her mother standing over her looking down to see if the job was finally done.

But being stolen from her father, being offered as a prostitute, being burned with scalding water, and being hacked at by a machete, all by her own mother— all of these were the least of her worries.

Because the real struggles in Mara's life were about to begin.

CHAPTER 2

Mara was awake for an hour before she managed to get her first eye open. The raging pain from her migraine, the cuts from the machete and the burning from the boils of her skin absorbed all of her attention, making it impossible for her to focus on anything else. She lay there, her back to the cold concrete, wondering if she was paralyzed or on her way to death.

Or both.

The dried blood from the injuries to her face prevented her from opening her second eye. Her left arm was broken, the bone shattered from the blow of the machete. But as painful as that was, it didn't compete with the ruined state of the rest of her body.

She forced her second eye open. The ceiling was blurry. The room was spinning. It was like there was someone pushing her down on a table made of nails. Her throat throbbed from the rising temperature from the fever her body was generating as an attempt to rid her of all the evils that had crept in during the last 24 hours.

Get up. Get up! She's coming back. She's coming back to finish you off. She'll be back with that machete and hack you to bits! Get going. Get—

The panic mechanism in her body kept sounding the general alarm, but what little strength she had left was being diverted to help her body heal. She wouldn't be able to get up now and run, no matter what. Her mind concentrated on trying to twitch one limb at a time. The rest of her, that faint part of her that remained on constant red alert after an attack like that, tried desperately to listen for any sound of an impending second strike.

The first struggle was to release herself from the false hope that help was coming. She was a day's journey from her father, which in rural Kenyan terms meant forever. He had no idea who took her, and even if he guessed that it was his estranged wife, he'd have no idea where to start looking. There would be no government assistance to find her. She would be added to a list of numerous people who had gone missing. There were no medical personnel on their way to help. And no neighbours who had heard the incident were coming to her aid.

Mara was alone.

She hoped she would be able to walk. She hoped there were herbs close by that could aid in her recovery. She hoped the injuries would not become infected.

And the best she could hope for from her mother was that she would be safely passed out and unable to commit further atrocities.

Mara wiggled her toes. They didn't hurt. That was a good sign. She curled her fingers. She swallowed and gathered the courage to lift her head. That was both courageous and a mistake at the same time. She was still naive enough to believe that she was okay. That her body wouldn't show the effects of last night's disaster. But even with one good eye there was enough that she could see to take in the full effect of the horror show.

Dried blood. Cuts. Bruises. Boils.

She felt light-headed and lay back down. A rush of fever ripped through her body. She felt like throwing up. She breathed in short bursts, trying to get back to what she had a moment ago. Her mind began to whirl around as she tried desperately to cope with the new pressures placed on her.

You have to force yourself to get up. If she comes back, you'll be dead.

But if I get up now I could injure myself further and pass out from the pain.

Better that than waiting here.

I'm trying. I'm trying as best I can.

Try harder.

This is the best I can do.

Do you want to do your best, or do you want to live? You have to do better than your best or you'll feel that machete.

She lifted her head again and kept her eyes off her body this time. The fever pulsed through her. She took a deep breath, managed to sit up and resisted the urge to pretend that this was all a dream.

She breathed in, feeling the sting in her left rib cage where the machete had connected with her. Reaching out to the chair, she pulled herself to her feet. Sweat poured off of her body. She felt like she was on a ship in an uncontrollable storm.

Mara reached for the door, stumbled, and held herself up by the wall. Then she heard the bedroom door behind her opening. She was too exhausted to panic. There was no burst of adrenaline this time. She turned and saw her mother standing in doorway wearing the strangest expression, as if to say, *What happened to you?*

It's been said the opposite of love is not hate; it's indifference. If that's true, then Mara's mother hated her with as much indifference as a person could ever develop. Her mother walked past her, out the door, and disappeared down the road, hoping to find another man to sleep with to get some much needed money so she could buy alcohol or other necessities.

When her mother was out of sight, for the first time Mara felt the life-altering feeling of being ignored. She tried to fight it as best she could.

You are pathetic and useless. You're not worth being loved.

Yes, yes, I am worth being loved. It's just that my mother is not well.

Your mother is fine. It's you that's the problem. Any decent child would be loved and respected by their parents. But you? You deserve what happened to you.

No, no, that's not true. I am a wonderful—

You actually believe you are wonderful? Wonderful children don't have their mothers beat them and leave them for dead.

I am a good girl, am I not? I am someone who should be loved, shouldn't I?

You're finished. You're nothing. There's nothing good about you.

But...but.

But what?

Maybe you're right.

Mara went outside to the bushes. There she found herbs to try and heal her wounds.

The wounds on the outside, anyway.

Finding food was a constant struggle. Her grandmother was no help. Life was one blur of beatings, a drunk mother, and an eternity of being caught in the same routine day in and day out without any indication that the next day, week, month or year would be any different from the one before it. But change did come when Jedidah decided to take Mara with her to the city of Eldoret. The plan was to work with her cousin, Mara's aunt, in a hair dressing salon to earn money. It seemed good enough. But, as Mara would find out about her mother, a change in location does little to change character.

They took a bus and found a rental unit in the area of Kapsoya. The initial impact was positive. Her mother worked. Work resulted in money. Money meant food. Food meant security. Security meant less anger. And less anger meant fewer beatings.

But old habits die hard. And when the novelty of a new location, new work and new friends began to wear off, Jedidah was left with the inevitable feeling that of the many things she could try to escape in life, she would never be able to escape herself.

At least not without a strong dose of alcohol.

So she drank herself into oblivion. There were times when she would leave and not tell Mara where she was going. Days, weeks, would go by. Month after month. Year after year. Mara would wait. Wondering what happened to her mother. It was difficult to determine which was better—living alone and wondering if your abusive mother was dead, or living with her and fearing the almighty machete would be used to finally finish you off.

Mara had been alone for weeks when she received word from a relative that her mother had died. AIDS had taken her life. Where she had gotten it was anybody's guess. She had slept with so many men, most of it under the influence of alcohol, that life was one long chain of abuse.

Mara sat on the mud floor of their rental unit. Tears streamed down her face. She felt the conflicting emotions of being angry at her mother for being so awful to her and being sorrowful that the woman who brought her into this world was now gone.

"Whatever you do, don't ever be like your mother," neighbours told her.

There was no work for her in the hair salon. No money for her to go to school. And no food. The African sun set, and the stifling daytime temperatures suddenly shifted to near freezing. Mara wrapped her arms around her body and rubbed her shoulders to keep warm. Rain poured down onto the metal roof with a clanging sound that echoed in the small room. Some of it dripped through and began to form a small puddle on the ground beside her.

Where am I going to get food? How am I going to survive? How will I get enough warm clothes to wear? No one will hire me. There are no jobs. There is no work. I can beg on the streets, but no one has any money here to give. What else can I do? What else can I—

You know.

What? I know what?

You know exactly how to make money. It is easy and it will make you rich.

I'm not doing that. I am not my mother.

Sure you are.

I am not!

More rainwater came in. This time through the bottom of the door. She stood up against the wall and watched as the water swirled in a pool at her feet. It had been days since she had eaten last. And the pain of hunger distorted her reasoning.

Yes, that's it. Just head out the door and you'll have food. You want food, don't you?
I don't want to do that. It's not safe. Look what happened to my mother. I don't want to be like her.

You aren't your mother. It's your life. And you have to take care of yourself. What other choice do you have? Stay here so that you can freeze and starve day after day? You'll be dead if you don't.

She preferred an alternative. She wanted something different. But she was in a slum and she had no one else—the very concept of having options was foreign to her. So she walked through the water to the door. Part of her wondered who this was that was doing this. The other part of her was driven by a need to survive that surpassed whatever logic and human decency was left in her. She left her rental unit and walked under the pouring rain to stand with some of the same girls with whom her mother had stood. Some were tall. Some were short. Some were in their thirties; some, like Mara, in their teens. They wore various kinds of clothes and used different tactics to attract customers. But all of them had the same set of desperate eyes. That dream of being loved for who they were, that hope of a man who would care for them at any cost, the desire to be valued for more than their bodies—all of this was long since forgotten.

She stood there completely unsure of herself. Unsure of what to say, what to do, or even how much to ask.

A man came down the street, and the competition started. The girls called out his name. He was a regular of sorts. He had his hand in his pocket protecting the tiny sum of money that would be able to dishonour any one of the girls. They crowded around him, trying to win his attention. He had been with them all, and he was about to pick the one nearest him when he saw Mara by herself. She looked up and made eye contact with him. He wouldn't be so bad, would he? *It's just one night. It's just one...*

She stumbled back through the rain to her rental unit. She had gone back with him and survived the ordeal. But when she asked for the money he refused. Not to be outdone, she pushed harder for him to give it. And when he smashed her head against the wall she stumbled outside and took it as learning experience to ask for the money beforehand.

When she made it back inside she saw that the rain had filled the entire floor. She stood against the wall, shivering, crying and wishing that somehow life could be different.

"You're not staying here anymore," her aunt said.
"What? Why not?"

It had been a steep learning curve, but Mara had succeeded in selling herself. For weeks she worked the streets at night and then slept the days away to try and recover from the sicknesses she contracted from her customers.

"You are turning into your mother. You're just as stubborn as she was."

"I have no other choice!"

"Sure you do. I will take you to school."

What? Did she hear that correctly?

"To school?"

As Mara rode the matatu with her aunt she was amazed that she would finally have a chance to learn. School? It was just so out of the realm of what she could expect. This was the turning point she needed. This was the break in pattern that would take her to new heights. It felt good. There was nothing quite like being able to leave the past behind.

Yet when they arrived at their destination, Mara's hopes were crushed.

It wasn't a school at all. Mara's mouth dropped open. She'd been had.

Again.

"This is a juvenile hall," her aunt said, as if that was the plan all along. Which, of course, it was, but still, it came out sounding so matter of fact, as if lying to Mara and shipping her off was no big deal. "They will look after you from here on. You tell them that your mother and father are dead and say that you have no other family to take care of you. This way they will have to take you in." She wanted to add, *And then we will finally be rid of you,* but she kept herself from saying it.

"How long will I have to stay here?"

Her aunt didn't answer. She just walked her to the front door.

Mara had heard rumours about juvenile halls. Terrible living conditions. Overcrowding. Fights with other youth. Horrible food. And guards so abusive that nothing was beneath them. But rumours were not going to be of concern to her.

Because she was going to find it all out for herself.

As they approached the door Mara nearly fell down. Before they had left, she had built up an image in her mind of what the school would be like. But on the matatu she downgraded that image with every intersection they crossed on the way over so as not to be disappointed when she arrived. Just before they showed up she reduced her image to that of the most basic concept possible. But school and juvenile hall are worlds apart. And there was nothing that could prepare her for what she saw.

A fading green roof sagged over a dull grey brick exterior. A tall fence surrounded the compound. They entered through the door, and Mara had the strange feeling that this would be the last time she would know what it was like to be on the other side. As far as she could see inside everything looked grimy and cramped. She saw youth in the distance. Their depressed faces made her wonder how long it would be before she looked that way too. She met a short, medium build manager who sat with her and her aunt and heard her situation.

"And no other relatives?" he asked, looking at her aunt.

"She has none. She stole 500 Kenya shillings from me, and she is a disturbance to neighbours."

The manager agreed to admit her. As he got up to lead her away, Mara turned to her aunt and whispered, "When will you come back?"

"What?"

"When will you come back to get me out? How long do I have to stay here?"

Her aunt's expression changed. Somehow she looked altogether different. Like she became a person that Mara had never seen before.

"We each have to live our own lives," her aunt said. "I will never see you again."

"What? What?!" Mara was furious. "I will tell them who you are."

"Go and try. They will never believe you." Her aunt leaned closer. A sinister grin formed on her face. "You are a thief, remember?"

Her aunt left without saying another word. Mara watched her go through the doors. The manager showed her to the mess hall.

"That woman. She is my aunt. I do not want to be here."

"You will make new friends here."

"Please believe me. None of this is true."

"Just obey the rules and all will go well."

She sat down in the mess hall. He brought her a meal of half-cooked beans. She took a bite and nearly threw up. They were crunchy with a suspicious pungent odour of being rotten. But hunger supersedes taste, and she finished her bowl, hoping she wouldn't bring it up later. She asked for a refill of her meagre bowl, but the manager denied it. As hungry as she was, it would not be fair to the others.

Mara followed the manager to the dormitory and was given a bottom bunk in the crowded room. It was late and the other girls came in for the night. When the manager left, Mara presumed she would be able to go to sleep. But the other girls moved the bunk beds aside and pulled Mara out of her bed. A tall girl with eerily similar cut marks on her arms and forehead to Mara's shouted at her.

"You are new? We'll see how strong you are."

Mara stood up. She saw scars on the girl's arms. She could relate.

"I don't want to fight," Mara said.

"That's not my problem. It is your problem."

Mara wondered what was better—living in a rained-out shack working as a prostitute or living in a cramped hovel with angry girls hoping to beat her unconscious.

The first hit caught her completely off guard. The rest of the girls cheered. The tall girl laughed as Mara tried to regain her balance. The second hit came clear across her face and sent her sprawling against the ring of girls.

"You are weak," the tall girl said. "Very weak."

Arrogance proved to be a problem for the tall girl. She turned to the others to gloat, but more importantly she turned her back on Mara.

Mara checked her lip and tasted her blood. "You want to fight?" Mara asked more to herself as she stood to her feet. "You really want to fight?"

The tall girl laughed. But she stopped laughing in a hurry when she turned around to see Mara jump on her, knock her off balance and pin her to the ground. She was about to throttle her neck when the other girls intervened to pull them apart.

The manager came in and shouted out instructions. The girls, out of fear of abuse or loss of food, or perhaps both, immediately put the bunks back together.

Mara got into her bed. The lights went out. But she stayed awake the entire night. Vigilant. Waiting. Every twitch of another girl, every sound she heard made Mara wonder if she was about to be attacked.

The following morning the manager took her aside. He brought her into a room. Concrete floor. Dull light. Why was nothing ever lit properly in this dingy place? A wooden table and two old chairs. He closed the door behind her. Mara waited to hear whether he would lock the door. That would clue her in real quick as to what would take place next. But all she heard was the door latching shut. Still, she had been with enough men to know what they really wanted whenever they asked to speak to her.

"Why are you here?" he asked.

"Because my parents are dead."

He nodded and took a deep breath. He looked into her confused and hurting eyes. "Why are you really here?"

Mara studied him, wondering if he was a man looking for a free favour from her or someone that she might be able to trust.

"My mother is dead. I have looked for my father but he is gone."

"Would you like to go to school?

"No."

"Why?"

"I don't want to."

That was a lie. She did want to go to school. Education was the way out. She knew that much. But she knew it was impossible, and she wasn't about to play along for a man who had other things on his mind.

"I am serious."

"You are serious?"

"Yes."

"When I am sitting in class then I will believe you. Until then, I don't believe a word you are telling me."

The manager took her to a court hearing in a small, modest room where a female judge reviewed her case. She asked routine questions that Mara answered truthfully. She figured honesty would be her best chance at trying to avoid prison. But the judge didn't look friendly, and Mara braced herself for what was coming next.

"This court is giving you to Mully Children's Family," she said. "You will go to school, and you will have a brand new start at life."

Mara was shell-shocked. The judge called the next case. Mara was lost. She gathered the courage to address the judge.

"What is Mully Children's Family?"

A man named Njoroge drove Mara from the courthouse to a large home in Eldoret that was surrounded by large bushes. They came to the large black gate that served as the entrance to the property. Njoroge honked. A watchman looked out from his post and opened the gate. They drove onto the compound, and Njoroge took Mara inside.

Mara had resisted the urge to imagine what she might see for fear of being disappointed again. But anything she could have imagined would have fallen short of what she observed.

A dozen young children sat on the floor singing a song with a young lady. Through the window she looked out into the backyard and saw what must have been a hundred children singing and clapping. When they finished their song a leader prayed with them, and the children then hurried to metal buildings. They were from different tribes. They all wore different clothes. They were all different heights and ages.

But their eyes. There was something similar in each of their eyes. A fire that she did not have. The young ones singing off to her side had it. The older ones in the backyard had it too. What was that? Was that…?

"Hello, Mara," a voice behind her said.

Everything inside her changed. In the instant she heard his voice there was something she hadn't felt before. There was peace in his tone. Assurance. How was that possible? She didn't even know who he was, hadn't even seen his face. But his voice. Somehow she recognized his voice even though she'd never met him before.

She turned and saw an unassuming man with a smile as big and as genuine as she had ever seen. It took her a moment to get the courage to look him in the eye. And when she did, she saw something that was even stronger in him than what she had already noticed in the eyes of the other children. It was more than confidence. It was more than compassion.

"I am Mister Mulli, and I would like to welcome you to your new home."

"Thank you."

"If you like you can call me Daddy Mulli," he said with a laugh. There was something so honest about it that without even meaning to it caused Mara to laugh too.

"I will."

"May I get you something to eat?"

"Yes, please."

"Come, sit down with me."

He took her into the kitchen and asked one of the girls to prepare a meal for Mara. The girl smiled and nodded. She welcomed Mara, introduced herself and left to go to the food storage for supplies.

"I am so glad that you are here," Mulli said. "And I am very glad to meet you."

"I am happy to be here."

Part of Mulli's strategy in rescuing children was to help them come to terms with their past. As difficult as it was to have children speak about what happened to them, it did give them the opportunity to express the burden that their lives had been to this point. When Mulli had explained that she would go to school, have new friends, have a place to sleep, food to eat and, as the judge accurately said, a new start to life, he asked Mara to share about the circumstances in her life that brought her to this point.

"My life…" Mara tried to get the words out but she was unable.

Mulli looked at her with such patience that she believed he would wait as long as it took until she felt comfortable to speak.

She struggled for words and then felt the peace that came with knowing that for the first time she was speaking with someone who actually cared to know how she was doing.

She relayed the series of adverse events that had happened to her. There was nothing positive. Not one thing. Life had been one long slide of disaster that started with her abduction and had just grown worse ever since.

Mulli listened with such attention that it seemed to her that the entire world had ceased to exist, that it was only the two of them left, and that nothing else mattered. When she was finished she wiped away her tears. She wasn't sure how Mulli would respond. Did he actually know what he was getting himself into when he picked her? Part of her wondered if he would throw her out on the street just like every other man had.

But instead, Mulli waited in silence until she found the courage to meet his eyes.

"I understand," Mulli said.

Mara felt another round of stinging welling up as her eyes began to moisten again. She had an instant bond with him. Suffering connects. And when she looked into his eyes, and not simply at them, she saw something she had never known before.

"I was abused by my father when I was a young boy," Mulli said. "I woke up and my parents abandoned me. I was forced to beg for food. There was no money and so I could not go to school. I worked very hard and later I became very, very wealthy. But you know, there are two kinds of success. There is success with things like money, with school or with a talent. But real success is not about those things. Real success is giving up everything. And that's what I did to help children. Children like you. And I welcome you here to my family."

Mulli gave her a hug. She dropped her shoulders and relaxed in the arms of a man for the first time in a long while.

The cook arrived and gave her bread—clean bread that smelled like bread—and a plate of beans—cooked beans that smelled the way cooked beans are supposed to smell.

Mulli prayed and gave thanks for Mara's safe arrival and for the food.

Mara took her first bite. Wow. Cooked beans and fresh bread.

"How is it?" Mulli asked.

Mara nodded. "Everything is good."

CHAPTER 3

It started out as a feeling of weakness. Tiredness. Like a flu that came and went. Mulli had been working incredible hours for years, and he thought at first that it might be from overexerting himself, if that for a man like Mulli were even possible. Twelve hours for Mulli was a short day. Fourteen was reasonable. On average Mulli clocked in sixteen hours. He'd been doing it for years. Ever since he got kicked out of school for not having enough money to afford the fees. It was good that he had brilliance and a strong work ethic on his side. His culture still rewarded him for his entrepreneurial spirit, even if the national policy of fee-for-education did not.

"Maybe you should learn to take a break," his wife, Esther, said as she sat down next to him. "Even the Lord rested, you know. And he had way more to do than you."

Mulli grinned as he leaned back on his chair from his desk. He had been studying for his Bible school classes late at night at his home in Eldoret. The children were already asleep, including Mara, who had begun to fit in well and was beginning to put distance between who she had been and who she was becoming.

With the home in Eldoret and the second location in Ndalani, the need to care for hundreds of children was becoming increasingly demanding on Mulli. To help prepare him for the challenges that lay ahead Mulli decided to go to Bible college for further training. The result was a schedule that would have been fit for five people, much less just Mulli. On Friday nights after college, Mulli would make the 450 km trek through difficult Kenyan roads that some-times doubled the driving time to Ndalani. There he would meet with the chil-dren, encourage them, work on building projects, and then leave on Sunday evening, when he would meet with the team in Eldoret before going to the Bible college. All of his responsibilities left him little time to study.

"You are right," Mulli said.

Esther looked at him with eyes that relayed their connection. There were few people that understood Mulli: how he thought, his passion for reaching children, his divine ability to come to the right solution to seemingly impossible questions, and his ability to do so quickly. But Esther understood him. There was a relationship beyond words that bound them together—a joy experienced by people who had come to the end of themselves, and a freedom that came with believing that they were born to serve.

"Tomorrow we will see the doctor," she said.

She had meant to say it as a question, but she was concerned in the way wives are when they sense that something is not right. She got up and stopped at the door, waiting for his response. Mulli looked up from his desk. He was better. Somehow having her in the room shifted his focus.

"All right," Mulli said.

Yet when she left the feeling of exhaustion returned.

The following morning, on the way to the doctor, Mulli recalled the time when he had been asked to come to a hospital to pray. The hospital cared for sick children who had been stricken with malaria, typhoid and other illnesses. Many were in danger of dying. Mulli prayed for every single child by laying hands on them one by one and asking their Creator to heal them. Nothing fancy, no special words, just a humble and confident request from a man who understood what it meant to be out of all other options except prayer. He left the hospital that day not seeing any physical change. He wasn't discouraged. He had prayed in faith. He had asked. He had believed. The results were not up to him.

Then the following day he received an urgent request. He returned to the hospital and was surprised by what he saw.

It was empty.

The nurse, out of breath and out of categories to try to understand what had happened, told him that the children had been tested and that all of them were completely well.

And all these years later, it was Mulli's turn to be the patient. When they arrived at the hospital Mulli met with a nurse who asked him to stretch out his arm. She took blood samples, sent them away to be tested, and later that day she called Mulli and Esther to discuss the results with the doctor.

That in and of itself was cause for concern. Doctors don't call people in if everything is fine.

Mulli and Esther shook hands with the doctor and sat down across from him. A desk, three chairs, a filing cabinet and a collection of medical books was all Mulli saw in the simple office. The window offered a view of a garden area outside, and Mulli would normally have commented on how beautiful it looked, had he not had other things on his mind. The doctor, in his late fifties, wearing a white coat and a concerned frown, looked through his glasses at the test results in his red folder to make sure that what he would be saying was accurate.

When he glanced up everything went quiet. All the pleasantries upon entering the office, the questions about each other's families, the inquiries into Mulli's work rescuing street children—all of it was done with the understanding that this moment was coming. The moment when the doctor would tell Mulli why he was being brought in. And then it came. *Is this the end?*

"You have diabetes," the doctor said.

Mulli felt the sting of transitioning from a world he knew to one he was not prepared to enter. He didn't want to hear this. Part of him wondered if this conversation was really happening. The doctor was kind and matter of fact and relayed the information with directness and efficiency. How was it possible that such critical news could be delivered in an unassuming office like this on an average day like this?

"It is serious," the doctor said. "But it can be managed." He placed the folder back on the desk. "With medication, you can lead a somewhat normal life. If you choose not to take the medication we will have to amputate your arm or leg depending on how it progresses. So I advise you to take the medication."

The doctor continued speaking, slowly and in a compassionate voice, like someone familiar with giving and receiving bad news. But Mulli did not hear him. His mind was elsewhere. *Did he say amputate? And what does "somewhat normal" mean? How will this affect the ministry? The children? There is so much to do. If I could barely get it done with being healthy, what are the chances now that I am ill?*

"Do you have any questions?" the doctor repeated. It was the second time he had asked. Mulli heard both times, but shock does things to people's response times.

Mulli asked about the medication, how effective it would be. But the big one about *somewhat normal* remained uncertain. He thanked the doctor and got up from the chair a different man.

Mulli and Esther walked back to the car in silence. The drive home that evening was quiet. Normally they discussed the children and the tasks to be done. Normally Mulli's mind would work through solutions to all the various emotional challenges the children were facing.

But these were not normal times.

And suddenly, Mulli felt mortal.

They arrived home, and it wasn't until Mulli was alone in the backyard that he began to process what was happening.

I have given everything to you, God. My wealth. My body. My life. I am serving you. I am being used of you to rescue street children. Why should I have this sickness? Look how much we have already accomplished together. Is this really fair? Does this really help to build your kingdom?

Mulli waited for an answer from God. The stillness felt unusual. Did the lack of response mean that God wouldn't answer? Mulli hadn't asked for anything for himself. Not in years. This ministry wasn't about him. It was about the children. But this illness was different. It was completely different.

Or was it?

Am I being tested? Why is this happening to me? I am praying for others and they are healed, but what about me? Demon-possessed children are delivered right before my eyes, and yet I am the one who is stricken with sickness?

Again, Mulli waited. He looked up to the incomparable African sky. The stars filled the canopy in an incredible show of dazzling lights that were only partially dulled by the glow of the city.

It's tough on me when you don't answer. This is when I need you, and you're where? Where have you gone? Hello? Hello, are you there? Lord, I know you are. Please answer.

Mulli sat down. He quieted his mind and focused his attention on God. But instead of hearing from God, he heard another voice. One he had heard numerous times in his ministry.

You're finished now, Mulli. You're sick and you won't be able to care for these children.

Yes, I will. With the Lord's help I will continue.

How? Look at you. You're fading with each day.

They that wait upon the Lord shall renew their strength.

You're a fraud, Mulli. You gave up everything and expected it to all work out. A challenge finally comes your way, and now look at you. You're terrified and you're wondering where God is. You're not quite the model follower you thought you were, are you?

I'm confused. That's all. I…I…

Mulli buried his face in his hands and experienced the pain that comes with realizing that he had been expecting his life to be smooth. He had expected life to go well for him. Challenges, yes. But challenges from the outside, not the inside. And the more he thought about it, the clearer it became. What right did he have for things to go easy? Was anyone entitled to assume a certain kind of life for following God? Did God reward faithfulness with a life of ease? He remembered the story of Peter on the boat in the midst of a storm. Jesus walked on the water and told Peter to join him. Peter got out of the boat and walked towards Jesus.

And then came what, Mulli?

He looked at Jesus.

After that. What happened after that? Where did he look?

He looked at…

He looked at what?

He looked at the waves.

Just like you. Your sickness is like those waves. You're no better than Peter. One storm and down you go.

Mulli felt the sting of regret. He had been successful in business beyond imagination. That was his boat. He had left that boat when he made the decision to sell everything. And he had walked on water by trusting God to help him every step of the way. There had been many waves before, and he hadn't taken his eyes off Jesus. Yet for some reason, this wave was unique. It had succeeded in distracting him.

Now you're done, Mulli.

I will fear no evil.

Spare me. You're afraid and you know it.

All things work together for good for those who love God.

As if. You being sick means fewer kids get rescued. That doesn't work together for good, and you know it.

Nothing can separate me from the love of God. Now leave me alone.

A lot can separate you from God. Is he here now? Can you feel him? Has he answered you? Of course not. He wouldn't answer you—

Leave me alone. I am not my own. I have been bought with a price, and I know that God knew all about me in my mother's womb.

That's right. He knew he would let you down right now when you need him most.

I said, leave me alone!

Sure thing. I'll be seeing you again, Mulli. Real soon.

Mulli breathed a sigh of relief. He felt a rush of confusion run through his mind. The solution was not clear. The purpose was not clear. There wasn't a lot of clarity in anything at the moment.

"God," Mulli prayed, "you are the owner of this world, and you created me. Father, may your will be done. Here I am; whichever way, whether I am healed or not, let my life glorify you. Give me an ability to lead the young people to know you. I am not going to blame you. My will is to do your will."

He looked back up to the stars. They seemed brighter somehow. Esther came out. She sat down beside him in her quiet, gentle demeanour.

"Are you all right?" she asked.

Mulli wasn't sure. This was new territory. He looked at her with eyes that were full of uncertain resolve.

"I will continue to trust the Lord," he said, putting his arm around her.

She looked beside her at the dormitories where the many children needing their help were sleeping.

"Are we going to be all right?" Esther asked. She had a tough time, at first, accepting that Mulli had given up their life of wealth for a life of rescuing street children. She had let go of her fear and trusted God to help her. And that's when she became enthralled by the adventure.

The adventure where she stood beside a healthy husband to do all this work. And now she wondered how this was going to go on.

"We're in God's hands," Mulli said. "And we are following him on the right path. Of that I am sure."

"But are we going to be all right?"

Mulli was quiet. He looked back at the stars.

He wasn't sure what to say.

CHAPTER 4

The pursuit of rescuing street children proved to be more a question of faith than of logic. Despite the cost of caring for hundreds of children, Mulli continued to go into slums to give children on the brink of disaster the opportunity to transform. The increase in children required the construction of larger classrooms, which required an increase in staff and food. Mulli had continued to sell off his possessions without the guarantee of any future stream of income, something unique and illogical to a former multimillionaire who had built an empire on sound business practices.

He served supper to the children who stood in a long line with their bowls in hand. One by one they came by, and he poured in a mixture of beans and rice. They no longer had the need to dig through garbage cans for food. No more waiting at the restaurant back door for the waiters to give them the best of the scraps. No more standing on a corner hoping for a man to take them in for the night in exchange for food. They had a new home. They had a new family. And the smiles on the children's faces were reassuring to Mulli of the changes taking place in their lives.

Mara laughed as she sat next to her classmate, relaying her thoughts about the morning. She sure could talk. Lots and lots and lots. An extreme extrovert, Mara could go on about anything forever. Her friends understood her. They giggled when they realized Mara was repeating the same story. But she didn't mind. It was one of the joys of living here.

It was okay to be a kid again at MCF.

Mulli saw the children as miracles all around him. They had learned that precious gift of being able to leave the past behind. Not overnight. Rehabilitation wasn't instantaneous. Yet Mulli saw them make the choice to forgive people who had committed unspeakable evil against them.

When supper was finished, the children went to practice in their choirs while Mulli went inside, humming the tunes the children themselves had written. It wasn't until he got inside that he saw Esther with a look of disbelief and worry on her face.

There were always pressures. Rescuing children was not for those hoping for a predictable life. Esther had become more and more accustomed to a life living every second by faith. But what Mulli saw in her eyes was something different. She had reached a point where her faith would be stretched past anything she had experienced to date.

And Mulli, too, of course.

"What is it?" Mulli asked in his trademark tone of calmness and reassurance.

She wanted to get the words out. She wanted to tell the man she loved and respected what was concerning her so deeply. But that was the problem. Saying it out loud would somehow make it real. As long as it was in her head, maybe it didn't really exist. Maybe it could stay a bad dream. Maybe it would just disappear on its own without anyone knowing.

Denial, however, wasn't going to work anywhere, least of all not in a home for rescued street children.

She took in a deep breath. Was she really saying it?

"My dear," she started. "We do not have enough food."

It was out. She felt better about that. But only momentarily. The peace in sharing a burden was soon overcome with the reality that the ship was sinking.

"How much is left?"

The fear in her eyes conveyed the answer.

Mulli walked to the food storage area and opened the door. He had seen it filled to overflowing. Bags of maize, beans, rice and vegetables. But this time when he opened the door it looked like the place had been robbed.

"There's enough for breakfast and lunch tomorrow," she whispered. "And that's it."

His knee-jerk reaction was to arrange to go to the bank first thing the next morning. Pull money out of the account and buy whatever they needed. But he knew their bank account position. He knew how much they had to spend.

Zero was a pretty easy number to remember.

"And what now?" Esther asked. Her motherly instinct for the responsibility of providing for her children kicked into overdrive. Panic knocked at her heart's door, and she wondered whether she had the power to keep it shut.

"Don't you remember when God gave me this vision in the beginning? Whenever we need something, we should turn to him."

"Where are we going to get the food from?" She spoke as a woman overcome with desperation. She could already see the children at suppertime staring at her with empty gazes. The horrific fear of letting her children down gripped her to such an extent that it was as if she were already there in the future, feeling the disappointment of her many children who would be sent away empty-handed.

"Don't ask me. Let's ask God."

That didn't help. It should have. But somehow coming to God now, at the eleventh hour, seemed irresponsible.

Sure, that's good. Go to God, Mulli. Where were you a week ago? Why weren't you planning better? Why didn't you organize yourself? God won't come through now. It's your own fault. This is the result of your poor organization. Use your head. God doesn't help you when you don't do your part.

Tears began to stream out of her eyes. Mulli hugged her and felt her body shaking with fear.

"Have we failed?" she asked.

She took in a deep breath, looked into his eyes, and went upstairs.

Mulli followed after her, unwilling to let his wife feel the weight of insecurity. She looked out their bedroom window.

"I gave up everything with you," she said. "I didn't like it at the beginning, but I did it." She wiped the tears from her eyes. She should have been able to go to Mulli for support. She should have been able to rely on her husband. But he felt a million miles away, and the man who had a love for street children that few could match suddenly seemed distant.

Mulli stepped closer to her and spoke in a soft voice that conveyed he was just as concerned as she was. "We are going to pray," Mulli said.

"Pray for what?" Esther asked, her mind out of options and her heart out of courage. "Is God going to provide something out of thin air?"

Mulli thought about her question. He didn't know. He didn't have an answer for that. It hurt him to see his wife suffering. He searched for something that would bring light to both of them.

"If it were always easy, how would we ever see God?"

She thought about it and realized his point. It was easier to keep a sailboat in the harbour. That would prevent it from being tossed around in the sea. But somehow deep down she knew that only in the sea could she know him in a deeper way.

"God wants to be real to us," Mulli said. "He uses many different ways to teach us to trust. And one of those ways is to bring us to a place where we *have* to have him come through. Where we have no recourse but to trust."

It sounded good. It should have been helpful advice. But it did little to calm those images of all the children looking at her.

Mulli closed his eyes and raised his hands. He stayed quiet for a while, not wanting to rush into a prayer but to first be clear in his mind that he was talking to the highest ranking person anywhere. "God, you are the one who called me into this ministry. You said you are the Father to the Fatherless. Today we have food. Tomorrow at lunch it is over. We pray for you to intervene. We pray for you to meet all our needs according to your riches in glory."

Mulli opened his eyes. He saw Esther wiping still more tears away. He hugged her.

Mulli lay down in bed. He felt the tug of war inside of him to continue to trust. But that nagging voice inside him grew louder and louder.

This is the beginning of the end for you, Mulli. Sure, God provides. And he did. He gave you businesses and he gave you money. And you wasted it. You threw it away. The logical thing that anyone including God would have done would have been to hang on to some of the businesses so that you could feed this growing army of children. But you misunderstood faith. There are consequences to bad choices. And now you're going to pay for it. Oh, and all those children are going to starve, too. Think about that tonight as you try to sleep. Think about being a failure in faith. Think about your illogical rationale. Think about all your children having to go back and starve in the street. Sweet dreams, Mulli.

It was early in the morning when some of the children heard the sound of honking at the black gate. They hurried to see who it was. The guard checked through the slot hole. He saw a truck with a driver and a woman seated in the front. The woman stepped out. Her eyes were as bright as the sun. Everything about her said genuine. Her smile grew from ear to ear when she saw a dozen children crowding around her. She greeted them with the happiness some people have that makes everyone around them feel good.

"Is this the home of Charles Mulli?"

"Yes!" the children shouted.

"Would you tell him to come? I would really like to talk to him."

The children raced off and found Mulli in the back speaking with one of the children.

"Daddy Mulli! Daddy Mulli," they shouted, running as fast as they could. Mulli looked up and smiled, feeling the rush that comes with seeing excited children. "There is someone here!"

"Thank you. Please tell them to wait. I am coming."

The children ran back as fast as they could. Mulli laughed.

Esther heard the commotion and came out to meet Mulli. Together they went to the gate.

"Are you Mister Mulli?" the woman asked.

"Yes, I am. This is my wife, Esther."

They introduced each other. Then the woman began speaking loud and fast. Mara would have been proud.

"A week ago I attended a women's fellowship meeting in our church," the woman said. "And a woman gave a testimony about how you sold all you had to help street children. I was so touched by this testimony. Last night before I went to sleep I felt the Lord speaking to me to give you food. So I brought this truck."

She led them to the back of the truck. She opened the door. Inside, Mulli saw that it was stuffed to capacity with sacks of beans, maize, cabbage, and on and on.

Mulli felt a powerful presence of peace run through him. Everything felt fuller. It was as if there were thousands of other people who were suddenly present.

"Thank you from the bottom of our hearts," Mulli said. He looked at the number of bags. It would last for at least three days. "You have really done something incredible for us."

As the children began to off-load the food, Mulli thanked her again. She pulled out a white envelope from her purse and gave it to him.

"It is I who should be thanking you, Mister Mulli," she said. "Why, when I was told to give you food I couldn't sleep all night. I was so excited. Wow, I get to help the famous Charles Mulli. I mean, for me, this is a treat. A wonderful treat!"

She continued talking with them as she walked back to the truck. She got in and waved goodbye. Then she started talking to the driver and off they went.

Mulli went inside and sat down with Esther. Her eyes had moistened over. She might not have been able to touch God. But she had seen him. Right in front of her eyes. She looked at her husband with a feeling of relief and encouragement. She didn't have the words to express what she felt.

She didn't have to talk to communicate.

"Wow," Mulli said. "This is really a miracle. This really proves beyond any doubt that God is with this ministry." Then he laughed. "There was really no food. You know? We had really no food left after today. We were really close to the end."

"I think I remember," Esther said, a smile coming to her face. "I was there to tell you about it."

"And the Lord himself intervened at the right time."

Esther leaned back in her chair.

"Yes," she said. "He did."

If the bags of food were an answer to prayer, then so was the envelope, which was stuffed with money. He used all the money from the talkative lady to buy food that would last them a few weeks. When all of that food began to run low and the pressure to find new income ran higher, Mulli went to the bank to close an account that was nearly empty. He hoped there would be enough money left to get them through the next day. He waited in line until a young woman in her early thirties called him to her wicket.

"May I help you?"

"Hello, how are you?" Mulli asked.

"I am fine."

"That is good. Thank you for seeing me. I was wondering if you could tell me the balance on this account."

Mulli gave her a piece of paper with the account number on it. She left, turned around a corner and came back a few minutes later with the sum written on a form. As she gave him the piece of paper Mulli prayed there would be enough for another day.

But when Mulli read the amount he gave the paper back to her.

"I'm sorry, there must be some mistake. Can you check again?"

Even though it was a simple request, she took it as an insult. "Sure." She forced a smile and left. When she came back her smile had vanished and she gave the same form back to Mulli.

"I'm sorry. But this cannot be correct. We deposited money about a week ago, and there was hardly enough money even then. We have since used up the money. There is no way we can have this much money. Someone has deposited it in our account by mistake. Please, can you check again?"

She said nothing. It was a symbol of her annoyance. She had had enough. But she went back anyway, and after a longer time she returned.

"It is your account. We have checked and confirmed that a large sum of money has been donated into your account by an anonymous giver."

"Really?"

"Yes. Really."

"Really?"

"I think I've answered that."

"Thank you very much," Mulli said. "This really is a fine day, isn't it?"

She gave a courteous smile, then turned to the person waiting in line. "Next?"

Mulli left the bank and checked the paper again. Incredible. He laughed as he walked under the bright sunshine.

It's not every day you walk out of a bank knowing someone has given enough money to feed hundreds of rescued street children for six months.

CHAPTER 5

How much longer could it go on this way? Mulli had already exhausted his personal financial resources, and the number of children continued to grow. Was waiting on donations as the only means of income the right approach? Was that really faith? Was trying to supplement donations an indirect sign of a lack of faith and not trusting God to provide? Mulli wondered. The situation was constantly difficult. Full of challenges. Lots and lots of challenges. He was confident that was how God had ordained growth in his servants. Not by miraculously calming the storms, but by divinely appointing them in the first place to give those who loved him the opportunity to draw closer to him.

Was he better off being like Elijah at the brook, trusting God to provide the proverbial ravens to bring them food, or was the more accurate biblical example for his circumstance that of the apostle Paul, who worked as a tentmaker and then used the money to help fund his missions work?

Mulli had prayed about the financial challenges during his time at Bible college. To depend only on foreign donations seemed dishonourable to him. There were people in the West working hard and giving of their resources. Shouldn't MCF do the same? Didn't Mulli himself have entrepreneurial talents that could be used? More than ever, Mulli was convinced that the responsible action was to chart a course for MCF to grow and export their own produce and use the sales to help fund the operation. To become part of the revenue solution. To begin to build now for a time when they could look after their own needs. They needed to pursue a new course of action.

They needed to push towards sustainability.

In a country without minerals, Mulli saw agriculture as the most fundamental resource in Kenya, famous for exports of tea, coffee, flowers and vegetables.

Mulli focused on vegetables because of his earlier experience in the field. The challenge would be formidable to say the least. The export quality control and consistency requirements required Mulli to lay out a strategic plan of finances, farming area, water supply, labour, community involvement, and of course favourable weather would be needed.

Mulli did all of this. But the first crops at MCF Ndalani suffered terribly from scorching temperatures. Mulli walked through the brown fields that should have been a vibrant green. Hundreds of his own children plus thousands more in the community were desperate for a successful harvest. All it would take was rain. Enough rain from heaven to transform the area. And yet, in spite of all their prayers, the land remained dry.

On his tour of Western cities Mulli laid out his platform to make MCF self-sustaining. It would be a long haul, but the end result would be better for everyone. He met with a group to discuss how funding MCF's farming initiatives would one day mean that MCF would be able to operate with a decreasing dependency on Western money. When he finished his presentation he smiled and asked the group of relief organizations and business people if there were any questions.

It was quiet, never a good sign in a Western audience. Then, finally, a man at the front cleared his throat.

"It's not going to work," he said.

"I see," Mulli said. "I apologize for not explaining it well. I am sorry. It is a new program—"

"I understood what you said," the man replied. "I just don't agree with it."

Mulli paused. A classic response to try to diffuse the man's antagonism.

"Maybe you could explain why you disagree with it."

"Because I've never heard of an African organization being able to sustain anything," the man said.

That hurt.

The man continued. "Purchasing tractors is a waste of money because there is no one in Africa who could repair or maintain them."

"These are good questions," Mulli said. "I can assure you that—"

"It's ambitious, Charles, but really, you can't get people excited about making you self-sufficient so that one day you'll be rid of their support."

Everything went still. Was that what this group was about? Wanting to maintain their involvement in MCF by keeping them dependent on their money? Were they content to contribute so long as MCF did not rise up and no longer need them? Mulli refused to believe that others thought this way. He prayed a short prayer in his mind, then looked directly at the man.

"What do you think? Is it better to help Africans stand on their own two feet or to keep them begging at your table for generations?"

If the room was quiet before it got even quieter now.

Mulli scanned the audience. Some of them looked at Mulli with blank stares, either not comprehending the idea of sustainability or not wanting to be part of it.

The meeting ended, and people, some of them anyway, politely thanked Mulli for coming. Normally a crowd would gather around Mulli afterwards to meet him in person. But not this time. There was an uneasy rush for the door.

But one of the businessmen stayed behind. He was kind, yet direct and confident in the way successful owners are. He recognized the same qualities in Mulli—it was as if there was an automatic kinship between entrepreneurs that crossed races and nationalities. It impacted him to see a man like Mulli, who once had bags of cash, humble himself to talk to the apparently mighty West, only to get turned down.

"You're on the right path," the man said. "This is the key for Africa."

"Thank you," Mulli said.

Even giants need encouragement now and again.

"It's a different idea, and different takes time to develop in people's minds. In the future people will push for organizations like yours to have a sustainability plan." The businessman stretched out his hand. "You're an inspiration," he said.

Mulli shook it. "Thank you."

"And don't worry. These people in here, they mean well, but they don't see what's down the road. They don't see the present as archaic. But lots of us will be on board. I'm with you," he said.

He was one of the few.

Travel is supposed to be a fun experience. But Mulli's flight back to Kenya was filled with sorrow. He hadn't expected that kind of rejection. Coming back from a business trip empty-handed was bad enough. Coming back empty-handed from a mission to help sustain starving children was far worse.

Even in the midst of doing precisely what God had called him to do, Mulli's life was full of struggles.

The next crop was significantly better, and Mulli took his vegetables to an exporter in Nairobi. A young man in the company was so impressed that he travelled to MCF to see Mulli's operation.

He stepped out of his car and looked at all the farms that stretched out as far as he could see.

"You could grow French beans. High yield and very high demand. But there is one challenge."The young man paused. His initial optimism of sure success was tempered by this new reality. "If you want to export, you have to apply for EurepGAP certification. No easy task, my friend."

"Can you tell me what is all involved?"

For a man who had risen from the ashes of destitution to among the highest in the country, Mulli was no stranger to challenges. But the standards imposed by EurepGAP and the thought of trying to compete against massive corporations made the task seem impossible.

The farming team prepared day and night. They went through all the required checklists to bring everything in order as best they could.

The EurepGAP auditors arrived on site and went through the entire operation. When they were finished they met with Mulli to provide him with the results. They reviewed the passing grade requirements and the various categories and provided Mulli with his score.

"Your mark is 10 percent," the auditor said.

If there ever had been a worse result than this, the auditor couldn't recall.

It was late that evening when Mulli sat with Esther and some of their biological children at the supper table. Grace, Ndondo, Kaleli, Mueni, Isaac and Dickson ate quietly, a rarity in their family. It was Mulli who broke the silence.

"This has not been a good day for us," he said. They stopped eating. They turned their eyes to their father. They recalled the day when he came home to announce he would be selling everything to help rescue street children. That day had shaken their lives and had been a catalyst to strengthen their faith.

Today would be something like that.

"We need to remember that all things are possible through Christ, who strengthens us. Sometimes we feel like giving up. Sometimes we look at a very bad result and we take that as a sign that we are to quit. But God does not give us easy things. He gives us tests. This is normal in life. Our response to tests is that we need to put our trust and faith in him, be obedient and do the right thing with no shortcut."

Ten percent. That's pathetic. Anybody could do better than that. Stop embarrassing yourself in front of your children. You did your best and you failed.

"We need to apply dedication, commitment, perseverance and endurance. We need to have hope, and we cannot forget that it will take much hard work that will most certainly exhaust our bodies. By the time you reach that wall and feel that you cannot go beyond, that is when the impossibility is destroyed by possibility."

He looked at each of them. So committed to the ministry. So committed to the rescuing of street children. So willing to consistently take leaps of faith.

"Are we ready to try again?"

Dickson smiled. "Well, we can't do any worse, can we?"

The table laughed. Life had come back to an otherwise brutal day.

They worked day and night to address the deficiencies and helped the field crew with all the aspects of the requirements. After a month of grinding through all the details, they invited EurepGAP back for another audit.

At the end of the day the EurepGAP auditor presented his report to Mulli.

"I am not exactly sure how an operation of your size ever expected to reach export status," the auditor said. "We deal with companies much larger and more experienced than you."

He handed Mulli the papers.

"Many people are applying for this status. And many are consistently failing," he said, "which is why I am so impressed to tell you that you've achieved 98 percent."

Mulli mouth dropped open ever so slightly. He saw the mark at the top of the paper.

"Congratulations."

"Thank you," Mulli replied.

"We would like to invite other farmers in the region to come here for a training seminar. You are the model example. Would you be willing to help?"

"Of course," Mulli said. "We are always willing to help."

"Then best of success to you. You are the first of your category to be registered."

The news raced throughout the area. The children and staff heard first and felt the thrill of success. Word spread throughout the community as a clear hope of future jobs.

Later that day, Mulli sat outside his humble home on the Ndalani property and looked out at a large rock. Esther came to sit down beside him. Her husband was always in deep thought. There was never an idle moment. And she had that precious gift of wanting to share in her husband's life.

"And?" she asked. "What are you thinking?"

Mulli smiled. "I am thinking about that rock."

"A rock? Very interesting," she replied with a smile. "And what great thoughts are you having about that rock?"

Mulli smiled. "Actually, I was thinking that this rock is like God."

Esther saw the setting sun casting a shadow around them. In the distance children hurried off to choir practice.

"He does not change," Mulli said. "He is the same, just like this rock. It has not changed since the first time we saw it many years ago. But the hopes and dreams we get from the Almighty God change things. Every time we obey, every time we refuse to quit, every time we push forward in his strength, we become more like him and we can be used of him to help others change."

They talked together about the day's events. Then Mulli got ready for bed. He was going to need his sleep.

Tomorrow was going to bring an interesting visitor to MCF.

CHAPTER 6

Mulli had only spoken with one of the three of them on the phone. He'd never actually met them in person. He waited at the Nairobi airport, wondering what they would be like. He'd heard that, like many people from around the world, they were interested in seeing Mully Children's Family (MCF). They wanted to understand how it worked and speak with children who had been rescued. Mulli watched as the next crowd approached. In the distance, three white males stood out.

Mulli stepped forward to greet them. The one on the left was average height, in his fifties, with a genuine smile, and introduced himself as Russell. The one on the right, James, was an accountant, slightly taller with glasses and a perfect haircut that had managed to stay in place despite the long flight. And then there was the guy in the middle.

Teagen the Australian.

Some people have the rare ability to walk into a room and have everyone notice them. Their bright personality. Their energy. Their engaging character. It's impossible to miss. That was Teagen.

"Is this the famous Charles Mulli?! Wow! Your reputation is as big as Africa! Is it ever a privilege to meet you, mate!"

"Thank you for—" Mulli started, but he was cut off by the exuberant Teagen, who shook his hand and continued.

"This is really amazing that you've taken the time to see us. I have been so looking forward to meeting you. I keep hearing about Mulli, Mulli, Mulli. The amazing man! And now I get to see you in person. I just had to come down to check out the operation for myself. It really seems too good to be true."

"You are most welcome. Please, can I take your bags for you?"

"No worries. We got them. I've been excited about this for ages. I can't wait to find out what makes this place of yours stick."

"Thank you."

They made introductions, then Teagen excused himself to go the bathroom. Russell needed a bottle of water. He asked the others if they wanted something—they didn't—and then he made his way through the crowd to a vending machine. That's when James, the one Mulli had spoken with on the phone about the invite, pulled him aside.

"There's one thing I should mention to you about Teagen."

"That he is a loud talker?" Mulli said, laughing.

"No doubt. He once talked for an hour straight. I kid you not. I'm glad I fell asleep on the plane."

Mulli smiled and chuckled. There was something so disarming about hearing Mulli laugh that it caused James to join in. He laughed hard, the hardest he had laughed in a long time. And over what? A guy who talked a lot. He wasn't exactly sure why he was laughing. He wouldn't have laughed at this back home. Wouldn't have laughed at this anywhere else. But somehow Mulli's joy was contagious, and he admired how a man who had gone through so much could be this happy. It felt good to laugh. It felt different. He looked at Mulli, feeling himself to have been suddenly transported to a totally different world.

"About Teagen," James continued. "He's not interested in faith. He doesn't believe in the Lord and gets quite upset whenever someone talks about it. He wants to hear about the work you do, but...I feel a little strange telling you this." James checked behind him then looked back at Mulli. "He gets really annoyed about anything to do with God."

Mulli thought a moment. "I'm not exactly sure how I can talk about my work without talking about God."

"I hear you. I—"

"All set?" Teagen said, rejoining them as Russell approached with three bottles of water, one of them already empty.

"We are ready," Mulli replied.

"Then let's get going!" Teagen grabbed his luggage and started down the hallway. "We have ourselves a stellar organization to look at!"

Mulli drove down the highway from Nairobi to Ndalani. Some of the road was repaved and made for easy travelling. Other parts of it were a thrill ride of sorts. It depended on if you liked or were terrified of driving inches from a thirty-foot drop-off. If Teagen noticed he didn't make any comment. But Russell and James sat in the back and held their breath on every turn. If either of them was tired from the trip over here, they were fully awake now. An hour before Mulli had asked Teagen about his business, and ever since, non-stop, Teagen had talked and talked, not only about his incredible construction business that he had built up from nothing, but about his travels and his adventures in life. For Mulli, it felt like he was giving someone the opportunity to not only be heard but to be listened to as well, which Mulli thought the man otherwise might not have had. Mulli laughed, and then, as loud as it had been in the car, it became quiet for a brief moment, and Teagen turned to Mulli and asked, "So I want to know, Charles, what got you started in all of this?"

Mulli glanced in the rear-view mirror and caught James' attention for a moment.

Mulli shared about his rise to the top of his business life in transportation, insurance, oil and gas, real estate and a tire and car parts dealership. Then one day he drove into Eldoret to update the registration on his buses. He parked his car, and street boys begged him for money to look after it for him while he was inside the building. But Mulli refused, thinking the money would be used by the boys to sniff glue. When Mulli returned, the car was gone.

"Wow! Those street boys sure play a hard game. You ever get your car back?"

Mulli had looked for it but never saw the car again. That started him thinking about the street children. *Why are they on the street? Why doesn't anyone look after them? Where are their parents? What happened to both parents that these boys have no home?*

"Now that's really something, Charles. I have to admit, I don't think I would ever have the guts to do something like that. I mean, who knew what was really going to happen, right? You could have sold all you had and then ended up with nothing. Bam. You could have been wiped right out. You could have been just as destitute as those kids. That thought ever cross your mind?"

Mulli shook his head. "I was too busy saving children's lives to worry about my own."

He glanced over at Teagen, and what he saw in his eyes surprised him. There was an instant, just a fraction of a second, when something dramatically changed inside of this extrovert of extroverts. It was there for such a short time that unless Mulli had looked at the exact right moment, he would have missed it altogether. It was as if the Outback multimillionaire showed the faintest glimmer of a desperate need for something he did not have. As if the curtain of everything he held dear was suddenly ripped open to expose his life for the unfilled theatre that he secretly thought it might be. As if for one moment he was stripped of all his incredible wealth, power and charisma and became just a regular guy who was faced with the reality of having nothing but himself.

And it seemed to Mulli as if Teagen had a glimpse into how empty his life really was.

But impressions are won and lost in a heartbeat, and as fast as Teagen had entered into that moment, that horror, really, of seeing himself for who he was, he got out even faster.

"You sure come up with the best lines, Mulli!" he said as they entered the Ndalani compound. "I mean, that was really good. That makes you think. Wow. I'm impressed."

But he was about to become more impressed with what he saw next.

As the vehicle came to a stop dozens and dozens of children ran up to the vehicle.

"Daddy! Daddy! Daddy!" they shouted.

Mulli opened the door as the crowd of children pressed around him, jumping to try to make contact with him. Mulli smiled and hugged them one by one, greeting them as he did.

But as compelling as the sight of rescued street children is, Teagen looked not only at them; he also watched Mulli's reaction. Watched to see what his face did when the children jumped all around him, reaching over each other just for a chance to touch him.

And what he saw made him pause for the second time that day, maybe in his whole life. He saw a man who had no money. No capacity to get on a plane and travel anywhere he wanted in the world. No ability to buy the nicest house, the fastest sports car or the best beach house. This guy was by all accounts penniless.

So why was he so happy?

Teagen saw Mulli as being different. It was unexplainable, yet undeniable, how content Mulli really was. That wasn't possible, was it? A man without financial success, without the ability to influence, without the power to chart his own destiny—he couldn't actually be happy.

Could he?

But that was the strange thing for Teagen. He saw that Mulli *was* happy. He was genuinely thrilled. Teagen thought his responsibility of running his construction company was intense. Yet Mulli had responsibility that far outclassed any CEO. Hundreds of children that he was accountable to help, to provide for, to love. Clearly Mulli had made a calculated move from the business world to the world of saving children's lives. But instead of receiving a big bonus at the end of the year, instead of being invited to the who's-who parties with all the other rich and famous people, instead of getting recognition and admiration from peers, he had kids from slums jumping up and down around him.

It seemed an odd trade-off.

A life like this should be marked with disappointment, shouldn't it? Leaving your great life behind to pursue what at best could have been considered a risky venture. Shouldn't that make you upset? Leaving you with a nagging grudge that *I could have had it all if only I wouldn't have made this move to the rescue ministry?*

But he didn't see that. There was no regret with Mulli. And that was the strangest part for Teagen.

He shrugged it off. *Good for Mulli. Good for him. He's done a good thing.*

Mulli introduced the children to the Aussie trio. And the moment Teagen shook one of the children's hands—a young girl with a smile that emanated through her shy and peaceful character—there was a shift in his thinking. It was so powerful that it was as if there was something that transferred from the child's heart directly into him. *What was that? What's happening to me here? What is it with these children? How is it that a man gives up everything and this is the result? Is this what his life is about? Is this what everyone here is about?* He had never entertained thoughts like this before. Giving money away. Losing reputation. For this? It seemed both brilliant and insane at the same time. He shook his head. *What is this place exactly? We're in the middle of nowhere. There's nothing around for miles. And yet I'm questioning everything about myself. I didn't come here for this. I came here to check out a...*

And just like that, Teagen forgot all about what he had just encountered. He greeted the children in his outgoing manner, watched them race off to school, then grabbed his bags and followed Mulli to the open guest dining area.

The children provided their guests with an African dance. Mara was front and centre. Colourful costumes followed by an a cappella choir and drama performances.

After lunch the foursome walked out to the farming area.

"So explain your plan to me, Charles. What's the vision? What's the future? What do you see down the road?"

Mulli paused a moment. Then he explained the greenhouse concept. He discussed the capital cost and how soon the increase in production would recover the initial investment.

Teagen looked out over the farming area. Like all good entrepreneurs he didn't see what was there; he saw was *could* be there. And that glimpse into the future excited him.

"I'll do it, Charles," he said.

Mulli wasn't exactly sure what *it* referred to.

"You send me a proposal that outlines what you're going to do, and I'll get you a big gigantic greenhouse so you can grow your French beans and whatever else you want to sell to Europe. I'm in."

"An entire greenhouse? That is quite a lot of money."

"Well, these are quite a lot of children." Teagen's voice suddenly went quiet. Was that a lull in the conversation? James and Russell had never heard him speak so softly. "And I think you can use the help."

Teagen talked all the way back to the airport. Business. Sports. Business. Africa. More business. When they arrived, Mulli went to the back to get their bags. Teagen grabbed them first, thinking that Mulli would gladly have taken their bags all the way inside if they would have let him. But they carried their own, and Mulli accompanied them to security. James and Russell went through first. Teagen was about to follow when he turned back to Mulli.

"I need to ask you a serious question."

Mulli saw the determination in Teagen's eyes. That confident man he met earlier had now been replaced with someone whose footing seemed to have been taken out from underneath him.

"Do you have any real satisfaction in this?" Teagen asked. "I have to know. You gave up everything and you claim to basically be at God's mercy every second of every day. That's a scary thing, if you ask me. But you were like me once. You had money." He leaned in. His eyes focused right on Mulli. It wouldn't have mattered if there had been an earthquake, Teagen was so desperate for a response that if given the option, he would have sold every last possession he had to get the answer to this question from Mulli. "Do you regret anything of what you have done, or is this the real thing?"

Mulli pressed his lips together, taking in what Teagen had asked. "You have been straightforward with me, and I want to be straightforward with you," Mulli said. "If money is not used to help someone, then it is just paper. Success is fleeting. And image is nothing. Years after we are gone, no one will remember us. And years from now, it will seem like we never even existed down here. My question to you is, what are you living for?"

The extrovert went completely quiet. He had nothing to say. For the first time in his life it occurred to him that everything he had been living for might actually have amounted to nothing. The question at first interested him. But now it was scaring him. Was there something more, something deeper out there? What was he living for anyway?

"I am glad you came," Mulli said. "Remember, it's okay to let go of the life you want to receive the life that God wants to give you."

That reached right inside Teagen. Got to that part of him he wasn't sure even existed.

"There you go again," Teagen said with a laugh, trying to break the tension.

"Another good line." He shook hands with Mulli and turned to leave. But then he stopped and looked back at him. It was as if something Mulli had said caused him to re-evaluate where he was going. And in that moment he was convinced that he was being faced with the most important decision he would ever have to make. His voice became quiet. Suddenly despite all his success he looked like a regular guy. "I'll give that some thought."

CHAPTER 7

The phone call changed everything.

The challenge of finding a way to make MCF sustainable demanded an increasing amount of Mulli's attention. During his business life Mulli could grow his empire by applying for bank loans and grants or re-investing his profits. But after surrendering everything to the Lord, Mulli did not have these options open to him any longer. The decision to let go meant letting go.

So Mulli needed to look for other means to finance his goal of MCF becoming self-reliant. He kept vigilant, knowing there was so much more that could be done if only he had the resources. It was difficult for him. A thorn in his flesh. He was frustrated that so much was within reach if only he had access to capital to realize his vision. The man who could once expand his business operation almost at will now found himself with a dream to expand his mission of changing children's lives, but felt himself hampered by not being able to make it happen. *Where is the money going to come from to fund the sustainability program? How can I find a way to convince people to give? Why isn't it working out the way it's supposed to?*

Around and around these thoughts went in Mulli's head, until a still, small voice spoke to him.

It's okay to trust me, Mulli.

He was suddenly at peace. It was as if a light had been turned on and the darkness suddenly vanished.

I am the Giver, remember? I own the world and everything that lives on it. I have all the natural resources and, most importantly, I have your life. I remember the covenant you made with me. At the bridge. I have not forgotten. I will take care of you, your family and all the work of your hands. For you to live is to be in me. You have dedicated your work one hundred percent to me, for my glory and for my honour. I will provide for your needs. I will reach out my hand to help you. Trust me for the unknown and the unseen. I am always in control, even when I appear not to be.

Mulli felt a wave of relief come over him. This mission was not about him. He knew that. It was about God.

So why shouldn't it work out?

Through prayer and God's favour, Mulli felt assured that God would bless him. He did not know exactly how it would happen, but he was confident that God would bring the sustainability program to a great accomplishment—that others would see the program's worthiness, and that it could be emulated by other groups so that hundreds of thousands could be helped.

Mulli drove from MCF Yatta feeling inspired the way people do when their souls have a renewed focus on God. He arrived at MCF Ndalani.

That's when the phone call came.

His assistant was calling to inform him that an email had come from a man from the West seeking to connect with him. She forwarded the email to Mulli, who read it that evening. The man introduced himself as Fred and indicated that he would like to volunteer at MCF. Mulli appreciated the kind gesture, but because of the number of volunteers already on site, there was no place for him to provide his assistance. Mulli thanked him for his email and replied that it would not suit.

A few weeks later, Fred emailed back, explaining that he understood the situation but wondered if it would be possible for him just to see the ministry first-hand and if he could help support any of Mulli's projects. Fred indicated he had read Mulli's biography and that it had inspired him to want to connect.

Even though Mulli had never met Fred before, and all he really knew about him was what he read in the emails, he decided to send Fred the descriptions of two projects. Fred reviewed them and agreed to fund a poultry farm project and sent the required money. Mulli purchased the chicks, equipment and facilities needed to make the project operational. The eggs were used to feed the children, and the surplus eggs were taken to nearby Matuu and Nairobi for sale as part of the sustainability effort.

A few months later Fred asked to visit Mulli to see first-hand how the project he had funded was making a difference. When Fred and his wife arrived at MCF Yatta they shook hands with Mulli and hugged him as if they had known each other many years.

Sometimes without even meeting someone face-to-face you can become the best of friends.

"Welcome to Mully Children's Family, Yatta," Mulli said.

"Wow!" Fred exclaimed, amazed that he was actually there. Actually on an MCF site. Actually seeing Mulli. "I am so excited to be here. When I got your email saying that I could come visit, it felt like I had received a letter from the pope!"

They toured the school and the farms and then sat down for lunch together with Esther. The four of them discussed the things people talk about when they want to know more about each other's lives. But then the conversation to turned to things of a deeper nature.

"So tell me," Fred began. The tone in his voice shifted. "What kinds of plans do you have in place to expand your sustainability program?"

Mulli was reluctant to respond at first. He didn't normally open up to people about his needs, especially to those who were new to him. But he found encouragement as he recalled the verse from Luke 11:9, "Ask and it will be given to you; seek and you will find; knock and the door will be opened to you." After a long pause, Mulli answered him.

He explained his plans to expand the farm operation and build a facility with new technology. This would help MCF compete with other businesses and farmers, not only in Kenya but also around the world. The plan would be to start with 10 acres of greenhouses with a goal to double this amount in the near future. Mulli had researched all the costs and gave Fred the number. It wasn't a small amount.

Fred liked the idea. Yes, it was a lot of money. But for him it would be money well spent. He turned to his wife to see what she thought. She nodded and told them that it would be a worthy project for their family to support.

"We're going to fund the entire program," Fred said, with a smile so big it reflected the total joy he had in giving.

It amazed Mulli. So many prayers. So many plans. So much wondering as to how it would all come about. And now, here it was. Mulli thanked them for sharing in his work. He watched as they got back into their car to make the journey back to Nairobi.

He felt as if angels had been sent to him.

Help to MCF came in many different forms from people far and near and in varying capacities. A local 75-year-old man who was not able to afford a car or even a bicycle brought a tin of maize to Mulli every month for six months. He was thrilled that children who were once on the street now had a home. He gave Mulli what he could, and he gave from the heart—that precious quality that defines people who love to give without the expectation of receiving something in return.

Whenever Mulli saw him approaching he felt a boost of encouragement. Here was another person who was doing what he was able to make a difference.

"I don't have very much," the man said as he smiled whenever the two of them connected. "But I am happy to give what I can. You gave everything to God. And God will reward you abundantly. You will never lack."

One time he came with a cash gift as well. It wasn't much. A few dollars. But it was what he had. And it was what he was willing to give.

And he did so with incredible joy.

Mulli and a friend of his drove two kilometres down the road from MCF Ndalani to visit Mulli's father and mother, Daudi and Rhoda. Daudi had been an abusive father and husband whose life had been transformed after Mulli forgave him. Now, instead of being an example of a disastrous relationship, Daudi and Rhoda were a beacon of hope to people who came to them for advice and counselling on marriage and other relational issues.

Rhoda told the story of how she nearly died when Mulli, her first child, was born. On December 31, 1949, she went into labour for seven days. In spite of her incredible pain, she could not afford to go to the nearest hospital, which was miles away down a long road in poor condition. There had never been any vehicles in her area and so she would have had to make the arduous journey on foot—an impossibility in her condition. Her husband, Daudi, was away in Nairobi looking for work. As was the custom, other women from the area brought her water from the river and firewood from the forest. They kept her company with great expectation of the child that would be born.

But on January 7 the pain had become so severe that Rhoda fell unconscious. All the women became gripped with fear as they thought Rhoda and her unborn child would die. Rhoda's sister-in-law, Muthikwa, who took care of Rhoda because Daudi had nothing to support his wife, and Rhoda's mother, Ndondo, sent a young boy to find Rhoda's father, Lila, to bring him to Rhoda's side to say his final farewell.

The boy found him drinking with friends. Lila came, wrapped in his blanket, carrying his gourd—a large carved-out fruit with a hard shell—filled with his traditional alcohol. He stumbled in singing some irrelevant song, half gone in his stupor. But things for drunk Lila became serious when he saw his daughter lying there about to leave this world.

"Will my daughter die?" he asked.

He stopped. So did the world. He stood there and felt the helplessness that comes with not being able to change the disaster unfolding in front of him. Even all the alcohol in his system could not prevent him from feeling the despair for the state his daughter was in.

In a strange move, he stepped forward and, taking in some alcohol, spat it on Rhoda as a blessing. As a father's last plea, he said, "Daughter of Lila, I would like you to give birth to a boy."

And, sure enough, at some point Rhoda came to and gave birth to Charles Mutua Mulli. The name *Mutua* means "a child who has lived too long in the womb." The women shouted with joy over the news.

As Rhoda relayed the story to Mulli it shocked him to notice how close he and his mother had come to death. How close his siblings had come to not being born. How close MCF came to not being in existence. Rhoda then told the story of how she and Daudi took Mulli when he was six months old to Nthoki, his great-grandmother on his father's side. As was the custom in their culture, Mulli was to be taken back to his ancestral land for blessing. Daudi and Rhoda travelled a great distance and arrived at Muuma Andu, which means *where the people come from.*

Nthoki was suffering from throat cancer when Daudi and Rhoda came to visit. "We have come to see you," Daudi told Nthoki, "and to ask for blessings from you and especially for our son."

"Let me hold this child," Nthoki said.

Rhoda handed Mulli to her. When Nthoki held Mulli in her arms she wept with joy, saying, "This child will be the blessing of our entire family, and whoever will be with him will be blessed. Thank you for bringing your son. May God bless you and bless this child abundantly as he continues to grow, that he will become a leader and a source of light to you and your family."

When Rhoda finished telling the story she turned to Mulli and looked at him with the kind of compassionate eyes that are reserved for a mother and her son.

"You must understand that whatever you are seeing in your life, even the person that you have come to be today, this is all by the power of God. You were blessed by your great-grandmother, and I believe you have received all that she had for the entire family in terms of blessings."

It made sense to Mulli. None of this was his own doing. Not the success of MCF. Not the children who were rescued. Not his confidence in God. He had been uniquely designed for this role. He had been blessed to be able to rejoice in great moments of victory, to stand firm when times of testing came, and to be a blessing to each person he met.

None of this was his own idea. He could not take credit for it.

And he was good with that.

Because he enjoyed the thrill of being able to walk in the works that God had prepared in advance for him to do.

And to be used by God to help others do the same.

Children in IDP School line up for lunch provided by MCF.

People line up for food from MCF at the IDP Camp in Eldoret.

Charles Mulli serving food.

Mulli praying with victims at the Internally Displaced People Camp Eldoret.

Charles Mulli with rescued children.

Rescued children at MCF.

People from the community employed at MCF.

Mulli at the IDP Eldoret.

The IDP Camp in Eldoret.

CHAPTER 8

It felt like someone had stuck a knife into her shoulder.

Esther lifted her arm to ease the pain, but nothing she did brought her any relief. She stood in the kitchen trying to stir supper and dropped the ladle. She let her arm hang down by her side and then sat down in a chair. She breathed in, hoping the increase in oxygen would help her cope with the throbbing that ran through her neck into her head.

But it only made it worse.

She stepped outside and smiled at the children as they waved to her on their way to class. Some of them ran up to her to give her a hug. She bent down and felt their little arms around her. As light as they were, the extra weight caused to her wince. They ran off, and Esther went to her bed and lay down.

Mulli came home and saw her in distress.

"Esther, are you all right?"

She was now. At least internally. Mulli had the rare gift of being able to enter a room and put people at ease. And no one knew that better than Esther. She remembered the first time she saw him. Her mother had fallen ill, and Esther, a teenager, took her place working in a field where Mulli served as the field clerk. He came by to record the names of everyone working that day. She looked up, and their eyes met. And in that moment everything changed. There is such a thing as love at first sight. When it happens you know it. An instantaneous connection. Even without any words being spoken, something deep inside each of them communicated to the other. And in spite of Esther's desperate financial situation, seeing Mulli that day brought her peace.

And oddly enough, it was the same feeling now.

She looked up at him as he came to her side.

"I am not that well," she said, understating the fact. "My shoulder is so sore I cannot even stand."

Mulli looked closer. Her shoulder had become completely swollen. It didn't look like a bite. An infection of sorts? An injury, perhaps? But did it really matter what it was? She was sick and needed healing. Mulli got down on his knees. Somehow when he was on his knees he felt a closeness to God that was strengthened by humility. He placed his hand on Esther's shoulder. He became quiet. Then he spoke to God as if he were standing right there in the room with them.

"Father, you see the situation. You know the pain my dear wife is in. I am asking you, God, to intervene. To intervene in her life and to heal her and make her well."

He expected her to get better. Believed that she would recover. Yet after he had prayed her shoulder remained as bad as it had been.

If anything, it looked like it had gotten worse.

He took her to a hospital in Nairobi, where x-rays, blood samples and countless injections did absolutely nothing to help her. The pain became so severe that Esther could not stand, could not walk, could hardly sleep, and the only thing left that she could do was cry.

At various times in the day she would call out for Mulli and he would pray over her, yet there was no change. Back and forth to the hospital, prayer after prayer after prayer, and the only thing that changed was the intensity of pain, which went from unbearable to excruciating.

"Why am I not getting better?" Esther asked one evening. She lay on her back. Motionless was best. Even the slightest bit of movement and the daggers would intensify. She looked up at the ceiling, blinked to get the tears out of her eyes and felt the despair people feel when they have exhausted every possible option and find no relief. No comfort. And no hope.

Mulli sat down on the side of the bed. He didn't just see his wife's pain. He felt it. Felt what it was like to be hurting. Felt what it was like to be in such agony.

"I don't know," Mulli said.

"Am I not praying right?" Esther asked. Desperation takes away every pretense, and she had reached the point where she was willing to examine any possible reason for the problem.

"Of course you are," Mulli replied.

"It's not enough."

"We are trusting in God. We are praying. But we are also believing. That is the key. Not just to ask. But to believe."

"Then why isn't it happening?"

She raised a good point. It caused Mulli to think back to when he had prayed for one of his rescued children, who lay dying in a hospital in Eldoret. He prayed for him, too, and then felt the life drain out of the boy right there as he was praying. And he remembered the countless other times when he had prayed for healing and saw people recover right in front of his eyes. There were no easy answers.

"We will continue to trust."

"Maybe I am not believing correctly?"

Mulli placed his hand on her forehead. He knelt down beside her as he so often had done. "Father, we are at the wall. We have reached the end. All I desire now is for you to take care of my wife. Now is the time. There is nothing else I can do."

He felt her wincing in pain. She clenched her teeth together and sucked in air as best she could, making a wheezing sound.

Mulli squished his eyes tighter. He prayed harder than any of the previous times. It felt like he was digging an endless tunnel. And then suddenly it was as if he felt a hand reaching through from the other side.

"God," Mulli continued, "my wife belongs to you. I only depend on you. You have healed many people, and I present this need to you with earnest prayer."

He was so intense in his prayer that it took Esther saying his name a second time for him to hear it. He looked up.

It's been said that when something happens repeatedly a person gets used to it, and it loses its initial thrill. But for Mulli, the wonder of miracles only grew in intensity. He had seen hundreds of miracles. Children healed. Demons cast out. People saved from hell. And every time it felt like he was just that much closer to the One he would be spending eternity with.

Which is why he was so amazed when he saw the relief in Esther's eyes.

She raised her arm, for the first time in months, carefully, as if unsure how to move it after such a long time of not being used. Normal felt strange. She breathed in, and just like that, the memory of her illness faded away and it was as if she had been well all along.

She stood up out of bed and put her other arm around Mulli.

"Thank you, God," Mulli whispered. "You have done this. You alone have done this."

"I too thank you, Father," Esther said. "I thank you for your help."

Mulli smiled, then he laughed.

Esther grinned. "Would you like to go for a walk?"

It was evening. Getting late. Time for bed. But Mulli agreed. Esther had been in bed long enough.

It was strange. All of it. No one had any idea what was happening.

One of Mulli's daughters, Ndondo, had been nominated by World Vision in Africa to represent Kenya. A choir was formed from 52 countries and travelled for three months, touring countries in Asia. They met prime ministers, talked about peace and reconciliation and had an excellent time. That was all fine. But it was when she returned to Kenya that everything started to go wrong.

She began to feel pain in her left eye. Nothing terrible, not at first. It was a nagging feeling like that of a headache starting. But the odd thing about it was that it spread. From her left eye it went to the left part of her mouth. It didn't hurt. She would have preferred if it did. She would have preferred anything to this. Instead of pain, she felt nothing.

It spread like ice water down her leg, immobilizing her. It was as if someone had flicked a switch to turn the left side of her body off.

Mulli and Esther took her to a hospital in Eldoret. They prayed the whole way there, pleading yet again for God to intervene. It would be so much easier if these disasters didn't happen in the first place. And as much as Esther's pulse raced and as much as it filled Mulli's mind, he had come to accept the unknown as commonplace. Somehow everything working out okay in life, and being trouble free had a tendency to make Mulli feel farther from God. A constant barrage of difficulties, his daughter's health being right at the top, gave him the drive to depend on God. And through depending on God, by choosing to trust and refuse the lies of the evil one, Mulli came to see the trials as the very means God would use to strengthen him.

Yet it was uncanny how, despite all the obstacles he had faced, when new trials came they seemed to be directed at places in his life where he was the most vulnerable.

When they arrived, the hospital placed Ndondo under observation. By the second day her speech was slurred. By the third day she was referred to a nerve and stroke specialist, who said the condition was so severe that she had to go to Nairobi for treatment. And by the fourth day her entire left side was paralyzed and she was unable to speak.

They brought Ndondo back to their home in Eldoret. Mulli was taking courses at Mission College at the time and went to the principal's office to explain that he needed time off while he took his daughter to Nairobi. He sat in a chair, looked at the clock and felt the way fathers feel when they wish they could trade places with their ailing child.

He took out his cellphone and dialled his friend's phone number. When his friend answered, Mulli couldn't get the words out. He bit his lower lip. He looked up.

"Hello, Sammy."

Mulli's voice quivered, and like all best friends, Sammy could pick out the concern in Mulli's tone. Those two words were more than Sammy needed. He didn't say anything to Mulli. Best friends don't have to. He just waited, hoping that he would be able to help his friend with whatever was on his heart.

"I need help," Mulli said.

"What do you want me to do for you?" Sammy asked.

Mulli tried to take in a breath. If it had been him who was half paralyzed instead, he would have felt a whole lot better. If he could transfer whatever it was in Ndondo's body into himself, he'd be relieved. But there was such a grief that Mulli felt, a tightness in his chest, that it made him wonder how he was going to get through this call.

"Can you pray for my daughter?"

"Of course," he said. Mulli had the distinct impression that Sammy would have answered that way regardless of what Mulli asked of him.

Mulli explained the situation. Sammy agreed to take his wife and a Nigerian friend to Mulli's home and begin praying for Ndondo until Mulli got there.

"Thank you," Mulli whispered. It was the best he could do given the circumstance.

Mulli hung up the phone and leaned forward to begin praying. Then he got off his chair, knelt on the ground, folded his hands on the wooded seat and pleaded for God once again to intervene.

Meanwhile, at the Mulli home in Eldoret, Sammy, his wife and his Nigerian friend met with Esther and Ndondo in the room where the children normally met for devotions. Ndondo stood as best she could, confused, worried, anxious, yet trusting that somehow God was there and that God was able. Sammy began praying for her, followed by Esther and Sammy's wife.

Back at the principal's office Mulli continued to pray for his daughter to be healed. It was a relief that his friend had come to his aid, that he had come to help him in his time of trouble.

The Nigerian man began praying quietly over Ndondo. But then he became louder and stronger as he quoted verses he had memorized.

"I am the Lord your God who heals you. Surely our sicknesses he himself bore and our pains he carried. By his stripes we are healed. And when evening had come they brought to him many who were demon possessed and he cast out the spirits with a word and he healed all who were sick in order what was spoken through the prophet Isaiah might be fulfilled, saying he took our infirmities and carried our diseases away."

Ndondo crashed to the ground. It was as if she had previously been held up by strings like a marionette, only to have the puppeteer suddenly removed. Her eyes closed and she began to kick out her arms and legs in a violent motion like she was being electrocuted.

The team continued to pray—those in person and Mulli, unaware of what was happening, back at the school. For over half an hour Ndondo shook uncontrollably. And then suddenly she stopped. Everything became still. Ndondo opened her eyes as if from a nap and wondered where the last 30 or so minutes had gone. She stood up, on her own, and shifted her weight onto her left leg.

The others watched in amazement. Her drooping eye was healthy again. Her lip didn't hang down anymore. She didn't have a limp. She looked well again.

Completely well.

Mulli drove back from the school ready to take her to the hospital in Nairobi. He came to the back door and saw Ndondo and the others sitting together.

"Everything is going to be fine," Mulli said.

"That is great to hear," Ndondo replied.

Her voice. It had been four days of not hearing it, and the second his ears registered her words his brain connected what had happened.

Again.

Mulli came nearer to her. "You are all right?"

She smiled.

Mulli raised his eyes. "You are all right!"

She smiled bigger. He ran up to her and hugged her. He felt her wrap her arms around him. Father and daughter. It didn't get much better than this. Didn't get much better than being able to feel God's work in his arms. Like the pages of the Bible alive and well right in front of him. Another challenge. Another miracle.

It never got tiresome.

CHAPTER 9

He was just as curious as everyone else as to why he was called to the classroom this early in the morning.

He had not been told very much, had not even been told who the others would be. He showed up, and there they were. All Mulli said to him the night before was that he wanted him to be there. There was no questioning. No thinking *What am I getting myself into if I say yes?* And no asking for more information as if what he might hear back would be a condition of whether he would accept. Without any hesitation, the young man just said "Of course" to Mulli.

Really, anything for the man who rescued him from being beaten to near death each night by his alcoholic father.

He had gotten up from his bed in his dormitory and made his way through the dark of the MCF compound. A heavy fog had enveloped the entire Ndalani MCF area, giving it the impression of a captivating medieval setting. He walked faster, wanting to make sure he arrived on time. He reached the classroom and opened the door.

That was the first time he saw them.

"Welcome, Felix," Mulli said.

Felix took a seat off to the side near the front. He waited as a group of a dozen of his grade 11 classmates gathered with him to find out why Mulli had called them here. Ndondo and Mueni spoke with Mulli at the front until the last person entered the room.

It became quiet. It felt different than other meetings. Before a choir or drama practice or even an exam, people talked, people felt a certain sense of anticipation. But this was different. Everyone was still. It was as if their consciences knew something important was about to happen, even though they had been told nothing.

Mulli cleared his throat, smiled, and in the moment before he said his first word, Felix had the unmistakable feeling that this would be one of the moments in his life he would remember forever.

"Thank you for coming," Mulli said. "I hope you all had a good sleep."

They nodded. Some slept better than others. Even many years after having been rescued, there were those who still had evenings when the memories came back. Those nights of being on the street. The beatings. The former addictions. The seemingly endless feeling of hopelessness. Every now and again flashes of their former lives would come knocking at their doors. *This is who you really are. You are worthless. You are nothing. Nobody who lived that kind of life could ever become something different.* But the counselling by Mulli and pastors at MCF had taught them to combat those impulses. Using verses to stand on, they defended themselves and resisted the temptation to give in to believing those voices.

Especially late at night when everyone else was asleep and their only comfort was turning to a God who would keep them safe in their new identity in him.

"I have brought you here because we have a special assignment."

All eyes focused on Mulli. If some of the youth had bleary eyes coming into the room, they were now all completely awake, wondering what their mission would be.

"We have worked very hard to help people here in Kenya. But there are many, many people who need to hear the gospel. And so I have selected you to join me in going to Tanzania, where we will minister to the people in the slums."

Everyone, Felix in particular, felt a sudden rush of anticipation fill the room, which was curiously accompanied by a sense of both adventure and apprehension that came with venturing into the unknown.

"This will not be easy," he said. "We must prepare. And the way we prepare is by prayer. God loves us. He is strong. But there is an enemy who opposes us in everything we do. And he is not overcome by our strength or by our mind or even by our will. Evil is overcome only through Jesus Christ."

As excited as Felix became over the news, there was an uneasiness that grew around him. At first he dismissed it as nerves. But the longer he listened, the more sure he became of the presence of an outside force whispering into his mind about the task he would be undertaking.

You won't make any difference in this mission. You aren't qualified. You aren't like the others. The others are good students. They are bright. They didn't do what you did on the streets.

"Ndondo and Mueni will teach you many verses that you will have at the ready. The attacks will come from many directions, and our only chance is the Word of God."

Felix could relate. This was their first meeting and already the assault against him had begun.

"Remember, when you are going into a mission you cannot have a double mind. You might miss having a comfortable place to sleep, you will be with different cultures, you will face challenges that you have not seen before. But like Jesus' disciples you must carry on. Check your heart to make sure you are in constant prayer. If you humble yourself during preparation, God will exalt you in the field."

As if. Not you, Felix. You will waste your time in preparation, and when you come to the field you will accomplish nothing. You will feel the emptiness of failure on your return trip. Can you really make a difference? Can you really pray and expect something to change? You? You of all people? Prayer is for holy people. Power is for the righteous. It is not for you. You are not special, Felix. You are average. And average people accomplish nothing.

"You are set apart," Mulli continued. "You are holy because God makes you holy. This began when each of you turned your life over to Jesus Christ. You had previously heard of Jesus. But it was not enough to simply know him. Even the devil knows Jesus."

That's true, Felix. I do know him. Do you? Do you really know him? How can you be sure that you do? Don't you just know about him? Can you really say that you are his? You aren't, are you?

Felix shifted in his chair. He tried to stay focused on Mulli, pushed himself to keep his attention on what Mulli was saying.

"You decided to give your life to him. And now you can be confident that what Jesus did for you he did for everyone. We want to bring this message of hope to the people of Tanzania. He died on the cross for you, and that is all we depend on. When we have faith in Christ and obey his Word we have nothing to fear."

Not so, Felix. You will be afraid. You will be terrified. You will come to know fear that you have never known before.

For two months the team met for prayer and worship each morning from 6:00 to 7:30. Then, each evening from 4:00 to 5:30, they prepared songs, practiced acrobatics and karate demonstrations, learned evangelism techniques and memorized verses. The team met for one final prayer, then boarded the van and drove 18 hours to Dar es Salem, translated as *the City of Peace*, which was ironic given that the Mbangala slum where they were headed was a picture of one of the most disastrous locations on earth.

They parked their van and walked into the slum. This was it. This was what all the preparation was for. Felix should have felt prepared. He should have felt like an athlete ready to take to the field after a long time of training. But instead, he felt unsure.

It's just nerves, he told himself. *It will be all right.*

No, Felix. It will not be all right. Do you have any idea where you are? Do you have any idea what I am capable of doing?

Greater is he who is in you than he who is in the world.

We'll see, Felix. We'll see.

Felix hurried to catch up with the team. He was no stranger to poverty. He'd lived and breathed it for years. But even among the poorest of the poor there are classes and distinctions. This was about as poor as someone could become. A consistent dull grey and brown depicted the entire slum. It looked like one desperate area was copied and pasted as far as Felix could see. In every direction, for what seemed like miles, the slum repeated the same image of a tattered sheet-metal roof with mud walls. Most huts didn't even have a door. Doors were for the wealthy. Here they just had tattered mats that hung down. There was little food. Maybe, maybe, one meal a day. Two meals a day were completely out of the question. Those who hoped that two handfuls of food each day could be possible dreamed of a realm so wealthy and so unimaginable that it could never actually be real.

The roads in the slum were barely wide enough for four people across to walk through. The ditches were filled with human waste and gave off such a pungent odour that it was impossible for the first few minutes to think about anything else. Plastic bags filled the ground, making it look like the slum was part of a massive garbage dump. Off to the side children drank from a stagnant pool of black water. Smoke rose up from fires used for making coal to sell for cooking.

But more than the dilapidated huts, more than the unforgiving and relentless odours, more than the disease-ridden and excrement-filled ditches that ran along both sides of the road, the most depressing part of the slum was the vacant and destitute look in the eyes of every man, woman and child in the community.

The people of the slum looked at the MCF team, staring at them with expressions indicating they had never considered that change could be possible. Hope was a foreign concept, a fool's gold for those who would take their eyes off the immediate need of survival to risk certain disaster by pretending that life could be different.

In the sweltering heat that worsened the stench, making it all the more difficult to breathe, the team visited people from hut to hut, speaking with them, giving them food, inviting them to the program they would be sharing. In the first day they served approximately 2,000 children with meals—a welcome comfort to many of them who were living with grandmothers because their parents had died of HIV/AIDS and they had nowhere else to turn. There were many sick children, some of whom were forced to steal or work as prostitutes to earn whatever meagre income they could to pay for food.

In a community that was largely Muslim, Mulli invited people to hear the gospel. He spoke in a simple church that was packed out and overflowing out the back, with still more people gathered outside near the windows, desperate to hear what Mulli had to say.

"Jesus loves you," Mulli said. "He is the Son of God, and he took your place and my place on the cross so that we could have eternal life. The Bible teaches that salvation is found in no one else."

Felix sat in the middle, watching the crowd. *How is Daddy Mulli able to preach like that? How is he able to speak and so many people listen?*

"There can be hindrances to us coming to know Jesus. Sometimes we think that we don't need him. Other times we may think that he doesn't care. Or we may think that he can't help us."

A man sitting near Felix began to grind his teeth. At first it seemed like nothing too far out of the ordinary. But the grinding continued, back and forth and back and forth. Felix angled his head to catch a glimpse at the man who was making that disgusting sound. And what he saw ran a chill down his spine. The man's eyes looked hollow, like they were shells with nothing but emptiness inside. His skin looked old even though he was middle-aged. He began to clear to his throat. But what started as the sound of a cough grew deeper, louder, more sinister. The sound of the voice coming from the man was so low that Felix wondered if it was normal. If it was a sound particular to this culture.

If it was human at all.

"I want to pray for anyone who has been troubled by evil spirits."

In the blink of an eye all pandemonium broke out. It was as if Mulli's words were the catalyst to let havoc wreak loose on the church. Felix heard the man near him scream in such a high pitched shrill that it froze Felix in his seat. The man shouted again and fell to the ground. People pushed back to get away from this maniac. Others ran to the door, desperate for a way to get out, thinking that whatever was inside the man might be contagious and come out and reach them, too. But Mulli, as if rehearsed, walked to the man. No fear. No panic. No anxiety.

Mulli bent down. The man's eyes had rolled back, leaving only the creepy whites to stare up at him. His faced contorted in different expressions. One moment he was laughing like a hysterical lunatic, the next he was crying with streams of tears, then he was filled with rage.

Mulli instructed the team to sing *There Is Power in the Blood*. At the first mention of the word *blood* the man went into such a convulsion that it seemed he was being stretched out on a medieval rack of torture.

"You demons have to flee in the name of Jesus Christ!" Mulli shouted.

The man rolled on the ground, struggling like an escape artist to break free from being bound by ropes.

Mulli kept shouting. Felix sang as best he could, feeling the security of singing praises instead of having to cast out a demon.

On and on and on it went. "Demons, you must leave him in the name of Jesus!"

And then, with a blood curdling scream that hurt everyone's ears, the man shook like he was experiencing a terrible convulsion. Then he stopped altogether.

Mulli laid his hands on the man's forehead and prayed, and the man's eyes rolled forward.

"You have been freed," Mulli said.

The man looked up at Mulli. He felt like he was a different person. It was as if an identity inside of him had been eliminated and he was only now remembering that he had once been someone else. He remembered the excruciating pain of seeing his wife and child die due to illness. To cope with the hurt he had turned to drink and had exhausted all his money on booze. He had tried to escape the unbearable depression that came because of a past mistake that could not be undone. He had felt that life was intolerable and that alcohol would be the only solace to deal with the ongoing doom in his spirit. *If only I would have picked a different medical clinic. Maybe the staff there could have helped my wife and child. If only I would have been smarter and taken better risks, I could have become successful and been able to pay for their recovery. If only. If only. If only.* That was when he heard the voice for the first time.

They are gone, and you will never be happy again. You will be all alone. Your wife and child were all that you had, and now you have nothing.

It had taken weeks, but eventually the voice was no longer that of someone else. That voice merged with his own, making it difficult to distinguish between his thoughts and the other's thought—if even there was a difference anymore.

For years it had gone on. The voice was like a guest in his home that had been there so long it was impossible to remember life without him.

But now he did. Now he remembered.

And he felt just as empty now as he did back then.

"Do you want to surrender your life to Jesus Christ?" Mulli asked.

The man hesitated. He wondered. He sat up and felt what it was like to think with a clear mind again.

"You need to know whom you are going to follow," Mulli said. "Will it be Jesus or Mohammed?"

The man opened his lips, but no sound came out. He took in a breath. He was about to speak when he stopped and a look of horror came over his eyes.

Jesus will not help you. He is just a man. A man like any other. He taught good things. But he cannot help you. He is just the same as any other choice. There are many options for you to choose, and they are all just as valid.

"Jesus said 'I am the way and the truth and the life. No man comes to the Father except through me,'" Mulli said.

The man nodded. He closed his eyes. Then he exhaled. His facial muscles relaxed. When he looked at Mulli again, he was finally rid of whatever was after him.

"I want to follow Jesus," he said.

Mulli knelt down beside the man. "Then pray this after me. Lord Jesus, I know that you died for me." The man did not answer. Mulli stopped and looked at him. "The Bible says if you confess with your mouth that Jesus is Lord and believe in your heart that God raised him from the dead, you will be saved. You need to speak the words," Mulli said. "Is that all right?"

The man cleared his throat. This time it sounded normal.

"Thank you, Lord Jesus, for dying for me," Mulli said. The man repeated it. Mulli continued, "I ask you to forgive my sins and to live in my heart and make me your child. Please put me in the Book of Life."

The man said it. The crowd, those who were brave enough to withstand the madness, watched, unmoving, as if they had been frozen in time. When they saw the man was in his right frame of mind, they breathed a collective sigh of amazement. Including Felix.

After the service the man who had been exorcised talked with Mulli. It seemed so nonchalant considering what had just happened. Two men standing together talking, as if the man had always been this way.

As the group left to return to their hotel for the evening, Felix approached Mulli.

"Daddy Mulli, that was simply incredible. The demon…it actually left. It obeyed you."

"That is the power of God."

"Do you believe anyone could do that?"

"What does the Bible say? What does it tell you?"

"It says that greater works than these will we do."

"That is the choice you have to make," Mulli said. "You can believe the Bible for what it says, or you can find excuses for why you think parts of the Bible do not apply today. Me, I know the entire Bible is for today. All of it. Otherwise, how would I face the challenges that come my way?"

"I don't think I could ever preach and have that kind of result."

Mulli smiled. He put his arm around Felix. "Life often does not come down to what you think. But it always comes down to what you believe. Tell me, what do you believe?"

"I believe in God's healing power," Felix said. "And I believe that you preached in a way that made a difference in that man's life forever."

"Good. I am glad you liked it," Mulli said. "Because tomorrow night it will be your turn."

The next evening, after a long day of serving people with food, with evangelism, with counselling, the MCF team continued to smile, despite their tiredness, and arrived at the church for the service. It had been a nerve-racking day for Felix. He was nervous yesterday because of the new surroundings. But now, he not only had the mission of caring for people in a foreign land on his mind but the responsibility of preparing for a sermon that he was not sure he was qualified to give.

They started the meeting, and after the singing the team sat down and Felix came to the front. He clutched his Bible in both hands and looked out to the crowd. Were there more people here now than a few minutes ago?

It won't work. You are not Mulli. You are regular. You will have no success here.

"I want to bring you a message of encouragement."

Just sit down and ask Mulli to come up. You are no help here. Don't embarrass your team. We all know your Daddy Mulli is more capable. If you want results, let him come to the front.

Felix opened his Bible. His fingers trembled as he searched for the right verse.

Sit down, Felix.

But Felix didn't. His mind suddenly felt confused. All those verses he had memorized were hard to recall. Even the simple ones seemed impossible to access. He found the verse.

"The Bible says, 'I am the Lord, your healer.'"

Felix spoke as best he knew how. And suddenly, that irritating voice vanished. Gone altogether. It was replaced with a calmness and confidence he had not know before. He invited people who needed healing to come to the front. Many came, including a woman in her fifties who had a terrible pain in her hip. She limped and struggled and made little progress until someone from the crowd stood up to help her.

"Can I pray for you?" Felix asked. She nodded. It was the best she could manage. She would have answered him, but the agony was too intense.

Felix laid his hands on her hip and prayed for God to take the pain away. In an instant the woman fell down to the ground and began to cry. She stayed that way for half an hour, until she stood to her feet. Someone came to her side to help her, but she let go of the person. She took a step to the side. Then she stepped to the other side. She bent down, waited to see if there would be any pain and then came up again. She smiled. She tried a short jump and marvelled that nothing hurt. Her smile grew wider.

Felix's mouth dropped open.

The woman jumped and then ran to the back of the church as fast as she could. She clapped in excitement. Others shouted and clapped. She thanked Felix for praying and then ran out, thanking God for healing her, as the others watched her in amazement.

After the program the team walked back together under the Tanzanian night sky. It was the coolest feeling for Felix. Here he was with other rescued street children sharing stories about how they had helped others on the street. Felix listened as he heard the joy from the others about what God had done. But not everyone was happy.

What happened with that woman tonight was just luck. Even the broken clock is right twice a day. It has nothing to do with—

Be quiet.

I will not be quiet. You are average and you are nothing and—

I am not listening to you. Goodbye.

That evening as Felix went to bed he thought about the woman who had been healed, about the man the night before who had a demon cast out of him and about the thousands of children who had been given food and medicine.

But mostly he thought about how an average guy like him could be used in such an extraordinary way.

CHAPTER 10

Exactly how do you decide which children you rescue and which ones you leave in the slum? It was never an easy decision for Mulli, and he had constantly turned the right to choose over to God. The awesome responsibility of a child's future would be too much for anyone to bear. There were over two and a half million vulnerable children, including street children, in Kenya alone who were being abused in every way imaginable, many of whom would never hear the words *I love you*, at least not in any meaningful way. They could be found in cities, in towns, around shopping centres, in slums. Twelve-year-old girls carrying their babies, begging for help, living in a world that only understood the cruelties of life. Young children pleading in the streets. They were everywhere to be seen.

For those who wanted to see them.

And for every child who was rescued a thousand more waited for their turn. Though most of them would never have the opportunity to go to school and study math or statistics, their life experience had taught them well about the nature of probability in that only a very few of them could count on the mercies of others.

Mulli knelt down at his bed and prayed for direction about which children to take into his family. He would be leading a team into Kipsongo today, a slum as dirty as and likely more violent than the one they visited in Tanzania. Mully Children's Family homes in Kenya provided an oasis to nearly two thousand children, each one of them previously on a collision course with destitution. But they had been rescued, and word about MCF spread. Children who were previously not chosen knew what was at stake when the man they called Daddy came to the slum.

If selling everything and risking all to start a rescue ministry for street children required Mulli to lean on the wisdom of God, then so did having a listening ear to hear his call about which ones to take.

And which ones to leave behind.

Having the unique combination of peace and confidence flood his soul, Mulli stood up and joined the rest of the team. Many volunteers from all over the world came to MCF to donate time, money and talents to the Mullis' work. A team from the West joined him as they boarded a van to Kitale.

The Kipsongo slum in Kitale is inhabited by a nomadic tribe, many of whom are addicted to strong alcohol like *chang'aa* and *busa*. Few of them go to school. They wear little clothing. Their faces and bodies are constantly dirty. The people have little understanding of hygiene. After losing a tribal fight in a hot and dry area of Kenya, the Turkana people came to Kitale to dwell in small makeshift huts made out of paper and plastic bags. With barely enough room to stand in, the huts were about as wide as they were tall, and any serious rain would seep through onto the ground.

People from surrounding villages and cities refused to lend a helping hand to the Turkana. They were seen as a cursed people, lazy, and ones who would only spend any handout on more alcohol, thereby making a bad situation even worse.

When people saw the Mully Children's Family logo on the van they came running out, shouting, "Mulli! Mulli!" When the team stepped out of the van, they sensed the difference between this greeting and the greeting the MCF children gave whenever Mulli came home.

The greeting here was of joy, but a different kind. There was urgency in their plea. And the excitement was not so much one of thanksgiving as it was of expectation.

Those making their first visit to Kipsongo were overcome with the destitution of the area. There is no preparation for the onslaught poverty makes on the senses, especially for those who have not seen it in person before. The smell was so bad that at the start some members of the team subconsciously breathed in short bursts through their mouths, trying to avoid the stench. The dirty, cramped huts were built so close to each other that it seemed as if a bulldozer had rammed them together to make room for still more people in the overcrowded slum.

At the mention of Mulli's name, people poured in from all directions for even the slightest bit of food or clothing that could make their next 24 hours that much more bearable. The crowd pressed around them with such expectation that it created a new category for the newcomers of how to understand poverty.

It was desperation personified.

And it was epidemic.

There was something deeper than the five senses that permeated the group. It wasn't something they could point directly to and say, *There it is.* But it was a feeling of uncertainty that gripped them all. They were in foreign territory. If something were to go wrong here, if one or more villagers decided to attack them, if a riot broke out and people began fighting, then the entire group of them could be killed, their bodies disposed of, and it would be a long time before anyone would figure out what had happened.

If ever.

The team set up and handed out bread and sodas. Mulli spoke with people as they were eating and asked how he could help them. Mulli normally rescued anywhere from two to eight or more children at a time. Sometimes he would sponsor children in a village to go to school or arrange to bring clothing to people or pay hospital fees for those needing medical attention.

Once they had finished eating, Mulli prayed for them. The MCF team sang a series of songs, followed by Mulli offering a word of encouragement. This was a difficult group to speak to at the best of times. Even as Mulli was preaching, people would shout out that they wanted money or more food. In spite of this, there were many who listened as Mulli shared John 3:16: "For God so loved the world that he gave his one and only Son, that whoever believes in him shall not perish but have eternal life."

Mulli saw a drunkard staggering through the crowd. He coughed as he pushed people aside. Mulli assumed he was trying to sit closer to the front, but the man came right up to him. He wore a torn shirt. His eyes were glazed over with a yellow tinge. And his breath reeked so badly of alcohol that Mulli had to stop preaching.

"I will be with you in a moment," Mulli said.

But the man refused to leave. He grabbed onto Mulli's sleeve and pulled.

"Let's go. Let's go."

"I am not finished yet," Mulli replied. "Please sit down."

But the man persisted. It was a dangerous proposition. In a slum like this someone could lead Mulli anywhere to steal whatever he had, kill him and dump his body in the ditch.

Mulli agreed to go and took with him some of the team members. He followed the man through a maze of huts that only a local would be able to navigate. The drunkard held onto Mulli, his breath a constant reminder of the shape he was in. The man kept repeating "Let's go, let's go" as if the words held power over life and death.

They arrived at a dilapidated hut. A stench similar to rotting garbage in the sun filled their nostrils.

"Inside," the drunkard begged. "Inside."

Mulli studied the man's expression. As drunk as he was, there was earnestness in those sickly eyes of his. Mulli bent down to go inside, and what he saw shocked him.

At the back of the tent he saw what appeared to be a blanket. But as he looked closer he saw a thin, bony skeleton image. It was so horrific that it did not even look human. Mulli edged his way closer. The body lay unmoving. A sick, disturbing sight.

Then an eye blinked. The faintest sound of a breath reached Mulli's ears.

O God. This child is still alive.

"Where is the mother?" Mulli asked.

A woman from the village pushed through the crowd to say that the mother was dead. The slum had no resources to help, and so the child was left to die. From what Mulli could tell, the child had hours to live. He laid his hand on the girl's head.

"God, I want to give thanks to you for having brought me to this area. I pray you will be glorified and that people will see your glory through this child. Bless this child and give your healing. And once she gets healed I pray that she will be a missionary to serve you. Save her so she may serve you. I pray for travelling mercies as I take her to Eldoret Hospital."

Mulli put his hands under the girl's neck and back. It felt no heavier than lifting paper, as if she weighed nothing at all. He pulled her up.

The child screamed in pain. It sounded more like a small animal crying out than a human being. Faintly, they heard her calling out, "Water. Water."

The woman provided a cloth to wrap the child in. As Mulli took her to the van he chose to rescue the daughter of the woman, a sixteen-year-old named Eunice, who would also prove helpful in understanding the language of the dying child.

Mulli thanked the drunkard, and the team drove off to Eldoret Hospital.

The team tried to provide her with water, but the child was so weak she could barely drink.

When they arrived the first clinical nurse saw the child and was too afraid to take action. She called the doctor, who came in and immediately took a blood sample and brought water for the child. People crowded around her, ready to help in whatever way possible.

Eunice looked through the rush of people, seeing only flashes of the young child as people moved back and forth.

"Her name is Lilian," Eunice said, wanting people to at least know her name in the event that the child would not survive.

"Water. Water," Lilian continued to plead.

Even the slightest move of her arm created tremendous pain for Lilian, causing her to cry out in agony.

"We are fortunate that you brought her in when you did," the doctor said. She worked with an incredible combination of grace and decisiveness. "Twenty-four hours later and this child would certainly be dead."

As Mulli watched he prayed again for her.

He had done everything he could.

He deposited money with the hospital to cover all expenses. "I will be back often to check up on her," Mulli said. "And I will pay any costs."

Mulli saw Lilian regularly. Many had guessed that she was two, perhaps three, years old when they saw her in the hut. They were all shocked when they discovered that she was actually eight. Her lack of nutrition and neglect had nearly destroyed her.

The process of recovery was slow but steady. Three months later Mulli took her out of the hospital and brought her to MCF. It was difficult for the other children because they saw how much pain she was still in. After a number of months she grew stronger and stronger.

On one of the recess breaks Mulli went to see Lilian. He looked on the playground where some of the children played a game throwing a ball but did not find her. He looked into her classroom but found it empty.

Then he heard the sound of feet against the concrete path running towards him. Just as he turned around, a young girl wrapped her arms around him.

"Lilian! Is that you? Wow, you are running really fast. How are you feeling?"

Lilian looked up at Mulli. He saw the faintest hint of a smile in her face. The muscles were beginning to respond; she had gained enough weight that a person wouldn't be able to tell she was once a skeletal creature rescued from the slum. "Good."

"How is school going?"

She looked off to the side. A mischievous grin came to her face. "Fine."

Mulli laughed. He bent down to be at her level. "And how is it really going?"

"Well, I have to keep studying."

Mulli laughed again. Lilian smiled as best she could. The healing would continue. She was making progress. She didn't need to laugh out loud just yet.

Mulli could tell she was laughing on the inside.

CHAPTER 11

Lukusan had an ideal start to life.

He was born and raised in the Kipsongo slum. Lukusan's mother died when he was three. It was suspected that she died of AIDS, though at his age he wasn't concerned with what exactly had taken her life. All that mattered was that she was gone, and that woke him to the reality that life was a constant set of changing circumstances that went from bad to worse.

He was fortunate enough to still have his father with him, at least until the age of four, when his dad was hit by a car and died instantly. Had Lukusan known that was going to be his last day with his father he would have made every effort to hug him one last time. To tell him that he loved him. To have something to remember about the man who somehow managed to work a job that was a three-hour walk each way and who returned each day to give Lukusan what little he could to keep his body going. But like every other day, he hadn't been able to say goodbye to his father that morning. A dad who left at 4 a.m. and returned at 9 p.m. was doing the best he could in a part of the world that had no safety net for the millions who had fallen down to the bottom.

He remembered the funeral. Sort of. It was foggy in his mind. He recalled just snapshots really. The entire day was lived in that strange place between the world that was and the world he wished he could have. He wished that the clock could be turned back and started over again. Wished that he could have a mom and dad or, not to be greedy, at least one or the other. But it was the part after the funeral that he remembered the most.

He wasn't sure what to expect. At four years old it's hard to anticipate what life will be like after everything you've known is suddenly gone. But what hit him was how everyone after the funeral hugged him and then they all just left.

Left him alone. Life was supposed to go on. As terrible as things had been for him, they were normal to those living in Kipsongo.

Welcome to life.

Lukusan went to live with a street lady. She used to work with his mother visiting garbage bins to collect the best portions of food. And seeing there was no money, Lukusan joined her. Day by day, bin by bin. He would reach in and hopefully find something that would carry him through that day.

The trouble was, every economy has competition, and a slum is no different. There were a lot of people after those scraps, and the two of them didn't always get what they needed. So she worked as a prostitute, trying to find enough money to be able to fill their stomachs and obtain enough cheap alcohol to clear her mind of the rank troubles of her life—a life that had proved to be a total curse from morning to night. They lived in a wretched, disgusting tent that was made up entirely of plastic bags. The bags were woven together over branches and tied down with ropes to provide at least some kind of shelter.

One morning when he was five the street lady did not come back. He waited for days, but she never returned. He never knew what had happened. Perhaps she moved on. Perhaps she saw Lukusan as a net drain on her food supply. Perhaps she died in an evening out with a drunkard. Either way, Lukusan sat there alone, in his tent, waiting for...he wasn't sure.

Exactly what is there to hope for when you're five and have nothing?

For the next two years it was as if Lukusan was caught in a vicious cycle where every day was just like the day before. He would beg on the streets, eat out of garbage bins and go to bed hungry. Day after day after day.

Street boys would often build a fire and play cards in the evening near his tent. Lukusan hung out with them, not saying or doing much of anything, just looking to spend time with something other than his own thoughts.

On a particularly cold night a fight broke out and the boys started throwing burning logs at each other. One of the pieces of wood struck Lukusan's plastic tent, and in an instant it burst into flames in a spectacular glow. The street boys ran off. Lukusan was too stunned to move. Neighbours came out to see the blaze, hoping it wouldn't spread and engulf the sea of plastic huts around them. It didn't. It just died down, along with the last of Lukusan's memory of anything belonging to his parents. Even though the stench from the plastic was horrible, Lukusan didn't seem to notice. He was more interested in trying to figure out what he would do now.

He could try to rebuild. It would take weeks to get enough plastic and rope together to make a new place. He could try to move in with someone else, which would be impossible. If someone had wanted him, they would have come to the rescue by now. That left the option of heading out to the slums and abandoning any sort of home environment. He looked at the smouldering plastic in front of him and then out into the slum in the distance and figured he would take his chances there.

Besides, seven was a good age to start out on his own.

Slum life proved to have a steep learning curve. He had to learn how to steal from vendors. Had to make friends with restaurant waiters to get the best of the leftovers. Had to find shelter on concrete floors beside stores in the chilly, rainy nights and survive beatings from guards who used wooden batons to smash his back to remind him that he was not welcome. But all the crushing realities of life became easier to deal with once he discovered the benefits of sniffing glue.

He had seen others doing it before and wondered what the attraction was. Finding a piece of bread in the dumpster was something, but when others found glue there was a genuine fight between the boys—like their very existence depended on it.

One evening while he was rummaging in the bin behind a hotel he discovered a small can of glue that was mostly full. He sat down under the roof and cracked the top off. He looked inside and brought his face forward. He breathed in a short burst and waited.

That was strange. Why all the fuss over nothing?

He did it again and felt nothing.

But when the vapour from the glue had a chance to mix with the realities of his mind, he felt a light-headed sensation he hadn't known before. It was like he had pushed pause on life. For only a short moment, a moment so brief that it left before he could make a memory of it, he became a different person. The anxiety of the loss of his parents left him. The fear of being beaten was gone. The chronic pangs of hunger disappeared, and he discovered the most coveted prize of all in a life on the street.

Lukusan could escape.

He pushed his nose into the can and breathed in so deep that it was as if he were transported to a completely different place. If only time could stand still here, it would all be all right.

That's it. Just relax. You are free here. You have no pain here. You can be a boy again without any cares in the world. You are always welcome—

"What do you have there?"

Had he not been high, Lukusan's reflexes would have kicked in instantaneously and he would have bolted into the slum night to escape what was sure to follow. But time travel is addictive, and switching from the place he thought he was in to the place he really was proved to be tougher than he thought.

There were three of them. Street boys he had never met before. The oldest one might have been twelve, but he was built like a fifteen-year-old. Broad shoulders, oily, stinky clothes. He stepped closer and grabbed the can out of Lukusan's hand.

Get up! Get going! Don't you know what's going to happen?

As the glue faded out and the world faded back in, the panic of reality suddenly overcame him. It was too late to run. It was too late to scream for help (like who was going to come anyway, right?), so the best play was to not fight over the glue.

"Fine," Lukusan said. "The glue is yours."

"That's right," the leader said. "And so are you."

He pushed Lukusan against the wall of the restaurant and in one violent motion tore off Lukusan's pants. He turned him around and shoved his forearm against the back of Lukusan's neck, pressing his face up against the cold concrete. The effect of the glue was all gone now and his mind was filled only with terror. He struggled against his grip, which only drew cheers of excitement from the trio.

Just let me live. Just let me live. Just let me live.

"What's going on here?" a man's voice shouted.

The gang leader stopped before he got started and turned to see a man approaching. The glow of light from the back alley prevented them at first from seeing who it was.

"You boys get out now!"

The gang leader looked closer. It was nothing more than a scrawny waiter. The street boys could have taken him. Easily. But fighting is sometimes more about confidence than about stature, and that thin little guy was about as confident and as determined as a man gets. The leader wasn't up to the challenge. He sneered and turned like he was about to leave. But instead, he clenched his hand and with lightning reflexes smashed his fist into Lukusan's jaw.

There are punches, and then there are punches. And the force of the blow the leader gave Lukusan was unlike anything he had felt before. The top of Lukusan's jaw shifted back with a disgusting crack. His body shot out a pulse of adrenaline that only seemed to intensify the pain. He fell to the ground as the street boys raced off. A rush of sweat poured out of him.

Where was the glue when you needed it?

The rest was a blur. It felt like the haze he experienced during the funerals of his father and mother. The waiter pulled him to a vehicle. A bright light from a doctor shone down on him. The sound of machines. And then everything went black.

He woke up in the hospital, alone, of course. When you don't expect anyone, it isn't a letdown when no one shows up. The pain was excruciating. It was impossible to think about anything else. The doctors asked him if he had the money to pay for the operation. Lukusan asked how much and they told him the amount. He was sure he had heard wrong, so he asked again and they repeated the amount. Even if Lukusan could get a job, which was about as likely as someone coming to offer him help, it would take him more than four hundred days to earn enough to pay the bill.

"So? Do you have someone who can pay?"

In a word?

No.

No, he did not. And the hospital enacted a strange rule whereby he would not be able to leave until he did pay. Fair enough. But nothing equals nothing, today, tomorrow and the next week. And finally by the sixth month the hospital let him go.

The return to the slum proved to be strange. After half a year the slum had taken on a different form. The players in power changed. Some had died or moved on and others were willing to fill the void.

He walked four days in the pouring rain to Eldoret. If he wasn't able to leave his life behind mentally, at least he could leave it behind physically.

But wherever you go, there you are, and Lukusan slipped into his familiar life of begging, digging for food in garbage bins, and crying himself to sleep on cold floors exposed to the elements.

It wasn't until a year later that Lukusan heard of his old street friends. Two of them had been executed by hanging. He wasn't sure of the crime, but whatever it was, it had to be brutal. Street boys weren't killed unless they had committed the sickest of evils. The other two were apparently in the area, but after days of searching he turned his attention back to the struggles of daily survival.

One evening he sat on a stool on a veranda and started sniffing glue, wondering where he would be in five years. There were a lot of things that could go wrong on the street. Thankfully there was glue to help set the world right, if even for a few minutes to sort out the future. The answer was obvious, even to him, but no one wants to believe that misery is inevitable, and so he cried his eyes out, relieved, without consciously knowing it, that it was still possible for him to feel. But as the evening wore on, and as the glue worked through his system, it began to dull the physical pain of his body while intensifying the emotional pain of his memories.

It was an odd escape. It used to work both ways. The glue caused the aches of the beatings to lessen and helped the pain in his life to disappear. But either his mind was becoming dependent on the addiction or he was unable to truly leave himself behind any longer, because when the watchman came out with his rubber baton and began to beat him, he made no attempt to leave. He just sat there. The whack of the baton smashed against his body over and over again, but he did not move. He'd feel it tomorrow. But right now, it was like someone else was being beaten. Like someone else was being yelled at.

"You rotten street child! Get out of here! Go back to your destiny on the street. You are meant for the slums and that's all you will ever be!"

The watchman grew tired from the beating. He huffed and puffed. Yet Lukusan just sat there. Staring ahead as if in a trance. Unaffected by the screams of the watchman. Unable to feel the blows of the physical onslaught. Unwilling to believe that a life any different from his own would ever be possible.

News in a slum travels fast. Especially bad news. Lukusan heard that street children had been going missing. While it was normal to have turnover in a profession as transient as begging, there were more and more disappearing into thin air. Four boys had been found in the football stadium. They had been killed, their bodies mutilated and hung out for everyone to see. The word on the street was that it was the work of devil worshippers.

Which is why Lukusan was so afraid of going to see a man who was meeting with street children.

"He gives out food," a street boy told him. "He brings us things and tells stories. My sister lives with him. She is going to finish school and get a job and help us."

"And how do you know this? Have you seen your sister? How do you know she is really with him?" Lukusan asked.

"No. This man is different. He wants to help."

"How do you know he is different? You don't know this. He's just a man like any other."

"But he isn't," the street boy insisted. "You can...you can..."

"You can what?"

"You can tell in his eyes. In the tone of his voice."

"That's nothing but superstition. You keep following him, you're going to be hanging in that stadium like the others."

"No. No, he is not like that. He was one of us."

"One of us? On the street? Begging?"

"Yes. He was abandoned and had to leave school. Now he helps children."

"Listen to yourself. Use your head," Lukusan said, which was really ironic given that both of them had graduated from sniffing glue to doing a cheap version of crack cocaine. "Nobody leaves the slums to become something better. And even if you could get out, even if you could get something better, you would never come back here."

"But he does. That's what I'm telling you. You will have to come for yourself. His name is...what is it? His name is Mulli. He will be back again tomorrow. You see this?" He pulled out a piece of bread from his pocket. "I did not need to steal this. And it has no mould. I got this from him."

"It is a trick."

"My stomach doesn't think so."

"I want you to hear me very carefully," Lukusan said. He focused on his friend's eyes, afraid that his buddy was being lured into something. "There is no such thing as people who help others."

And yet, in spite of his apparent conviction, Lukusan held out the faintest hope that maybe, just maybe, there might be some truth to what his friend was telling him.

CHAPTER 12

He watched them from a distance. Better to have a quick escape ready than to get too close and risk being captured. He saw his street friend in the crowd. Right near the front. Listening to a man speaking to them. That was crazy. Why would anyone be that trusting with a stranger?

Lukusan stepped closer and leaned against a metal hut. His stomach was empty. His legs tired. But there would be no sitting down. If he did, it would take longer to get away if there was trouble from these people who were handing out food. Besides, all of this was a ploy. It had to be. Why in the world would anyone give food to a street child?

Simple.

They wanted something in return.

But that was just the thing. These people didn't *seem* like they wanted anything in return. They looked different. They smiled. Not the fake *I have to smile because that's what's expected of me* skin-deep kind of smile. These were genuine smiles. They weren't being told to smile. They were smiling naturally, because of something going on inside them.

Especially that man who was leading the whole thing. He was unique. He stopped speaking and went to deliver food to a young boy who approached him. That would have been nice. A meal would go down really good right now.

Lukusan took a few steps closer and leaned against another metal hut. He was closer, but still far enough that he could turn back. The gust of wind blew in around him, and the sun seemed brighter than it had a few minutes before.

"My name is Daddy Mulli," the man said to the crowd of children. "And I am so glad that you have come."

His voice carried to where Lukusan was standing. People nearby stopped to listen. It was as if a hush had come over the busy area of the slum.

"I know many of you have had a difficult life. I had a difficult life too. I was abandoned by my parents and had no food to eat. But God looked after me."

That caught Lukusan's attention. *God? Who is that exactly?*

"God created you," Mulli said to the children. "You are not here by chance, and none of us is an accident."

Someone who made me?

"God loves you very much. He wants to be your father. He wants to give you his life."

Someone who loves me too?

Something inside Lukusan stirred. He'd never felt this before. Didn't even know he had the ability to sense this. He'd been high on glue and drugs before. Especially crack cocaine. They had nicknamed it *brown sugar.* That was an experience. But this was way different. This impacted him at his core, at a place so deep that he wondered how a stranger could be able to reach him there.

"God has a good plan for you," Mulli said. "He knew you when you were in your mother's womb."

That spoke to Lukusan. While he wasn't yet sure if he believed any of this, to think that someone knew about him through all of his troubles, that someone was with him during those hazy funerals, those nights on the streets, gave him reason to think hope might not be as irrational as he once thought.

Mulli indicated they would come back next week, and when he finished speaking the children made a mad dash for his vehicle. They crammed around the truck, pleading for a chance to be taken off the street and be given a home. Mulli took three of them with him. And in that instant, something involuntary in Lukusan urged him to want to go too.

It all seemed so authentic. So true.

Too good to be true, in fact.

Impossible. There's no way. There's no way that kids are being saved from this world.

But when he saw his street friend getting into the truck, Lukusan's heart changed. The two boys made eye contact. One being rescued, the other staying behind. Lukusan watched as the truck pulled away and disappeared down the road.

Did he just get his ticket out of here?

That evening, Lukusan returned to his familiar potato sack blanket and his spot on the concrete floor. After trying to ignore the pangs of his stomach and his rank desire for crack or a good sniff of glue, Lukusan tried his best to fall asleep. But what stayed with him more than the chill of the night air or the constant gnawing of his body craving something to eat were the words that Mulli had spoken that evening.

God has a good plan for you. He knew you when you were in your mother's womb.

Maybe, just maybe, there was someone out there who had been watching over him all this time.

Life is risk, and Lukusan made up his mind. He had his face smashed in here in the slum. He had been beaten countless times. Had been eating out of garbage. Lived in perpetual danger. And all he had to look forward to was more of the same.

He'd give Mulli a shot.

Anything was better than this.

He went back to the area where Mulli had been the week before, and sure enough, just as promised, Mulli returned. Lukusan took in a deep breath. He glanced behind him and then to the side. There were lots of escape routes if things got ugly. If Mulli wasn't who Lukusan thought he was, he'd be able to escape. He approached the MCF team and saw people handing out food. He stood in line.

Seriously? This can't be happening. Someone is giving me food? Just like that?

When it was his turn to receive food he stood in front of Ndondo, one of Mulli's daughters.

"Well hello there!" she said in a voice that was both energetic and kind. "This is for you." She gave him bread and a soda. "What is your name?"

He hesitated. He just wanted the food. "Lukusan."

"That's a great name. I'm so glad you've come. Welcome," she said with a smile and a laugh.

Lukusan stuffed the bread into his mouth. Wow. Now that was something. This was good bread. No mould. No soggy pieces. This actually tasted like bread.

He sat down with the other children and heard Mulli speaking to him. No. No, that wasn't it. Mulli didn't speak *to* him that day. It was deeper than that. Mulli spoke *into* him. Like he was connecting directly with that part of him that actually defined who Lukusan was.

"No matter what has happened, God can help you. No matter how confused you might be about what is happening in your life, God can make all things new. No matter how many troubles you have in life, these can all be used for good. I want to encourage you to put your trust in Jesus."

When Mulli finished speaking, pandemonium broke out. The street children shouted and pressed around him. They knew what was next. The great selection. Some would get to go. The vast majority would have to stay. There was only so much money to go around, and that meant that only a certain number of kids would make the jump from here to there.

Where and what *there* was, was not clear to anyone. Just that it was anyplace other than here.

And that in and of itself was enough.

Mulli said he could take a dozen this time. Lukusan pushed through the crowd, shouting with the others, hoping to get noticed. Mulli picked the first six almost immediately. They were young, younger than Lukusan, and they smiled with huge grins when they were seated inside the truck. They were home free.

It was chaos, really. Six remaining spots for all of these children. It was like trying to get on the last lifeboat of a sinking ship. It got really loud, and by the time the eleventh child was picked it was panic time. The kids shouted not so much out of affection but out of desperation. No one had any illusions about what was in store for the losers.

Mulli glanced at Lukusan, who felt a shot of hope rise within him.

And then Mulli picked the boy next to him.

The blood drained from Lukusan's face. The other kids tried to draw Mulli's attention, but he started up his truck. Lukusan's mind raced. What to do? What to do?

Whether it was real or brought on, Lukusan wasn't entirely sure. But he started crying. And not just a small sobbing either. He cried as loud as he could to get Mulli's attention. The truck pulled away and started to drive off. Lukusan ran after it, shouting at the top of his lungs for help. He cried all the louder, but the truck got farther and farther away from him.

Then he saw hope in the way of red brake lights from the truck.

The truck came to a stop. Mulli stepped out.

The tears dried up, and Lukusan ran even faster and reached Mulli.

"All right. All right," Mulli said, hugging Lukusan.

That was new. When was the last time he was hugged?

When was the last time he was touched in a positive way?

Mulli help him on. Lukusan sat down in the back with the other boys. The truck took off, and Lukusan watched as his putrid life in a slum faded away and then was out of sight.

Mulli saw the disorientation in Lukusan's eyes. The kid wasn't a hundred percent there, and it told Mulli that Lukusan was a user. That meant MCF Eldoret would not be the place for him. It was near the city. And the city meant drugs. If you're going to rehabilitate a child, you have to rehabilitate his environment. So Mulli moved Lukusan down to MCF Ndalani. No city nearby. No dealers. Too far to be tempted.

It was the perfect place for a recovering drug addict.

When Lukusan arrived he was shown the school, office of his counsellor, dining room and dormitory. That surprised him the most. He stepped inside. His mouth dropped open. He stared in disbelief.

Beds. Blankets.

A roof.

It was paradise unimaginable.

Lukusan sat down to eat with other boys and girls. Boys and girls with smiles. Like the smiles he saw on the MCF people that he met in the slum. He began to make friends with his new brothers and sisters. It felt strange that his focus on life would now shift. Before, he spent his entire day searching for ways to get food. Now, food was going to be provided for him and his day could be occupied with things other than trying to survive.

It was at night during the first month, after the lights were out and he was in his new bed with a warm blanket, with no rain coming down on him and no watchmen beating him and no street boys hurting him, that the first thoughts of the old life crept into his mind.

You don't really want to be here. You want to go back. I know you do.

No. No, that's not true. I am safe here. I have a family here.

Family? Your family is dead. Don't you remember? And what did you do to escape the pain of their death? That's right. The glue and the crack cocaine. What did you call it?

No. I'm not going back. I have a future here. I had nothing on the street.

What was it called? There was a special name for it.

Go away. I want to stay here. They love me here.

Something sweet. White candy, was that it?

Stop. I don't want to go. I'm not going. That's final. I'm not going.

It felt so good inside you. Made you invincible. Made you a man. Black candy?

Stop. I'm not listening.

Brown candy? Was that it?

Lukusan let out a sigh. He remembered. The sniffing of glue was one thing. But then there was something much better. Much more powerful.

Brown sugar, Lukusan remembered.

Yes. The brown sugar.

Lukusan made slow, steady progress. Transitioning from a life of desperation to one of organization was not easy. He studied hard in school. Loved sports. He enjoyed his new friends. He spoke with his new Daddy Mulli whenever he was in Ndalani. Those times were always special. They would meet under the shade of a tree near the Thika River.

"And how are you feeling?" Mulli asked.

"It is going well," Lukusan replied, shooing away the thoughts of addiction to brown sugar.

"Are you having any thoughts about the old life?"

It was uncanny how Mulli seemed to know exactly what question to ask and when to ask it.

Tell him. Tell him you're struggling. Just be honest. Get it out in the open. He'll help you.

No, he won't. You have to be tough. You can't show any weakness. If you tell him you want drugs he will throw you out, and you know it.

I don't think I can hang on much longer.

Then tell him.

"I'm doing all right," Lukusan lied.

"You're sure?"

Lukusan nodded. They continued talking, but the moment he left, Lukusan felt an unbearable sense of dread.

It was after class on a blistering hot afternoon when he met up with two of his MCF friends. They too had been using on the street and felt the incredible pull of temptation to go back. Lukusan had tried to ignore it, but ignoring it only made it stronger. They had reminisced about the times in the street—oddly enough they emphasized the 1 percent that was okay about the street, like playing cards and being able to do what you wanted when you wanted, but disregarded the 99 percent of life on the street that was characterized by hopelessness, fear and pain.

When Lukusan went to bed that night he turned to see the look in the other boys' eyes. It communicated enough. They had a connection without saying anything. It was a like a code between those who had been on the street. A desire. A calling. A need.

They wanted to go back.

Lukusan shook his head. This was madness. Going back? Wasn't that exactly the place he wanted to leave? He lay down on his pillow and closed his eyes.

And as soon as he did, he was greeted by a familiar foe.

Rules. Rules. Rules. How do you stand it here? This is no life for a boy.

It works. I'm getting better.

Better at what? At having your rights taken away? You're not getting better.

I just need to concentrate longer and it will get better. I don't want you.

Sure you do. You want the glue and you know it. You want the brown sugar.

That was actually correct. He did want the brown sugar. It was strange how little difference there was between thinking about something and actually doing it.

It was good. But, but…

But it would be so good to have it again. Oh, the freedom of the street life.

But it was dangerous.

It was back then. But you're tougher now. You have strength and you are smarter and you will be able to handle yourself better.

It was tough, but there were good times.

And there will be many more. Are you ready?

It will be risky.

Risk means adventure. Every boy wants adventure. Are you ready?

And it will mean I can do what I want.

Exactly. Whatever you want. You will be your own boss. Won't that be great?

Yes. Yes, it would be.

Are you ready?

Lukusan got out of bed while everyone else was still sleeping and touched his friend on the forehead. He woke up immediately and reached out to grab Lukusan's hand—an instinctive response he had learned while on the street.

"I'm leaving," Lukusan said. "Are you in?"

"What? Now?"

"I have enough money to get us to Nairobi. In or out?"

The scary thing was there wasn't any hesitation. No questioning about how he got the money. No thought about whether this was right or wrong. His friend just raced out of bed. And when Lukusan spoke with the other friend, he got out too.

They snuck out of the dormitory and ran as fast as they could to the nearest MCF farm to avoid detection. They hurried along the edge of the property all the way to a back road, checking behind them to see if they had been spotted. They walked down the road and breathed a sigh of relief. They were in the clear now. They had made it. The future was wide open.

He could put MCF behind him. Sure, it offered food, clothing, shelter and those kinds of things.

But ahead of him lay the irresistible promise of a wonderful life on the street.

Lukusan was free at last.

CHAPTER 13

There was no hesitation.

Mulli's reaction was so immediate, it was as if he were expecting it.

As soon as Mulli heard the words through the phone from the MCF teacher's mouth he started looking for his keys.

"When did they leave?" Mulli asked from his desk in Eldoret.

A boy in MCF Ndalani from the same dormitory had informed a teacher that he had noticed Lukusan and two others boys were not there when the rest of the boys woke up. He also complained that he was missing money.

"Sometime during the night. I can't say for sure," the worker said.

"I will be there right away," Mulli said. "Thank you for informing me."

Mulli hung up and met Esther in the kitchen. His entire day had been planned out—everything that he had to do between now and catching his flight this evening. But that all changed with one phone call.

"Getting ready for your trip?" she asked, and then noticed his expression. There was a singular, focused look about him when someone was in trouble. She had come to recognize it over the years. His entire demeanour blocked out everything else except one thing.

His lost children.

"Change of plans. We need to go to Ndalani."

"Ndalani. You will not have enough time."

"Three boys have run away. I fear they may be heading for drugs in the towns or maybe even Nairobi."

"You will not be able to go to Ndalani and then make it back in time to the airport."

"There is always time," he said.

His flight to North America was set to leave at 9:30 p.m. The list of things he had to get done before then was so long it might have taken five Mullis to complete them all. But there was something strangely unique about Mulli's mission to save children and his supernatural confidence in the providence of time.

His flight was perfectly scheduled to coordinate with a number of activities from the moment he landed. Any delay and meetings would be missed. They both knew it and were hard pressed to make this all work. The children were their priority, and they had to get this solved as soon as possible.

Why was it that kids ran away at the most inopportune time?

They made the trek from Eldoret towards Ndalani. Mulli estimated how fast a child could walk and how far they could have gotten by now. He factored in the amount of money they thought was stolen from the boy in the dormitory. The math wasn't friendly to them.

They could have gotten on a matatu and been anywhere by now.

When they arrived in Ndalani a group of children raced up to them.

"Daddy! Mommy!" they cried out.

Hearing the joy of the children who were rescued from a slum and who were now thankful to God for what he did for them made Mulli think how close that kind of love must be to God's heart. Yes, Mulli had a flight to catch. Yes, he had three boys who had been duped into going back to the street to fill their broken cisterns with drugs. The needs were imminent.

But there was always time.

There was time to meet the pressing needs that were around him. To affirm the love he had for the children around them. To assure them of his undivided and consistent compassion for them.

No need to feel rushed.

No need to feel panicked.

There was Someone looking after his schedule. There was Someone who was ultimately in control, even if at times it seemed like he was more distant than the sun and moon and galaxies beyond.

There was time to hold children who were crying out for his affection.

He hugged them and called them by name.

Every. Single. One.

The worker hurried up to Mulli and Esther and relayed the details. The best bet was that the boys had taken the back road through the farms to avoid detection. They would have connected up with the road that would lead them to Thika.

From there, the sky was the limit where they would go.

The clock was ticking. Mulli and Esther got back into the vehicle and drove off. They stopped frequently. Mulli got out to ask people if they had seen

Lukusan and the other two boys walking down the street. Many of them knew Mulli. MCF helped not only children in the MCF Ndalani site but also the myriad of people in the community. He gave jobs to hundreds of people, most of whom would otherwise have no income and no means to get better. MCF was not only a beacon of hope to children.

It was a lifeline for the community.

Even for those who would walk 20 miles for a chance at getting to their medical clinics.

They continued on to Thika. Mulli and Esther got out and spoke to people in the stores and on the street. Finally, success. One of the boys, James, had stayed behind. He wanted no more part of running away. He got tired of listening to the voices in his head telling him that a life of drugs and sniffing glue on the street would be better than a home where people loved him.

"They left here two hours ago," James said.

"Did they have any money with them?" Mulli asked.

This was crucial. In two hours with a matatu they could easily be in Nairobi. And if they reached Nairobi…

"They had no more money."

Thank goodness for poverty. The boys would be on foot.

Mulli arranged for someone from Ndalani to come and pick up James. Then he and Esther got back in their vehicle and drove towards Nairobi.

Mulli scanned the highway in one direction, Esther the other. Maybe there was still time to catch the flight. Maybe there wasn't. He had lost track of time. It was odd, really. There were donations waiting for him in North America, as there were in many countries throughout Europe, as well as in Australia, Israel and other places. But two of his sheep had gone missing.

That was reason enough to leave the other 98.

There. There they were. On the other side of the highway. Walking in the same direction Mulli was travelling. He saw the two boys walking side by side. That was them. Sure it was. You could spot Lukusan's swagger anywhere. It was clever. They boys travelled in the opposite lane of traffic because if anyone from Ndalani was coming, they would be on the other side.

Which would give them time to escape if a car suddenly stopped.

And that's exactly what happened.

Mulli hit the brakes as he saw them and slowed down as he drove past them. He pulled over and committed a no-no by driving in reverse.

"What are you doing?" Esther asked. But she didn't press the point. When a man like Mulli got passionate, only the end of the world would have any effect on him. And when it came to the safety and well-being of his children, even the threat of the end of the world would not be enough to deter him from reaching out to help them.

Cars honked at him. They were in the right. Who backs up on the shoulder of a major highway? It was craziness, really.

But it was consistent.

Who sells their multimillion-dollar empire to help street children?

Mulli opened the door.

And that's when it could have all ended.

Passion is the outcome of self-sacrifice. "Until we say 'here I am,' we cannot be used of God," Mulli had said to the church leaders when they kicked him and his rescued street children off their property for fear that they would corrupt the good, holy children of the church. How odd, Mulli thought, that grace had the potential of becoming suddenly exclusive once it was attained.

But one of the potential drawbacks of passion is that it can override logic.

Logic tells you to look both ways before crossing the street. And Mulli should have, but his love for his kids superseded all that and Mulli ran straight across the street without looking.

My lost sons.

It made him do the unthinkable.

The van should have hit him. Clear on. That should have been the end of Mulli's story. But the driver was good. He swerved at the last possible second. It was close. Really close.

So close that the van, travelling at breakneck speed, literally brushed the glasses clear off Mulli's face.

The driver drilled the brakes.

Mulli suddenly realized his mistake. He stopped. Shocked. He should have been dead.

The driver opened the door and let out a barrage of expletives. Every possible swear word he could think of flew out of the driver's mouth.

Lukusan and his sidekick bolted. It was now or never. Either they would have a life filled with a future of love, education and a family—or a life of drugs, beatings and eventual disaster.

Why was it that the easiest choices were the hardest to make?

But desperation and addiction can play strange tricks on a person's mind, and the boys ran as fast as they could.

Mulli took off after them. He caught the first boy soon enough. Mulli had run a five-minute mile many times in his life. And even at his age, he could still outrun the majority of MCF kids.

"Why are you running?" Mulli asked. "Why are you afraid? I am looking for you. You should be happy that someone came to look for you. Who on the street is coming to look for you?"

In that instant everything changed for the young boy. His mind was suddenly cleared of the delusion he was in. It was as if a veil had been lifted and he saw the situation for what it was.

"I..." reality was crashing in on the poor boy. He felt the stupidity of his actions. "I'm sorry, Daddy."

"Everything is all right. You go and stay with Mom and everything will be fine."

The boy left. But everything was not all right. A mob had gathered. It was similar to the way the renters had gathered around Mulli to burn him to death years earlier when they refused to pay him their rent. He had prayed then, and God had supernaturally delivered him from the wrath of others. Now he prayed for the same solution.

They looked mean. Intent on beating him to death. That's how it was in Kenya. Even with all the street children, if people suspected Mulli of trying to steal a child he would be beaten and burned alive right before their eyes. Mob justice might not always have been correct, but it was always decisive.

Ashes proved that.

"What are you doing?" one man said. He was tall, extremely black, with yellow eyes that screamed sickness, muscles that defined every inch, and a club that would kill Mulli with one viscous blow.

There wasn't much point in running away. They had formed a ring around him. And any one of the people surrounding him could do him in.

Dear God, you know why I am here. I am here to bring your children back home. Please help these men to understand.

"You are going to die for stealing children!" Yellow Eyes said again.

He raised that sickening club in the air. It was reminiscent of the time Mulli's father was tied down with ropes by the tribal clan and one of the young men raised a stick in the air and was about to bring a crushing blow down on his father to punish him, maybe even with death, for beating Mulli's mother.

But Mulli had intervened, much to everyone's dismay. And now his father, Daudi, was a productive member of MCF instead of being a cripple, or worse, at the hands of the tribal council.

He hoped this mob would be as understanding.

"Wait!"

That was enough. It was a stay of execution. But it was one chance. One shot. One opportunity between here and there.

The safest bet was to deny the whole thing. Leave Lukusan to his own fate and get back in the vehicle. Or he could find Lukusan, but that might risk having Lukusan deny Mulli as his father, and the result would be a quick, horribly painful death on the side of the highway.

"I am looking for my son," Mulli said. "I rescued him. He was a street boy hooked on drugs. He has run away, and I want him back."

And just like that the anger of the group subsided. Yellow Eyes lowered his club. It felt like a bomb had been diffused. How was it that a mob could go from being ready to kill to being ready to listen so quickly?

"He is right around here," Mulli said. "I know it. I saw him go into the tall grass. Can you help me find him?"

Yellow Eyes and the others, including nearby university students, helped him look through the tall grass beside the highway.

It was Mulli who found Lukusan. Crouched down in the tall grass. Terrified of a certain beating.

"Lukusan?" Mulli said. He hurried to him and hugged him.

That wasn't exactly what Lukusan was expecting.

"Is this your father?" Yellow Eyes said, showing a hint of his club to prove it was still in his hands.

Lukusan started to cry. He wasn't sure if it was because he was relieved at being found or because he would not be going through with his plan of leaving a life at MCF in return for an existence on the streets.

"Is this your father?" Yellow Eyes said again. He was just as ready to accept it and move on as he was to beat Mulli to a pulp.

"Yes," Lukusan said. "This is my dad."

The crowd dispersed. Mulli and Lukusan remained.

Father and son.

"Why?" Mulli asked. "Why did you run away?"

Flight. Schedule. North America. Donor meetings to help keep everything going. You're going to be late.

There's always time.

"I wanted drugs. I wanted the old life. I stole money. This was all wrong."

Lukusan cried more. As Mulli led him back to the vehicle, Lukusan heard a familiar voice.

Walk back with him to the vehicle, and once you cross the street, run back and hurry onto the matatu. When they kick you off at the next town for not having money, you'll be in another town and you can get your brown sugar.

Be quiet! I am not listening to you. You are what got me here in the first place! I am your friend.

No! Daddy Mulli is my friend.

He is not.

He is. Now leave me alone!

Until next time.

Lukusan rode back with Mulli and Esther. It felt good to be with them. To be accepted. To be loved in spite of his unwise decision. They arrived at the main office at MCF Nairobi. Lukusan ate until he was full. Mulli sat down beside him in the kitchen. The sun had already set. The stars had rolled in. One faint light from the ceiling cast a perfect glow on both of their faces in the otherwise dark room.

"I am sorry, Daddy," Lukusan said.

"You are most forgiven."

"I wanted the city," Lukusan said. "I know it is wrong, but there is this craving. It is in my mind. I wanted to go back."

"Lukusan, you are my son. When I asked you how you were doing, why didn't you tell me about your struggles?"

Lukusan remembered the conversation. Why had he pushed Mulli aside?

"I don't know."

"Just come talk to me. I will listen to you. I am your dad. I love you. It is me who should fight for your rights. I will always help you to put you in the place where you should be."

Mulli smiled. Somehow his smile put the whole world right.

Lukusan smiled too. "All right."

Mulli hugged Lukusan and arranged for a vehicle to take him back to Ndalani.

He got his things together and headed off for the airport. All those things he had to do? They would have to wait. They weren't pressing. And why would they be by comparison?

His boy had been found.

Mulli made it to the airport on time. An hour to spare, no less. More than enough time to pray in preparation for his trip. What a whirlwind day. What a day of the unexpected. As per usual. There wasn't always enough time to do everything.

But there was always time for the essential.

There was always time for his children.

Even when there were over two thousand.

There was always time.

CHAPTER 14

Her name was Anika, and she had reason to be concerned.

She looked well enough on the outside. She smiled. She had friends at MCF. She did well in school. But even on the best of days it was with her. It was there to greet her when she woke. It was there to sing her a bitter lullaby when she went to sleep. The thought was never more than a heartbeat away.

Children with abusive parents never forget.

It wasn't so much the memories of her father beating her that would come back. Those would show up from time to time. But she had poured out her heart to Mulli, about the pain of being punched by her father and of living in the constant torment of wondering how bad it would be tonight. Mulli would listen as if she were the only person in existence in that moment, and she would feel the relief that came with knowing that she could share her grief without the threat of being interrupted. It hadn't erased the memories. But it had changed their meaning. Somehow the hurt, fear and humiliation from the beatings were replaced when she forgave her father for what he had done.

She grew up in Mavoloni, an area behind the hills of Ndalani. When word reached Mulli that she was in danger he brought her to his home. Later, her father, Bennett, came to work at MCF as a casual labourer. It was a step in the right direction. But when Bennett started to receive wages, his life's compass lost its bearing. The money bought him the ability to make poor choices, and Bennett headed for the booze. The joy of the drink and the ability to escape gave Bennett a new lease on life.

And every night, his wife and children lived in fear.

Even though she was at MCF, Anika had the constant feeling that her family could be in mortal danger from the man who should have been their greatest protector.

It was a clear evening after choir practice under a sparkling starry sky when she walked back with her friend Thumika to the dormitory. They were a match of opposites. Thumika was tall, liked sciences and talked a lot. Anika was shorter, preferred languages and spoke only when in a small group. When Anika talked in confidence with her friend, it was an indication that everything was all right.

But on evenings like this, when Anika said nothing, Thumika understood that she was having a difficult time. They walked together, not saying anything, not needing to, the way friends do when they are able to connect without having to speak.

The children around them continued singing as they crossed the small bridge from the classrooms to the dormitories. But neither Anika nor Thumika said or sang anything.

At least not until they reached to the dormitory.

They got into their beds, pulled the covers up to their chins and rested their heads on the pillows. There was nothing to be taken for granted here. They knew where they had come from. They knew what real life was like for the majority of people. They had no illusions that the world should be easy or that someone, anyone, owed them something. Their bunks were pushed close together, and with everyone else in the room of twenty girls talking, it gave them the opportunity as best friends to have their late night conversations.

"Do you believe that prayer changes things?" Anika asked.

They didn't look each other in the eye. Best friends don't often need to. They had an instantaneous connection, as if the other person knew what one was going to say before she said it.

"I know that it does," Thumika replied. "But I don't always feel that way."

"I pray and pray and I just don't see anything changing with my father. Am I saying the wrong words? Does God not hear my prayers?"

Thumika rolled over on her side. This time she did look at Anika, who gazed through a window at the stars over the mountains. Just beyond them her family would be getting ready for bed.

She wondered if they would sleep in safety tonight.

"Don't give up, Anika. Our job isn't to answer prayers. It's to offer them in faith."

"But I feel like I am praying and no one is listening. If there was the slightest change, if there was an indication that my father was getting better, I would have more confidence in praying. But I just sit and wonder if this is doing any good at all. And then I think that I am doubting, and then I worry that my prayers are for sure not going to work because I'm not asking in faith and…I just get confused and disappointed."

Her heart was heavy. She lived in that tension between knowing something to be true and not being able to see those beliefs reflected in real life. She tried to dispel the notion that she could sense danger. That she could feel the rage already beginning in her family's hut. She shook her head as if doing so could somehow erase the thoughts from her mind. The room felt still. As if a silence had suddenly come over everyone.

Had it gotten quieter, or did it just seem that way?

"I'm worried," she continued.

Thumika wanted to say, "It will be all right." But she was smarter than that. Things didn't always turn out all right. Some prayers were answered, some delayed, some denied. But through it all she was learning that precious possession of diligence, and she hoped her friend would see it too.

"I want to encourage you," she said. "I am agreeing with you for your father to change. For him to give his life to Jesus Christ."

"But what if he doesn't?"

"We can't focus on a result," Thumika said. "We can only focus on asking God to do his will."

"Thank you," Anika said, trying to dig down to her well of faith in the hopes of finding sustained courage. "But I still have this overwhelming sense of dread."

They prayed together for Anika's father. For him to change. For him to find peace with a God who was in control, even when he appeared not to be. They went to sleep, and Anika hoped that closing her eyes would be enough to close out her fears.

But deep down inside she knew better.

And based on what was about to happen in that small hut just across the hills, it was just as well that she was here, at MCF, far enough away. She would be safe here.

But it would be a different matter entirely for the rest of her family.

It had been another rough day for Bennett. The poor life is not an easy life, and Bennett had to make critical entrepreneurial decisions every day that determined how well his family would survive. How would he spend the few Kenya shillings that he had? He could use them to buy seeds for planting, or he could use them to buy medicine for his wife, his second wife now—the first one he had to leave. What use is a paralytic wife anyway? Or maybe it should be spent on buying better harvesting tools. The list of choices was endless. But in the end, the best option for Bennett was a trip to the bar. He'd spend his money on booze. His wife and kids would go to bed hungry. But, big deal. They would put on a nice smile for everyone to show that everything was just fine. If it looked good from the outside, then it was good enough for Bennett.

He approached the hut late at night. He was drunk, as usual. The children were already asleep, on the floor; there was no money for beds. His wife sat on the floor in front of them. That was her way of protecting them. A last line of defence.

When he pushed open the door his wife felt such a jolt of fear that her body ached from the resulting rush of adrenaline.

"Where is my food?" he shouted.

Tough to answer, really. He had spent the food money on booze, so strictly speaking his supper was already in his stomach. Only it was there by way of alcohol and not an actual meal. But explaining that to Bennett, sober or drunk, wouldn't help.

The three children began to wake. They left the realm of dreaming where they could escape the realities of life and entered a nightmare that had become altogether familiar. They huddled together, shaking, feeling like throwing up from the fear.

She watched his eyes. Hopefully they would indicate he was exhausted. But they darted around the room like a madman's, looking for something. Sweat dripped off his forehead. That was different. She hadn't seen that before. He gritted his teeth together. The hut became cold. Bennett stared right into her. His eyes seemed altogether different. And it made her feel scared right to her core.

He breathed so loudly that it filled the entire room. And then, in a gross low voice he spoke to her. She heard him say the words, but the voice didn't sound like his. Either way, what he said sent a chill down her spine. His tone was so convincing that she believed she might already be dead.

Without breaking eye contact with her he reached beside him and picked up a machete.

"I am going to cut you up, woman," he said.

Her motherly instinct kicked in. She decided to make a run for it outside. As counterintuitive as leaving her children at a time like this might have seemed, she was doing the right thing. When a woman knows her husband she can read his instincts. And she knew he wanted her more than the kids. Fleeing would draw him out of the hut. He was a fast runner, and it would mean she'd get hacked to death on the farm. But at the very least it would give the children a chance to get out.

She figured it was better he get her than all of them.

He swung the machete at her. But he missed completely and hit the frame of the bed. The children screamed. The mother, however, didn't have time for fear. She only had time to run.

One last time.

She bolted past him out the door. She was quick and just beat the blade whizzing past her head on the way out.

Come after me, she pleaded. She raced into the night, hoping for and at the same time fearing the sound of his feet running after her. But she got her wish, and Bennett took off after her with his machete in hand.

It's working. It's working.

She might be a faster runner than him now that he was inebriated. The trick was to run fast enough to not be cut by his machete, yet slow enough so that he didn't give up the chase and go back and finish off the kids first.

There was a science to dealing with a homicidal drunk.

Her knee gave out for no particular reason. Maybe it succumbed to the shock of what she was going through. Maybe she stepped awkwardly. Either way, she hit the ground. She stumbled to get back up. It was bizarre. It felt like a dream where you have to run, you absolutely have to get away, but you just can't.

She looked back and saw the flash of the blade. He swiped at her. She pushed herself away, and it grazed the back of her neck. She got up and continued running. The children ran out of the hut and hid themselves in the bushes. Even in Kenya it gets cold at night, and the children crouched down, shivering under the cover of brush and darkness, watching their father try to hack their mother to death.

She managed to get a few steps ahead of him when he swiped wildly at her one last time. He missed again, and then dropped his machete. It was too much effort to go after her anyways. He exhaled, the alcohol finally won out, and he collapsed to the ground.

She hurried back, taking the wide route around him, thinking he might get up any moment and continue the assault. She grabbed some clothes from their hut and came out to see him back on his feet, stumbling towards her. She bolted for the bushes, grabbed the kids, and ran with them to the road. She checked behind her and saw her husband, or what she thought was her husband, make it to the hut and fall down inside.

She took the children an hour down a dark road, a risky move this late at night because of the high potential for muggings. But she figured the risk of being mugged or raped on the highway was better than being outright killed. She checked behind her continually to make sure her husband wasn't coming after them and watched the bushes for any hint of thugs looking for an easy take.

They reached the home of Mulli's parents—Daudi and Rhoda—who took them in. She relayed the story of what happened. As Daudi listened he realized she might as well have been talking about how he treated his family those years ago before his life changed forever.

The next morning she went with Rhoda to see Mulli. He had observed her expression in hundreds, thousands, of other people. It's the look of having reached the absolute end. No more options. No more thoughts. No more plans. She had no place left to turn.

Mulli listened to her. He cancelled his plans for the day and told her to return to safety with his mother. Then Mulli called MCF Yatta and asked the supervisor to send Bennett to him. When he showed up he was smiling, upbeat. To the untrained eye he seemed like a genuine, caring person. It was eerie how beneath this shell of congeniality lay a murderous drunkard.

"How are you?" Mulli asked, gesturing for Bennett to sit down.

"Good," he answered. He sat down. His smile was too big to be considered real. He wrung his hands. He swallowed. He shifted in his chair. But he kept his smile.

"And your family?"

"Good."

"Really?" Mulli asked.

"Well, we've been having a few small problems."

"Do you know where they are?"

"No."

That didn't seem to bother him. They were gone. For a split second he wondered if perhaps he had killed them all last night.

"What kinds of problems?" Mulli asked.

"Well, I sometimes drink a little bit."

"Is it a problem?"

He paused. The moment of truth. He repositioned himself in the chair as if doing so could somehow make saying this easier. "Yes," he admitted.

Mulli continued to question him, hoping that by having Bennett think through his actions it would lead him to understand how awful he truly was.

"Alcohol is ruining your family. This is a terrible sin against your wife and children. You have probably tried to stop before. Has it worked?"

He stopped smiling. Truth can hurt. And it was getting to him. He stopped wringing his hands. Sweat formed on his forehead.

"I can't stop," he said, his strength completely gone. He felt like a child again.

"This cannot go on. You know it and I know it."

"I agree," he whispered. "But I have tried. I have really tried. I just can't let it go."

"I would like to tell you the way in which you can be free. Would you like to hear it?"

Bennett looked into Mulli. His glassy eyes indicative of his hangover pierced Mulli with all the hope he could muster that somehow he could have what he was not able to do for himself.

"If you admit that you have sinned and ask God to forgive you and give your life to Jesus, he will come into your life and begin to make you into the person he wants you to be."

"That's not possible."

"Nothing is impossible. Not for God. You can be changed."

He began to cry. He wasn't sure what the tears were for. Remorse? Embarrassment? But either way, he had reached the end of himself—that precious place that few people get to. He wiped his tears. He saw himself for the despicable person he was, but more importantly, he saw himself as someone who was not going to be able to get out. Not on his own.

"I want to be forgiven and meet Christ," he said.

Mulli prayed with him. Nothing fancy. Nothing wordy. Strange how such a simple prayer spoken from the heart is the basis for the greatest event.

Lord, I have wasted my life. I have sinned against you and my family. Please forgive me because of what Jesus did on the cross. I give my life to you and ask you to make me your child.

Mulli assigned two MCF pastors to walk with Bennett to see his wife and children at Daudi and Rhoda's home. When his wife saw him she didn't recognize him. Physically he was the same man, but outer appearance counts for so little in an overall person. There was something completely different about him. No anger. No drunkenness.

No machete.

Just a peace in his eyes that was so unique she felt captured by what she saw.

They waited in silence. Attacker and victim. He bit his lip. Looked his wife and children in the eyes and said, "I'm sorry."

It was a start. They talked the entire afternoon. The condition for them being able to live together again was that they would come for counselling for two months and become involved in a local church, which they agreed to. Then Bennett, his wife and children went to MCF to visit Anika.

She was studying in the form 3 room, also known as grade 11, when a friend came in to tell her that her dad was looking for her. Normally she would have put a bookmark in her textbook and carefully closed her notebooks before getting up from her desk. But this was not a normal occasion, and she stood up and hurried out of the classroom, past the incredible array of red and blue flowers that glistened in the spectacular sunshine, and ran down the path towards her father.

They hugged each other. He felt different. She pulled back. A quizzical expression came over her face. She studied him.

"Anika?" Bennett said. "I have something I want to tell you."

The following Sunday, the entire MCF school met for church in a new building that was filled to capacity, with people sitting on wooden benches, including Bennett, his wife and his three children, who sat down near the back.

After the opening songs, Anika came to the front. Being an introvert is never easy in front of a large crowd, and this was no different. She glanced out at the sea of faces looking at her. In the back she saw her family. And right behind them—she had to look twice to confirm—she saw the face of a white man. His colour alone made him stand out in the otherwise African crowd. She focused on her father, then on her mother and siblings. Then she looked to Thumika sitting at the front. Anika smiled, and for a moment she forgot how nervous she was in front of everyone.

"Praise the Lord," Anika began as a common greeting in the group setting.

"Amen," everyone called back to her.

"Praise the Lord again," she said.

"Amen."

"Today I want to share with you about how God answers prayer." She looked out at her father. He had seen the light. Finally. How many years had that been? "I was very discouraged about why things were not changing in my family. My family life was terrible, and I prayed with my friend Thumika for many years, ever since I came here, that my family would be saved. And many times I thought this was going to be impossible."

Mulli listened as she spoke. It was one thing for him to believe in the power of prayer and to experience God first-hand. But it was something different and just as special when he saw one of his children giving testimony to how God came through.

"My father gave his life to Jesus this week," she said. That got to her. It was real now. She had said it out loud. Then she explained what had happened. She chronicled the violence and how her father came to ask forgiveness.

The white man at the back later got the translation of what Anika had said and thought it to be mind-bending how less than a week before the man who had been sitting in front of him was trying to machete his wife to death.

"I just want to encourage all of you. Don't give up in your prayers. Keep on praying. Even when you think nothing is happening. Be encouraged that God still hears and God still cares about you. Even when it hurts and you're not sure if he hears, he does hear."

She sat down and everyone clapped. Mulli came up after her.

"Maybe you have been listening today and you have heard God calling you to give your life to Christ. Maybe you have made mistakes and you have caused harm to others, or maybe someone has caused harm to you. The only path forward is forgiveness and faith in Jesus Christ. You can really trust him. He loves you even when it seems like there is no hope. So I want to ask you. Even now as you are sitting there. Do you want to give your life to Jesus Christ? Do you want to say 'Yes' to him and follow him? Do you want to leave your old life behind and accept the life of Jesus Christ, who died on the cross for your sins?"

Mulli paused. He watched the crowd. He felt no impulsion to hurry. There was no awkward silence for him. The room of more than four hundred was quiet. And then, Bennett's wife stood to her feet. She spoke in a voice so quiet, so effortless, yet it carried over the entire room.

"I want to get saved," she said.

Mulli nodded, and she walked all the way from the back to the front. The only sound in the room was that of her feet against the concrete floor. She stood beside Mulli, who gave her a grin of approval, conveying his complete assurance to her.

"Let's pray," Mulli said as he began to lead her in a prayer of salvation.

Everyone folded their hands and closed their eyes.

All except Anika. She kept her eyes open.

She wanted to see the miracle first-hand.

CHAPTER 15

It was cramped, but it worked.

Philip and his brother, Kepha, curled up underneath the seats of a matatu. The passenger van had eighteen people jammed into the space, which served well for the seven- and eight-year-old boys. They were small enough to sneak on and hide until they got to their destination.

They didn't have the luxury of worrying about school or a home life. Those options had long since disappeared. Their father was gone, and their mother had decided to abandon them a few months before to find greener pastures working as a prostitute in Tanzania. That left the two boys with a choice between starving with their grandmother or living the dream of desperation on the streets.

"Hey! What are you street boys doing?" a man at the sliding door shouted. It was his job to encourage would-be travellers to take his matatu and to collect their money. It was also his job to get rid of freeloaders.

The driver stopped. The boys got out from under the seats. Hard to believe boys who looked this innocent could have done something wrong. Their clothes were old and dirty. Philip's shirt was faded red. Kepha's, hard to tell. Too many rips and stains. Not that colour mattered. Not to them.

Some of the passengers laughed. But the man at the door grumbled something under his breath, hard to hear exactly what. The boys could guess. They'd heard it before. *Useless street kids. Rotten, good for nothing…* They stepped out into the bright sunshine.

The matatu took off.

In front of them they saw the brownish haze that covered the entire slum. It was as if someone had flown over the area and sprayed it all with the same dreary colour. The rusted sheet metal roofs stretched out for what seemed like an eternity of poverty. It was hot again today. That was bad news. It would make their food supply in the garbage cans rot that much faster.

They had no place to sleep. No parents to care for them. No other friends. But they knew nothing different. And to them, a hopeless struggle of daily survival was the best paradise they could hope for.

They jumped over the ditch that acted more as an open sewer system. They didn't notice the putrid stench. Not anymore. Strange what you get used to when you're around it for so long. They walked down the crowded street to the market. Everything imaginable was for sale. Shirts, shoes, pants, souvenirs, chess boards with figurines carved as animals. The storefronts lined the street on both sides as far as they could see. Every shop owner called out or waved a sample of merchandise, trying his best to lure prospective buyers.

It was Philip who saw them first. Cool long-sleeved shirts that would sure do wonders to replace the junk they were wearing. He stopped and eyed them closer. Kepha looked as well. Without either of them saying it they understood what the other was planning. They stood off to the side while the shopkeeper spoke with a customer. Instead of using the smash and grab technique, they stood by quietly, hoping to blend in with the traffic around them.

Philip touched the shirt. Wow, that really was a great shirt. And clean, too. When was the last time he had a shirt that free from dirt and grime? He'd look good in it. He slipped it off the end of the table as if to want to examine it more closely. Kepha did the same. The shopkeeper should have been more careful. Because when he turned to see the boys, they had already bolted away from the shop.

"Stop! Street boys!"

Philip and Kepha raced down the street. They had a good lead on the owner. But when people nearby heard the shop owner calling out they suddenly became an army of one and tried to stop the boys. They reached out to stop them, but even at such a young age the boys were good runners and dodged around them like football players in a crucial match. Their pulses pounded in their bodies. They had motivation. They knew what was coming if they got caught.

They turned the corner down a quiet alley and looked back to see that they had escaped. They breathed a sigh of relief.

And that's when they ran straight into the arms of two watchmen.

No parents and no relatives meant that Philip and Kepha were put into the juvenile centre. Bad food, mean guards, tough kids. It was a trade-off whether the streets or juvenile was worse. On the street you could find a place to mind your own business. But in the claustrophobic children's prison, you couldn't escape. If someone wanted you, they'd find you.

Every day was the exact same thing. Over and over and over again. It was boredom beyond description. No future, no fun and no father.

They had been in the endless day-in day-out routine for months when they heard that a man who rescued children was coming. They crowded into the mess hall for a look at who it was. Statistics were not on their side. This detention centre alone held four hundred children.

They saw him in the distance. For a man with hundreds of children he didn't look like he was anything out of the ordinary. Kind, humble, unassuming. Yet there was an undeniable confidence about him.

It was like the whole room went quiet when he entered. It had never been so still.

The man and the warden walked down between the tables and came towards them. Their eyes locked onto him. Was he looking at them or at the boys the next table over?

But their dream would come true when the man stopped in front of them.

"Hello," Mulli said.

The boys' mouths dropped open.

The warden prepared the charges to be taken to the court, where the Kenyan government would permit the children to be taken to MCF. When they arrived they were put into school, joined choirs, played games and took part in evening devotions. It was all going along so well.

But when they got into their teens, the boys took a turn for the worse.

Theft was the big problem. When people from the West came to MCF the two boys would try to find ways to steal from them. Philip even managed once to take a woman's passport. They would run away from MCF, only to be found and brought back. Mulli spent countless hours speaking with the boys. Philip in particular. They would meet in the quiet of the evening, under a metal roof with open walls around them, sitting on plain wooden benches. Father and son.

"How do you feel about your life?" Mulli asked.

"I know it is wrong to leave. I don't want to be on the streets."

But he did. That was the big problem. He did want the street. It was as if it were a craving that had gotten into his blood, and despite the logic against it, the pull to the old life was unmistakable. He wanted the protection of MCF but he didn't want the rules. He wanted the joy of the stealing and getting high but didn't want the consequences.

"Do you understand that being on the street is harmful for you?"

"Of course." He nodded in a way that made it seem he was trying to act convincingly, as if his body language had to convey what his true self didn't believe.

"God will help take that desire away from you."

"I know. I know." He smiled. Another decoy tactic. It was a half smile, really, and the lacklustre appearance of his eyes only served to incriminate him all the more.

It seemed impossible to get through to him. Philip would say *yes* with his mouth but *no* with his heart. There were moments of genuine regret, but it was so temporary, so fleeting, that in spite of all the encouragement he seemed bent on not really wanting to change.

Mulli gave as many opportunities to Philip as he did to all the rest. Ironically, he spent more time counselling Philip and Kepha than other children. He poured out his heart for them. Yet they felt like dried-up trees that, no matter how much you water them, refuse to grow.

Philip and Kepha ran away again from MCF. And again Mulli did his best to track them down, as he did with any child who left. They started out making the same bad choices, which felt so good to them because it seemed like they were in control. But the boys got sucked deeper into their life on the street. And for some strange reason a dead-end existence of theft, drugs and violence on the street outweighed the benefits of a life filled with growth and purpose.

The boys were in and out of remand homes on drug trafficking charges. Mulli would track them down and visit them in prison. Philip especially would be remorseful. But Mulli had seen this time and time again. Philip would be released, only to fall right back into his defiant ways. Instead of coming back to MCF at Mulli's earnest invitation, despite all the chances he had already been given, and even though Mulli encouraged him to come back, Philip chose to hustle drugs and sat in a revolving cycle of temporary freedom, crime and prison.

"Please keep praying for me," he would tell Mulli each time he was back in prison. It was like he had two personalities. One that realized how pointless it was to reject MCF—the best offer he'd ever get, and one that loved to roll around in the mud after he had been cleaned up. He would flip back and forth between these two people, becoming one and hating the other, and then switching to become the other and hate the former.

Sure, the kid had been given chances. He had been handed the opportunity to change. Anybody would hold Mulli faultless in his efforts to help Philip. But none of that entered Mulli's mind. He didn't understand why it was so difficult for someone to want the light. He didn't understand why someone would knowingly head down a path of calamity.

There was so much Mulli had to be thankful for. There were so many children who had already been transformed through his work. But even the greatest have moments of deep sadness. And as Mulli stood on the Thika River he felt the unbearable pain of losing a child to his old life. He had done the best he could. He loved him. He prayed for him. He cared for him. But none of that helps when the child has gone astray and doesn't want anything more to do with the people who sacrificed so much for him. Mulli felt the unbearable burden of anguish a parent feels over a wayward child. It did more than simply hurt. Losing Philip, and the others who went back to the street, did far more than cause him pain.

It crushed Mulli.

He wiped the tears from his eyes. Life had many more questions than answers. And joy did not mean he would always understand everything. It was what it was. He prayed for Philip and then returned to the other children.

There was still much work to be done.

CHAPTER 16

It was during the night that she remembered it the most.

Nduta lay awake in a small one-room hut in a slum in Eldoret. Evening was always difficult. Daytime was slightly better. At least during the day there were distractions, like having to look for food, worrying about her father beating her, and wondering if she would have any hope of a life other than what every generation before her as far back as she could remember had experienced.

But when night crept in, Nduta was left with only her memories to keep her company. She saw images of her mother. They appeared in and out of her mind without any control on her part. She saw her father beating her mother. Saw her mother falling into depression. Deep, dark moments where she did nothing more than stare ahead and wonder how bad the encounter with her husband would be tonight. Her mother became mentally unstable and died. That left Nduta and her sister to stay in the care of their alcoholic father. He married again. But it would have been better had he stayed single. Nduta saw a horrific flash in her mind's eye where the stepmother, as crazy as she was, took out a stick and knocked her baby sister on the head, killing her.

Each night, Nduta saw these scenes replay in her mind. Daytime and night-time were two sides of a bad coin she had come to know as life. One side provided confirmation of how awful her past had been. The other assured her of how awful her future would be.

She was forced out of school because her stepmother was too short-sighted to see that an education now would pay for itself later. Instead Nduta worked in a field. Every day of every month, no days off, for half a dollar a day.

Her father was kind enough to give her the dregs of his finished alcoholic drink as her only food source. He certainly wasn't going to eat them. Who would stoop so low so as to eat the leftovers of booze? And he would certainly never stoop so low so as to provide for his new wife or Nduta. Besides, real men don't provide.

They get drunk.

He came home that night hung-over, as usual, but he began to beat the new mother, which was unusual. A torrent of rage came over him. The more he drank, the worse it got. Once he hit his new wife so hard that it broke her arm. Instead of helping her, he left her and Nduta alone in the hut and went to another woman.

Nduta tried to help her stepmother as best she could. It was bad enough for her to take the beatings. But it would become worse if her stepmother's secret got out. Neither of them wanted him to know that the stepmother had diabetes. That would spell disaster for them.

Exactly why would he stay faithful to a woman who was not healthy?

The stepmother fell asleep. Nduta lay down on the ground. It felt colder than normal. She hadn't had any dregs to eat. She was terrified of her father coming home. And she was beyond exhausted, both physically and mentally.

And it was when she reached the absolute bottom that she heard the voice for the first time.

I can't handle this anymore. I can't live like this.

I'm fine. Everything will be okay.

Who are you? I don't know who you are.

Who am I? Who are you? You're nobody. There's no one else here. I am the only person here.

That's not true. I'm here. I'm here in this hut.

Fine. Fine, okay? We'll both be here.

I don't want you here.

Of course you do. I'm the one that makes everything safe. Whenever you don't like something, you can just become me. Okay?

Really?

Of course. Who wants to have a drunk father and live in constant fear of him coming to beat you or do something worse? Who wants to believe that the only food they have is the leftovers at the bottom of an alcoholic's drink? You can become me whenever you want.

How do I do that?

You've already created me. Whenever it gets difficult, you can decide to live in me. That way the girl who is getting hurt will actually be someone else and you will be safe.

But how can I know that I can get back?

You can get back to your other self whenever you want.

Are you sure?

Of course. Trust me.

Nduta opened her eyes. It was then that she realized she had dug her fingers into the ground. She took them out and only then realized that she had been sweating. Who was that person talking to her inside her head anyways? It first it felt scary. But there was one thing she could not ignore.

For that brief moment Nduta was able to do what she had dreamed of doing as far back as she could remember.

She could escape.

He was nice enough. He looked good to her, and most of all she could tell that he liked her. As warm as the Kenyan sun can get, there was nothing that compared with how good she felt to have someone pay attention to her.

She noticed him while she was working in the field, earning what little she could to keep from starving. Their eyes connected, and he was brave enough to come over and speak with her. He was taller than her. He spoke kindly. It was easy to like him.

He represented everything that her father wasn't.

They became friends and spent a lot of time together. He gave her money to help her afford something real to eat. For the first time that she could remember she smiled. It felt good. Like there was a whole different way to live. He managed to break her out of her pattern of thinking.

And then, as quickly as he came, he disappeared from her life. Vanished. Just like that. She blamed herself for something she had said or done, or not done, to send him away. She wondered what happened but couldn't come up with any answers.

But she did find out. About eight months later. She worked in the field, and co-workers began asking if she was fat or if she was pregnant.

"I'm not pregnant," she insisted. But the instantaneous rise in her blood pressure and a sudden grip of panic betrayed her confidence. Her body knew, even if her mind refused to believe it. She tried to thrust this all aside. Push it into the deep recesses of her brain.

Where are you? Where are you? I need out. I need out right now. Where are you?!

But try as she might, she began to feel the walls of her terrible existence come even closer together. And she sensed all the anguish a 13-year-old feels when she realizes that there will be no going back.

I'm right here. I'm right here for you. You're not pregnant. You're home with your mom and dad. They're taking you to the park. Isn't that great?

Yes, that's excellent. I always enjoy going to the park with Mom and Dad.

And your sister. She's right beside you. All of us can go together.
That's better. That's much better.

The doctor informed Nduta that her hips were not wide enough to give birth. The only relatively safe way would be a C-section. Nduta didn't know what that meant. She was having enough trouble getting to the point of natural birth. Her brain didn't allow her to think past that option.

It will all be okay. I'll be here for you. You don't have to go through this if you don't want to.

She nodded. It was the best she could do, sitting halfway between this sane world and the one she was visiting more and more often.

She remembered going in for the surgery. She remembered seeing the doctor and the nurses. And that was the last thing she recalled. She didn't really need to check out of the hospital physically now. She could do so mentally. And that meant that she could leave and become anyone she wanted, anytime.

It's finished. It's all over. Isn't that great?

Who are you? What do you want?

Don't you remember?

I've never met you before. There was someone else here before. That person wasn't me. I was playing in the park.

No, you weren't. Your sister is dead. So is your mother. And your father doesn't want you.

That's not true. We can go to our car and go on a trip to the coast. Mombasa.

You're not going anywhere.

Yes, you said I could. You promised.

Who are you? Who are you really?

I'm 13 and I attend a private school. I'm liked by all my friends and I…No, I'm nothing. I'm hated by everyone…No, no, I have a great boyfriend and he makes me feel good.

She lay in the hospital for three weeks. Unable to speak or hear, Nduta was constantly disoriented. Reality was a distant memory, a fictitious invention that had no bearing on the real world.

A nurse came in to see her. Young. Genuine. Her compassionate smile alone melted the concern of any other patient.

Except Nduta.

Nduta's eyes circled around the room. Out of focus, then in focus.

"Nduta, you have a child. A baby girl."

Normally that would be cause for celebration.

Not for Nduta.

In that moment, in that instant when she received and processed the information that she was now a mother, something clicked in her fragile mind. And whatever deep end she was on the verge of going over, the news of being a mother pushed her that much closer to the edge of the precipice.

It was not clear to her whether she got pushed or whether she voluntarily jumped herself, but either way, she checked out and landed in a place that was familiar only to her mentally unstable mother.

They are out to get you. All of them. Get them! Get them!

"You are out to hurt me!"

That scared the nurse. Nduta's eyebrows contracted. Her jaw became tense. Body language training or not, the nurse felt the change in character.

"Doctor," she whispered, overcome by the fear of the change in Nduta's expression. "Doctor," she said again. This time with more desperation.

But she wasn't fast enough. Nduta whipped out her hand and caught the nurse on the side of the face. There was so much force in that slap that it sent the poor nurse sprawling to the ground.

How did a 13-year-old learn how to hit like that?

Nduta got out of her bed.

You see, you have to stay in charge. They will hurt you.

Why are you doing this? These people like you. They are trying to help you.

I don't want any help from either of you!

That creeped her out. Exactly how many people were there inside her mind? For sure not just one. She thought two. But was it three now? Could she really pick and choose between three different people?

The nurse on the ground didn't have time to wonder. Blood oozed from her mouth. Dazed from the hit, she got to her feet. That compassionate spirit was gone now. It was all business.

"Help!" she shouted.

And it came running.

A doctor and three other nurses burst into the room.

Stop them. Stop them all.

Let them help you.

How are you enjoying the park, sweetheart? Do you like it here?

Nduta lashed out at the doctor. She slapped away as if she were a non-swimmer panicking for survival.

"Get ropes!" the doctor shouted. The nurse with the bleeding mouth gathered herself and took off down the hallway.

The rest pushed Nduta onto the bed. They forced her down. Each one took a limb and pinned her to the mattress.

I have to get out. I have to get out!

You're not going anywhere. You're mine. And you have what's coming to you.

I would like some more ice cream, Father. Can I get some more?

You'll never get out of here. You're trapped for life. Struggle all you want. You're captured. I own you. And you have no means of escape. End of the line for you. How does it feel?

Please, please Mom, don't hit my sister.

Get out! Don't you see what they will do to you?

They tied her down as best they could and then called for medication to stabilize her.

But Nduta didn't hear any of it. She was off in some other place far away. It should have been a relief. But her break from reality had become a bit confusing to her. What was once a fun dissociation from this world had become a collection of competing voices, most not her own, in another place. Wasn't she supposed to be able to get out whenever she wanted? Wasn't she supposed to be able to come and go when she needed to escape reality?

Yet little did she know that while walking towards the door of escape there was one set of rules, but once through the door those rules all changed.

And she became so messed up that she had no idea which voice inside her head was really her own.

CHAPTER 17

Time stops during intense suffering. The clock shuts off altogether, and there's no way to regulate whether getting through the pain is taking forever or just a split second. That's how Nduta felt lying tied down in that hospital. Voices would come and go. Some were from actual people, nurses and doctors working around her. Other voices were from people that existed only in Nduta's mind. And as much as she wanted to be rid of them, it felt like an eternity to get the slightest hint that sanity might someday return.

The first sign of relief came when she opened her eyes and realized the sun was bursting in through the window. Even though incredible light dazzled her otherwise empty room, the strange thing was that she didn't so much see or feel the sunshine, but she *heard* it. She heard the sunshine around her. Somehow the voices quit. There was no one vying for her attention, real or imagined. Just her and light. And for a moment her world went completely right, making her wonder if her time in the hospital had only been brief.

Which is why she was so surprised to hear that she had been in the hospital for weeks.

The doctor came to see her. She sat up, trying her best to get used to her surroundings. He talked with her about her condition. She listened as he spoke, but her mind drifted off. Whether he was giving her good news or bad news she couldn't tell. What she could tell was that she felt a rush of relief in knowing that this was the only voice she could hear.

Sanity can be relative; still, the doctors determined that she could go. Not because she had passed a test to prove she could cope with life—that was yet to be determined—but because the hospital bill was piling up and it was clear that she had racked up a debt so high that it would be impossible for her to ever repay it.

So she left and returned to the hut, where her stepmother was looking after her child. When Nduta held her baby in her arms she felt the indescribable sense of connection. Not just of two people feeling close, but of two people feeling the same. And yet only moments later, instead of dwelling on the joy of giving life and the sense of fulfillment that it had brought her, she felt the unbearable grief and dread that perhaps without any desire on her part she might have somehow genetically passed her struggles with sanity down the bloodline to her child.

And it caused her to feel the most incredible sense of regret that she might have unwittingly contributed to her baby's future demise.

It was bad enough that she was at the end of the rope and walked a fragile line between being able to function and being tied down in a hospital bed. But worse still was the terrifying guilt that she was not able to overcome her struggles, and her punishment might be to see it visited on this precious child, who did not deserve to start out in life with such a setback.

Being poor in a slum is bad enough when a person is single. But being an unwed mother who now has to find enough money to support herself *and* her child was something that gripped Nduta with such pressure that it pushed her to make decisions that were driven by a necessity for survival at any cost. She took the quickest way out to relieve the stress. She had no education. Had no one who would help her. Had no skills to offer.

But she had herself.

And so she went to the streets to sell her only product.

The first time out was the most difficult. There was a lot to learn. Where to go. How to approach a man. How to negotiate the price. Exactly what was the going rate anyway?

She took care of her child during the day, and at night she took her chances with men captivated by their own desires.

It was both humiliating and dangerous to go through with it. Yet the promise of money and the warped but well-intentioned desire to use the money to feed her baby helped her push through the ordeal. When her first shift was done she gathered herself together and held out her hand for the pathetic, but critical, amount that was to follow. They had discussed the price beforehand. That much she knew. He had already been so intoxicated that he gave her a price, and even though she didn't hear it she was just as happy to take whatever he was offering. Something is better than nothing. But when it came time to settle the tab he didn't give her anything. At least not any money. Instead, he punched her with such force right on the cheekbone that her feet lifted off the ground as she flew backwards and crashed into the sheet metal wall in his dingy, stinky, filthy hovel.

What's a girl to do when the world shuts her out, when her family aban-
dons her, when her sanity becomes as reliable as a lazy worker who shows up
when it's convenient, and when the very lowest form of debasement of selling
herself to the cheapest bidder results in not being paid and also being punished
for requesting it?

She got up. Stunned. Was her cheekbone cracked? He screamed at her, and
she stumbled to the door.

Don't worry. It will all be okay. Just come back to me now. You can be safe here.

The man screamed at her again to get out. She found the door handle,
opened it, and collapsed into the Eldoret night.

She staggered back in the dark. Depression surrounded her. She hurt
everywhere. But somehow she made it back to her child and collapsed on the
floor. As she lay there on the ground, shivering and in pain, she thought to
herself that she had now exhausted every possible opportunity for hope and
had nothing left to try.

She got up the next morning and quickly wished she would have stayed
asleep. Her father was home, sober—that was rare—and her stepmother, too.
There's a look desperate parents in slums get when they are being pressured to
make even the little they have go ever further. It was bad enough that Nduta was
here. But the child, too? That was too much to ask.

"Have you found work yet?" her father asked.

He knew the answer. Everyone knew the answer. But he wanted her to say it.

"Not yet."

She had been close, of course. She had worked, but didn't collect the fare.

"And now you expect us to take care of you?"

Her temper flared in an instant. She tried her best to calm herself down, but
desperation does strange things to a person, and if she had had the strength she
would have beaten him senseless right then and there.

"I am doing my best," she said in a tone that conveyed both her anger and
her complete sense of worthlessness.

"You're not trying. And there is no hope with you!"

That was it. Whatever semblance of self-control she had left was not enough
to hold back the wave of fury that followed.

"Don't talk to me that way!" she screamed. "You have never helped me!
Never! All you do is drink, and you don't care what happens to me!"

"You stupid woman!" her father screamed. He let out a slew of expletives
that conveyed everything he thought was wrong about her. And the worst part
was that she believed every word of it. They shouted back and forth at each

other. He hated her. She just wanted to be loved. And the resulting argument just kept escalating.

"Leave me alone!" she shouted back in an ear-splitting shrill. "If I die in a car crash, don't even come to get the bones and bury them. Just let the dogs come and eat them!"

And with that she picked up her baby and left to go nowhere.

She carried her child for hours. Even though she had no destination, the feeling of movement gave her the temporary impression that she was making progress, however invisible it might be.

You can come back to me anytime. You can. You can just ask me to be your friend and we can become the same person again.

It was tempting. It was very tempting. But it hadn't worked out so well the last time.

No. Go away. I don't need you.

Sure you do. You need us. You do.

Us? Who is us? I thought...stop it! Stop talking to me!

She turned off the street and into a field, hoping the change in direction would clear her mind. But it only served to make things worse.

She stopped at a deep well and sat down. She looked down and saw the water far beneath her.

How am I going to live? How am I going to care for my child?

I can get help.

But no one is there to help you.

Then I will get work.

But you have no skills, and the only work you could do you tried last night. How did that go for you?

I can beg.

Sure, you can beg. You can beg like all the others. You can join the thousands and thousands who compete every day for the smallest amount of money.

I have to get out of this situation, and I'm out of options.

The world was closing in on Nduta. Tighter and tighter and tighter until she had no more room to think. Desperation clouds out the luxury of being objective, and Nduta was ready to do anything to escape.

But you are not out of options.

Yes, I am.

Really? What do you see at the bottom of the well?

Nothing?

Are you sure?

It's so far down I can't see anything. It looks like water…there's nothing there.

Oh, but there is.

What?

You know what.

No, what is there? I just see water.

It is your escape.

Her baby cried, and she clutched her closer to her.

My escape?

Just jump in and this will all be over. You will have nothing more to fear.

She didn't want to entertain those thoughts. She wasn't going there. She wasn't going to let her mind—

You want out? This is out. This is your freedom.

It could be all over, couldn't it?

Yes. Finally, you will be done.

But it would not be right. This is not right.

Right from whose point of view? If you want freedom, you have to do what is right in your own mind.

That was a bit of a problem. Exactly who did *your own mind* refer to? There were so many varying tenants occupying her mind that it became difficult to know which one, if any, to listen to.

Just step over the edge and everything will be fine.

She peered down the well, and for the first time she felt the sudden burst of horror in thinking that she might actually do it. She took in a deep breath.

That's it. It will all be over.

She hoped it wouldn't hurt. It was bad enough to be in agony after prostituting herself; she didn't want to have to go down in pain. She lifted her leg to climb over.

That's it. That's—

"Nduta?"

It's nothing. Keep going.

"Nduta, are you all right?"

Nduta turned around. It was the strangest thing. Whatever world she was just in vanished, and suddenly she was back in the middle of a warm day sitting by a well.

She recognized the woman. She lived down the road from her. What was her name again?

"I am fine," Nduta lied.

The woman sat down next to her, touched the baby's cheek, then put her hand behind Nduta, just to be sure she wouldn't lean back and finish what she had started.

"Nduta, you don't need to do this."

At first she felt embarrassed for coming that close. Then, a unique rush of fear came over her. The bottom of the well meant the end of this world for her. That she understood. But what exactly was waiting on the other side? What happens right after a person exits this place? That, she had no idea about. And it terrified her to realize that for the first time she had given thought to the next world, and whatever lay out there, and worse yet, that she was completely unprepared to meet it.

Why am I on this planet? How did I get here? Where am I going? Is there some-one out there who invented all this, or was this all just an accident? And what went wrong so that I have to live this way?

"I don't know why I am here," Nduta said. "I don't know the purpose of this. I don't know the meaning of life," she said. And saying those words sur-prised her.

"I used to wonder the same thing," the woman said.

"You did?"

"Oh yes," the woman replied. Even though her skin was tough—evidence of the scars her body and soul were carrying—there was compassion in her that Nduta had not seen before. "For me, the meaning of life is to be in a relation-ship with God."

God, Nduta thought. *Who is that exactly?* But she had a pressing matter of survival on her mind, and whoever God was did not matter to her as much as how he might be able to help her.

"My father hates me," Nduta said. "I can't go on like this."

The woman waited. She had the rare wisdom of knowing when to listen to someone even when they weren't saying anything.

"It is no value to kill yourself because of your father," the woman said. "God can help you. The child can live and become something. Don't let your father stop that."

That sounded good. Nduta wanted to believe it. But was it really accu-rate? Could the child really live to become something? What was the real probability that the child could have any different kind of life than she had? Or her mother had? Or her grandmother? Or anyone in her family tree for that matter?

"God can heal you from the painful memories of your past," she said.

Sometimes amnesia can be the greatest gift. And for an instant, for just a split second, Nduta forgot about her past completely and felt the freedom that came with being able to leave the ball and chain of her old life behind.

It occurred to her that if she could live in a moment like this forever—one where she knew there was someone who loved her and offered her a future, where she wouldn't have to look back, wouldn't have to hear voices—that a life like that would be the best thing that could ever happen to her.

"This is all fine and good," Nduta said. "But who's going to help me right now?"

CHAPTER 18

From the outside looking in, MCF could seem like an entrepreneur's dream come to life. It could give the illusion that a man's hard work and leadership can transform a dry, hot and undesirable location like Ndalani into a flourishing village. The rescued children, the dormitories, schools, farms, medical facilities, the hundreds of thousands of planted trees—it can all look like a brilliant achievement by a man's ambition. His hard work. His ability.

But Mulli had no doubt about where the power came from.

And how to make himself available to it.

The demands on his time were incredible. Children who needed attention. Financial strains that regularly pressed him to the brink. Spiritual attacks that always managed to come at the most inopportune time. Yet despite everything around him, despite the apparently logical solution of staying focused only on the execution of the work, Mulli would often slip away to the riverside to pray. Sometimes alone, sometimes with Esther. To be with God.

To strengthen the relationship with the Person who made it all possible.

It was ingrained in him. Yes, there were countless children in desperation who needed help. Yes, there were projects to build. Yes, there were hopeless communities that needed to be sustained. But all of these, despite being the most the noble of intentions, were not the work.

Prayer was the work.

All the rest was the result.

Those who heard about Mulli, about the rescuing of hundreds and hundreds of street children, who marvelled at the transformations, who saw the changed landscapes, could see the outworking of the organization. But the very core, the absolute heart of the ministry, was both so simple and so profound that to some it seemed a trivial act that couldn't possibly affect the outcome.

Mully Children's Family didn't come down to brilliant planning, though it certainly had it. It didn't come down to dedicated individuals, though people at MCF gave of their talents in disproportionate passion to the ministry. It didn't even come down to skill.

All of it boiled down to a man and his God.

A man on his knees, like all great men of God, who had a conviction in his spirit, through good times, bad times and confusing times, that the power of God alone was the difference between the cheap facade of well-meaning intentions that would fade away and true, everlasting change that would impact people's lives forever.

Like on the first day when he came to Ndalani with Esther to dedicate the property to God. They spent the entire day praying. At first it felt like nothing out of the ordinary. But after an hour, there was a breakthrough. A suddenly deeper connection that made time seem irrelevant. They had stayed that way for hours. And when they opened their eyes, it was as if they were in a completely different place. Like they were looking not at what was, but at what was going to be.

The property was not large enough to accommodate all the children, so Mulli prayed about the land, claiming both his and the neighbouring properties for God. The owners came to him one after another, telling him they could not sleep because they were sure they were supposed to sell the land to him, that they felt they were denying poor children a place for training by hanging on to it. He purchased the lots from them, expanding the territory to be able to make room for farms, schools and the sports grounds.

When money was difficult the natural reaction would have been to shut down programs or reduce the number of children. But Mulli continued on. Even when he had exhausted all the finances Mulli went out to the slum to rescue still more children, only to find out that a friend from the West had contributed a large amount of money that arrived exactly when he needed it.

Divine intervention can sometimes be confused with probability. One person's reason for faith is another person's reason to doubt. But for Mulli the evidence was not just in the answered prayer; it was in the ongoing conviction that despite the results he was being carried by God.

But sometimes, God did not steer Mulli's ship out of storms.

Rather, he steered Mulli directly into them.

Mulli came down to the river alone. Esther was in Yatta, the MCF home about half an hour away from Ndalani. He sought direction from God on a number of pressing matters. And as he was praying, he sensed another person creeping into their conversation. Like a mighty and sneaky python it waited until Mulli was most vulnerable before it struck.

You don't really believe God will answer you, do you? God doesn't answer prayer. He does whatever he wants. Your prayers don't change God's mind.

The effective ongoing prayer of a righteous man accomplishes much.

We'll see. I almost got you, Mulli. I've been close in the past.

Greater is he who is in you than he who is in the world.

Which really surprises me, coming from a man like you. If God really is greater, then why for every one child that you have rescued is there still well over a hundred more digging out of garbage cans? Look around. Who is winning?

The battle belongs to the Lord—

Okay, enough. If you're not going to look at the facts around you, look at the facts in your past. Those tenants back when you used to run your business? The ones who refused to pay, whom you went to see and they got so riled up? Remember? They were about to put tires around you and burn you alive. I'm wishing they had.

The Lord delivered me from your hand.

But he doesn't deliver everyone. He only delivers some. Even the Bible is full of people who prayed and God did not help them. That's how it is with everyone else. You're a false example.

The results I leave up to God. My job is to be faithful.

I'm planning something right now, Mulli. It's going to be worse than anything you or this country has ever known. I'm coming for you, Mulli. And I am going to finish you off once and for all.

Mulli continued to pray, pleading for God's help. When he opened his eyes it was beginning to get dark. He felt a chill in the air.

He decided not to worry about the future. He did not know what was coming, and he would not ruin his life by fearing what might be.

Though he had the unmistakable conviction that something truly out of the ordinary was on the horizon.

CHAPTER 19

Medical teams from the West regularly came to volunteer their expertise at the clinics at MCF. Doctors and nurses worked into the evening seeing the children, MCF workers, and also people from the community—many of whom walked miles, days, just for a chance to stay in line. The chance of receiving free medical care was simply too good to pass up.

Mulli walked into one of the clinics to get an update on the progress. It was late. The team should have been tired. They had been at it for days. Many of them took their holiday time to come to a hot, dry climate and put in even longer hours here than at home in order to serve people they would likely never see again. They had joy in their service, working to address the desperate health concerns of the endless number of people seeking relief.

The single light in the main room of the small clinic cast what little glow was needed to see the patients. Mulli recalled some of the many instances when God had supernaturally healed people. If he had to record every time he had seen God working, it would take months, maybe years, to recount them. Yet the God who was healing people miraculously was the same God who used doctors and nurses at the MCF clinics to help patients.

If God can and does heal supernaturally, why doesn't he do so all the time? Mulli didn't spend time on questions that ended in circular reasoning. On the one hand, there were apostles in Acts who saw miraculous cures, and there was Luke, the medical doctor who wrote about them.

Somehow the supernatural and the natural worked together under God.

Mulli took a moment to watch the team working under a faint light to help hundreds and hundreds of people. It touched him that people would come such long distances and be so generous as to give everything they could to help people.

Mulli thanked and encouraged the two doctors and the nurse who were still working. When he turned around to go back to the entrance, he suddenly stopped. In front of him stood a ghastly figure. At first his mind wasn't completely sure what he was seeing. It was a human being, wasn't it? It was hard to tell. So frail. So depleted of energy.

The room went completely quiet. There's a stillness that comes when people see someone in terrible agony. There before him Mulli saw a woman so weak and so pale that she might as well have been a ghost.

Her face was sunken in. Her hair, what was left it, lifted with every passing breeze from the outside air as if it weren't really attached at all. Her mouth hung slightly open as if to indicate that she no longer had the muscle strength to pull her jaw shut. Her hands hung down as evidence of her exhaustion. She stood just off-centre, leaning to one side, like her mind was no longer interested in spending whatever precious energy it had left to have her stay upright. But in spite of her fragile and creepy appearance, in spite of the arresting shock of sensing the unimaginable pain she must be in, it was the condition of her eyes conveying that she knew the end was near that gripped Mulli the most. There was no light left in them. Instead of having the radiance of a person shining through them, they were just empty shells as dark as the black night from which she came.

She had two children beside her. A son and a daughter. About six and five years old. One on either side. Their faces were tired and dusty from the long journey. They hung on to their mother, both as an instinctive reaction children have when they are in a new place and in a desperate need to connect as long as they could with their mother, who they were sure would soon be leaving them.

Mulli and a doctor hurried to help her. She was so frail that it seemed she would fall apart at any moment. They laid her down on an examination table. She felt some relief, like her long trek had now reached a critical point. Yet even though she had come all this way, Mulli had the distinct impression that her raging illness was not the true concern on her mind.

She stretched out her hand as best she could as a faint indication that she wanted to speak to Mulli. Her skin was so cracked and worn that it seemed she had already been dead for a number of days.

Mulli bent closer. Her speech was so laboured that it seemed she had to redirect every ounce of power left in her to get the words out.

"You are Mulli?" she asked. The best she could do was a faint whisper.

Mulli leaned in. "Yes."

Normally, Mulli would have asked her for her name. He would have asked where she was from. He would have thanked her for coming. But when it gets so close to the end like this there are very few things that actually have to be said.

Mulli had seen many women's lives ruined by HIV, though none as destroyed as this woman before him. The pattern had been repeated by millions. The husband was unfaithful. He would come home and give it to his wife, who in turn would pass it on to the children. The woman before him now had made that giant leap of accepting her condition. She was done. It was only a matter of time now. And yet, she had pressed on to MCF as a beacon of hope for one reason.

"My...my children." She started off well. But what was taking her body was also taking her mind. She faded out for a moment, like there was a power outage in her brain that came back just as suddenly as it had left.

Mulli leaned in closer. "Yes," he whispered. He turned to see the young boy and girl.

"Will you take care of them?" she asked.

"Yes," Mulli said.

And the moment he spoke those words there was an unmistakable sense of relief in her expression. If she had the strength she would have smiled. If she had the ability to thank him she would have.

But instead, all she could manage was a brief close of her eyes in gratitude for Mulli granting a dying woman her last request.

Mulli prayed over her. The children stood by, wondering if this was the moment they would become orphans.

The doctor recommended that she be transferred to a hospital. Mulli agreed.

He knelt down to look the boy and girl in the eye. He introduced himself, and the shy children gave him their names. When he asked where the father was, the boy shook his head, confirming what their generation experienced far too often.

"Your mother is very sick," Mulli said. "We will be taking her to a hospital. Your mother has asked if I would look after you, and I would love to take care of you."

Mulli touched them both on the shoulder.

"Your mother has brought you all the way here to help you. Would you like to come and thank her?"

The children didn't know what to say. Didn't know what to do. The woman in front of them was still their mother, just not the person they remembered. Their mother had been a happy, energetic woman with a vibrant smile. That woman was gone. She had been gradually replaced day by day with someone else. And now, their mother was just a distant image. What remained was a struggling person who somehow looked more at peace here at MCF than she had in a very long time.

The mother reached out again to touch her children. This would be the last time. And when she let go of them a tear came from her eye. Whether it was grief over saying her final goodbye or relief in knowing that they would not be left destitute, the woman touched Mulli and then closed her eyes in exhaustion and drifted off to sleep, having fulfilled her responsibility as best she could.

Mulli took the children outside. He knew what it was like to be without family. To have that sudden awareness that all of life was about to change.

Mulli held their hands. He prayed with them, gave them supper and then introduced them to the care workers who stayed in the dorms with the young children. The boy went to his dorm for the night and the girl to hers. The girl pulled the cover over her body and rested her head on the pillow. It was all new. New people. New place. New bed. The bed was truly new because she had never had one before.

But the interesting thing was that despite not having known anyone at MCF, despite not ever having visited this place, and despite not ever having met Mulli, she had the complete conviction that she was in a familiar setting.

Exactly how could someone come to a new place and feel like she had been there her entire life? It wasn't so much about coming to a different location as much as it was about leaving the old place behind to become part of what she had somehow always been meant for.

She closed her eyes and felt the sorrow that came with knowing even at a young age like hers that she was losing her mother. Yet as she drifted off she felt the peace during despair that came in knowing that she was loved. That she was going to be all right.

That, strangely, she was home.

CHAPTER 20

"Where would we take them?" Mulli asked. "There isn't anywhere to go."

The Mullis gathered together in Ndalani for a time of intensive planning. The situation had turned from serious to desperate. At first, the rains were late. A few weeks isn't the end of the world. But what started out as a delay turned into an all-out drought. MCF Ndalani is located in Eastern Province, which was one of the most affected areas. It had become so severe that the president declared the drought a national disaster.

The grass, trees and everything else that should have been green turned the same dull brown colour as the slums, which spelled discouragement for everyone. The mighty Thika River dried up for the first time as far back as anyone could recall. People began to die. A mother passed away shortly after giving birth to twins, who then also died because of the lack of food and water. The entire region around MCF suffered to such an extent that people existed in the constant anxiety of not knowing when or from where their next meal might come.

As usual, Mulli went to his knees. He prayed for God to send rain. A bold request considering the enormity of what he was asking. But Mulli's faith never caused him to see the size of a problem. Instead, his faith actually looked *through* the problem at God. And despite the growing and seemingly insurmountable crisis around him, his focus on his Father comforted him with a perspective that enabled him to see the relative smallness of the problem in relation to the greatness of his Creator.

He gathered the MCF children and the workers together and pleaded with God for his intervention. They stood on the empty riverbed, their feet touching the dry land as a bitter reminder of their critical condition and their imminent need for intervention. Normally the children would be swimming here. Normally a torrent of water would have been rushing past them.

They gathered by the hundreds, pleading for God to send down rain on their parched land, trusting God to build a bridge of providence between this world and the next. That evening they built a large fire in the middle of the river bed to keep everyone warm as they continued their prayers through the entire day and into the night.

For three consecutive days they prayed. The young. The old. Men and women. They prayed not simply for their own needs but for God to bring enough money to buy food for all of MCF and for the community of Ndalani and Yatta with a population of over 40,000.

It was a lot to ask. Clearly this was an unreasonable prayer. Wasn't it? Wasn't prayer just for the things a person could reasonably expect God to accomplish?

Or was prayer also for those things that were outside the normal range? Was it okay to be courageous in prayer?

Or did that just set someone up to be disappointed if it didn't come through?

Either way, this true burden from God was impossible for Mulli to ignore, so he prayed for his God to provide.

God, I pray that you will visit your people with a hand of blessing. That you would provide a handful of grace in giving people food.

When Mulli opened his eyes he thought about his MCF family, about his Eastern Province area, and about his country, Kenya. But then his thoughts extended to Africa as a whole and to the world in general. He wondered about what divides people. What classifies one person as prosperous and another not? What is the defining line between the rich and the poor? Is it money? Is it a car? Is it a home? Is it the ability to go on a vacation? Is it a second pair of clothes? A bed?

As Mulli looked out at the mass of people gathered in the barren river he concluded that ultimately the world was divided into two categories—there were those who had enough to eat and there were those who did not.

There was no downpour of rain. No indication that it was even on the horizon. Still, the Mullis made the decision to stay in Ndalani and trust the Lord to provide. The land was desolate.

They had no other option but God.

Instead of hoarding their resources in the storehouse, Mulli began a feeding program for students in the other surrounding schools. An additional 2,000 children came every day for a cooked meal at no charge. On top of feeding the MCF children this placed an incredible burden on the MCF food supply. Some of the villagers doubted how long MCF would be able to continue giving out that much food and secretly believed this would spell the end of Mulli.

A sea of students from all over ran to MCF at lunchtime in the expectation of having something to eat. It was an awesome sight. A packed street full of children lining up with eager hands for their only meal of the day. They sat down and filled an entire field. Mulli took the opportunity to address the youth, who became quiet as soon as he spoke.

"I am so glad that you have all come," Mulli said. "Did you all get enough to eat?"

A thunderous roar of clapping and cheers erupted. It reached right inside of Mulli. All those happy faces of children having a place to eat. Mulli knew what it meant to beg for food. Now he stood in front of this crowd of children that he had fed who shouted their appreciation.

And in that moment Mulli felt the complete affirmation of what it meant to give up everything to follow God.

"God loves each and every one of you," Mulli said. "He has given you this opportunity to go to school. I want to encourage you to study very hard and keep focused on your education. And remember to respect your parents and your teachers. Whatever happens, be faithful to God."

MCF's friends throughout the West contributed to the famine relief, allowing MCF to purchase a water tank vehicle to transport water from their Yatta site to Ndalani to offer drinking water to more than 4,000 people in the community.

Each day people came to MCF in the hopes of receiving something to eat. On one day the throng of people that travelled down the dirt road to MCF Ndalani was so great that it created a trail of dust that workers saw from the MCF site. Some people had travelled as far as 20 kilometres. Some on bicycle. Some on foot.

The workers came to inform Mulli. As he walked with them through the trees he came to the playground area of the MCF site and began to hear the sounds of the great crowd that had gathered. When he came through to the clearing he couldn't believe his eyes.

Every inch of the field was covered with people. Thousands crammed onto the property, hoping that what they heard about a man who fed the poor was true. There were so many bicycles everywhere that it almost looked like a manufacturing company had set up shop right at MCF. About ten thousand people had made the arduous journey, some of them taking the entire day to travel.

Mulli organized the staff, tractor drivers and stronger boys to transport bags of maize, beans, oil and salt to the greenhouse. Mulli gave thanks, and the MCF team handed out food. The mass of people lined up. This seemed fine at first. But ten thousand is a lot of people no matter what the event is, and some of the crowd began to feel the angst of possible disappointment from being near the back of the line. People started pushing and shoving to try and gain better position. But Mulli assured the crowd that everyone would get something to eat, a promise he would have appreciated hearing when he was young.

At first it was odd to see grown-ups struggling for position. But given what was at stake it was understandable to Mulli. It was an instinctive survival reaction when existence was threatened. There were so many people and only so much food. The less food there is, the more people worry about what's going to happen to them. It was true in this drought-ridden area of Kenya. And it was true on the global level. Mulli was convinced the basis for most wars was competition over resources.

Four hours later everyone had received something to eat, and people went home thanking God for getting them through another day with enough to eat.

Mulli made special daily preparations for the older women and those out of work in the community. Whenever Mulli would meet someone new he would open with his trademark greeting, "Have you eaten?" And that would give Mulli the opportunity to serve people and to ensure that no one left MCF, the former desert turned oasis, hungry.

There was a consistent God-given uneasiness in Mulli's heart whenever he saw the crowds of hungry people approaching him. Whether it was the thousands who came down dusty roads to see him, or a child eating out of a garbage bin in a slum, it compelled Mulli to do something. He didn't just see people; he saw into them. He didn't just notice their problem; he felt their need. He didn't just perceive them as people without food; he saw them as extensions of himself. And it wasn't until people had enough to eat, when they were leaving his table fed, that Mulli felt true peace.

He went to bed thinking about how all the terrible struggles he had in life—being beaten repeatedly by his drunk father, having to go day after day without eating anything—had ironically been the catalyst for him becoming the man he was today.

And as he drifted off that evening, the pressures and rewards of the day fading away to make room for tomorrow's, he thought mostly about the verse where Jesus said, "For I was hungry, and you gave Me something to eat…and…to the extent that you did it to…even the least of them, you did it to Me."

CHAPTER 21

They both came from poor backgrounds. But the lack of money was not the source of their fighting.

His name was Mavoli and he had begged Mulli for a job. Mavoli came from nothing and often went without food. He was desperate and in the interview he made a good impression. He was on his best behaviour, of course. Still, he admitted to Mulli that he and his wife were having trouble. Mulli made the best call he could based on the information he was being presented with and hired him.

Mavoli's wife's name was Lucy, and she was relieved to find out they would finally have an income to support their two young children, a girl and a boy, four and five years old.

They had been having trouble. That was true. At least, that was *sort of* true. In reality, they were having more than trouble. They were having a disaster. Their evenings had often ended in vicious fights, both verbal and physical. Fists flying. Bitter screaming. But they put their best foot forward and entered MCF under the pretense that money would make it all go away.

He taught in the school, and the children took to him. That part went well. But a little yeast gets into the rest of the dough, and it was in the evenings that their home life, or lack thereof, came out in full force.

MCF workers normally stayed in one-room residences that were connected in a larger one-storey building. The roof and dividing walls were made of sheet metal, which was practical. But the protection against sound transmission was next to zero. One family's problem became every family's problem.

Lucy complained about everything. He hadn't turned out the way she had hoped. He didn't treat her the way she wanted. And even though it was a totally depressed economy and even though he had persevered to get a job, the money was still not good enough.

Apparently beggars could be choosey.

Handling criticism was not Mavoli's strong suit, and listening to her go on and on about how awful he was pushed him towards the line. It was midnight, and she was shouting at him. Great time and place for an argument. He told her to be quiet. She kept at it. Then he told her to shut up. But that just infuriated her all the more. He could have chosen to walk away. He could have chosen recourse. But he didn't. With a reaction that was almost instinctive, he brought his hand back, then whipped it forward and hit her across the face so hard that it spun her around and sent her crashing against the metal.

She was equal to the task. She wasn't going to take that. Not from him. She gathered her strength, picked up whatever was left of her respect, and turned to attack him, with both hands aimed at strangling him. He grabbed her by the wrists and held her away. She thrashed at him with her head, and the whole thing turned into pandemonium in that tiny metal room.

One of the fathers from the dozens of other families who heard the escalating mess hurried to the disciplinary committee chair and got him out of bed. He came to Mavoli and Lucy's door. He knocked. They opened. And he saw them infuriated from another fight.

She claimed it was all his fault. He claimed it was all her fault. Back and forth it went. He accused her. She accused him. But in all the ruckus they had completely forgotten about their children. The two young ones had seen the whole thing again. It was nothing new. They'd already seen this movie many times. They listened as their mom and dad tried to argue over who was right. But children don't always know or care who is right. The finer points of an argument are usually lost on a child. All they see is the fight. All they hear are the screams. And all they feel is the insecurity that constant fear brings.

The disciplinary head managed to get Mavoli and Lucy quieted down. They became rational again. And as bizarre as it seemed, the mood in the room changed, and they agreed not to fight anymore. It sounded okay.

But they'd all been here before.

The disciplinary head left. The two of them said nothing. Not to each other. Not to the children. They just lay down and waited for the fury pounding in their hearts to subside. Mavoli was the first to drift off. He had already put the whole mess out of his mind. Big argument. Big deal. Just close your eyes and the promise of the new day coming should somehow erase what had just happened.

But Lucy didn't have it so easy. Going to bed angry never helped anyone. And so she lay there, fuming, trying to do the impossible task of clearing her mind of something that was consuming her with rage. She could try to let it go. She could try to put this evening and all the others out of her mind. But like a recurring headache, the bitterness against her husband wouldn't leave her. And by the time Lucy finally did get to sleep, she had secretly plotted how she was going to get him back.

The fighting continued between the two of them, big surprise, and Mavoli had to answer to the disciplinary committee. He tried to find the connection between her incessant arguing and his explosive temper. Fighting was not tolerable. He had to find a way to live in peace with her.

He spoke with Mulli, who encouraged him to rely on the Holy Spirit to change him. He also challenged Mavoli to pray for his wife. He was the man. He was in charge. And ultimately he was responsible. Mavoli understood and promised, again, to do better.

It was only one case in a list of issues Mulli was dealing with. While the vast majority of workers—both teachers and field staff—were gifts straight from God, some were challenging in every sense. Hiring people who turned out to be underperformers always affected the organization in negative ways. When he was in business a bad employee would cost him money. But now the stakes were infinitely higher. Children rescued from the streets who had deep psychological, emotional, physical and sexual scars needed adults whom they could depend on. Teachers weren't just teachers. They were pseudo father and mother figures as well, loving the children in and outside of class. And when one of them dropped their responsibility by treating a child with neglect or referring to them even in haste as a *chokora*, a street child, it would wound that fragile child. It was far worse than if said to a child who grew up a loving home, who would likely have the internal confidence to withstand such an accusation.

Mulli faced increasing pressure to organize such a great number of people. This wasn't a company. It wasn't an organization. It was a home. He needed to have impeccable integrity and a good name for the home to run and to win the hearts of the children, donors, government and surrounding community. His number one challenge was to protect the name of the home, which was increasingly difficult when it came to workers who either did not carry out their duties well or would not treat the children with love and respect.

After one of the evening devotions Mulli was walking back to his outdoor office when he saw a child sitting by herself on the ground. Her knees were pulled up under her chin, her back against the outside wall of the kitchen, and her head buried in her hands.

"Hello, Doris," Mulli said.

Doris was ten. She'd been rescued from a slum near Eldoret. Her parents had pushed her into the streets to earn money in exchange for giving her a place to sleep at night. They figured it was an even trade.

She stopped her crying but she didn't look up. She suddenly felt awkward. "Is everything all right?" Mulli asked.

She wiped her tears. This time she made eye contact. "I am fine," she said.

But Mulli did not want children who were suffering to hide their pain. Covering up hurt in the short term only led to serious problems in the long term.

"You can tell me," Mulli said.

But still she refused. She had learned many things on the streets. One of them was that you did not make enemies. And telling on a teacher would certainly come back to haunt her.

Mulli knelt down beside her. He was gentle. He was firm. "Doris, I am your father. And I am now asking you to tell me exactly what happened."

Mulli put everything else on the back burner. All of the meetings, challenges and issues he had to address suddenly disappeared, and it was just him and his daughter. Doris told him what happened, and Mulli went to the member of the kitchen staff who had talked down to her about being nothing but a former street child. He encouraged the worker to make things right, which he did by asking her for forgiveness. Just as he was finishing the conversation, another worker came to ask for his help intervening in yet another dispute.

The following morning Lucy watched as her husband walked down to the street. She had had enough of his anger. Enough of his presence. She didn't need to change. He did. She wasn't to blame for this mess. He was. She had a right to tell her husband what she thought of him. She had a right to shout at him whenever she wanted. This was all his fault.

She had gone to the village the day before and bought a small can of gasoline. He wanted a fight? She could give him one. No problem.

She followed him at a distance. Glancing behind her she saw that no one was watching. It was the perfect crime. She hid the can in a sash she swung around her body. In her pocket she had a pack of matches. She touched the bruise on her face from last night's beating and felt relieved in knowing that it would be the last time.

He turned and saw her. She smiled at him. That should have tipped him off. Exactly when was the last time she had ever smiled in his presence? She greeted him, and as they walked along they talked about the irrelevant things people talk about when their relationship is in shambles and they keep up the pretense by exchanging nominal questions and comments that only further reveal their disdain for each other.

If he had been paying better attention he would have seen her reaching into her sash. She opened the lid and dropped it on the ground. She didn't care. She wouldn't be needing the container again. The sound of the lid hitting the mud should have been the second clue that something wasn't right. But he didn't put it together.

Though he was about to.

As fast as she could she emptied the contents of the bottle over his back.

His slow reaction time could be attributed to the reality that a man should-n't have to be on guard against his wife dousing him in gasoline. It was the smell that finally tipped him off. But by the time he made the connection it was too late. As he turned around he heard the strike of the match. He caught a glimpse of her eyes. In that instant he saw someone he did not recognize. Out of the corner of his eye he saw the flame. And as the match left her hand he was sure he saw an expression of complete satisfaction come over her.

The instant the match touched the gasoline an incredible flash of fire and heat erupted around him. Lucy had done a good job of pouring the gasoline all over his back so the fire would engulf him more completely. She had rehearsed this mentally over and over again, and her training did not disappoint.

The horror of the moment paralyzed him for a split second. He actually debated whether to beat his wife for such a stupid act or to fall to the ground to try and save his life. In the end, logic won out and he dropped to the dirt road. He screamed as the flames burned through his shirt and began scorching his back. He smelled the stench of burning clothes and then for the first time smelled burning skin.

As much as it hurt he scraped his back against the mud and succeeded in extinguishing the flames. He felt his heart pounding so hard in his chest that he thought it would burst from all the fright.

He breathed in short bursts, relieved that the fire was out. Then he jerked his body around to see his wife. Did she have any more gasoline in there?

The container was empty. And so was the look on her face.

The matter was brought to the authorities, and she was arrested. She had previously attempted to stab her husband to death. Now it was fire, which made Mavoli wonder what she could possibly be planning for him next. Mavoli was suspended for ongoing violence against his wife. Their children stayed at MCF. Mulli and the other teachers paid particular attention to them as they struggled to cope with a violent father and murderous mother.

Then, a few months later, after she had been released from jail, they came back looking for work. Mulli met with the disciplinary committee.

"What do we think? Should we take them back?"

There were four others in the room. It was hard to tell which one was the most shocked. Though if the wide eyes of disbelief belonging to the head of the committee were any indication, he was the most baffled by Mulli's suggestion.

"Bring them back?" He wondered at first if he had actually heard Mulli properly. "A woman who sets her husband on fire has serious issues," he said. He looked to the others for affirmation. "Doesn't she? I mean, are we serious about bringing this lunatic back?"

The other three agreed with him.

Mulli was quiet and measured in his response. He waited, making sure he had heard each of them. "The spirit with which we challenge people is important," he said. "I have discovered that my position in the management, vision and mission that God gave me is to see that those who are bad and are struggling in life, and who have given up hope completely—they need someone who can forgive them as we have been forgiven by God. It is hard to do. We have all been disturbed by their behaviour. We, however, need to balance ourselves. When we do, we are able to get a solution to the problem. The strength to be able to listen, to act without emotion and to be kind to others is paramount for us."

"But Mr. Mulli," the disciplinary head began, "can we really allow these two back? Are we not putting others at risk?"

Mulli raised his eyebrows. It was a good point. "If I was to fire every worker according to their deeds, many by now would have had to go. The important thing is not them working in MCF, but how their lives have been impacted and transformed by their stay and experience at MCF. This happens through forgiveness and the love that is shown them. The children are safe. It is a quarrel between the two of them. And through love they can be won over."

That changed their minds. There was something so convincing about anything Mulli said. The four others in the room found themselves agreeing. And how did that happen? Weren't they just talking about a woman who had attempted to murder her husband not once but twice? Wasn't this as clear-cut as possible?

Evidently not.

They came to one mind and agreed to allow Mavoli and Lucy back to serve.

They were grateful for the opportunity to return. Mulli's kindness surprised them. Yes, he was a good man. But this good? It was far past what they expected or what they could have imagined. Mavoli was an excellent teacher; the children loved him—he had that going for him. But change would not come without effort.

Mavoli and Lucy were counselled. They formed friendships with others. They learned to surrender and not insist on their own ways. They read the Bible. Relinquished their rights. Prayed for each other. And found ways to care for each other.

And with many prayers, and over time, the fighting completely stopped. In fact, they became a model to newcomers of how to serve as husband and wife at MCF.

And the children came to feel the confidence that comes with growing up in a solid family.

CHAPTER 22

It was a tough evening working the streets.

Offering herself as a prostitute was bad enough. She had been doing this so long that the humiliation of having to sell her body for something to eat shouldn't have bothered her as much. But having to stand out shivering in the cold evening with her breath already visible in the near freezing temperatures made it all the harder to keep up appearances. She put on a smile as best she could whenever a prospective customer would pass by. But the moment he would shake his head and move on, her smile would disappear and she would feel the degradation of whatever semblance of respect she still had left.

No matter. Life had taught her not to give up. There were other men out there. And so with every passing potential customer she would dig down deep into her crushed spirit and draw strength for the next skin-deep smile she would have to manufacture. At 13 years of age she could already act the part. And she was still young enough to attract decent money from indecent men. All the same, she hoped she could reel someone in soon and call an end to this awful night.

But that's not how things were going to happen.

She stood on a dark street corner in Eldoret. There were only a few streetlights, and what little light they gave off cast an eerie shadow on anyone passing under them. She managed to position herself under the sign of a bar to provide enough illumination to highlight her youthful appearance. That way she would have an edge on trying to attract whatever customers might be coming out.

Up ahead she saw two people approaching. Her heart both jumped and fell at the same time. It was work, so that meant money. But on the other hand it was still work, and that meant having to go through with this. Again.

As they came closer she realized it was a couple. Not good. So she stepped back and pretended not to notice them.

But they didn't return the favour.

The couple was dressed up. Heading out for dinner. And their exciting evening out was now dampened temporarily by having to pass by a rotten street girl.

The man put his arm around his wife in a sign both to the street girl that he was taken and to his wife that he wasn't looking. The woman pursed her lips together in a vain attempt to hide her disdain. They had just about passed her when the woman turned around and let the street girl have it.

"You filthy black devil!" she shouted. The man tried to pull her away but there was no stopping her desire to impart every piece of vileness that she felt in seeing what she believed to be wretched scum. "You stand there and try to steal husbands away! You are rotten and disgusting! You awful sinner!"

The girl wouldn't look at the woman. No eye contact. Not for years. She looked down at the ground. Others nearby noticed the commotion, and she felt their stares and condemnation.

"Let's go," the man said.

But she continued. "Get off the street, you filthy malaya!" It was hard to determine which was worse, being called a black devil or a malaya. *Malaya* means prostitute and conveys the notion that a person is a dirty adulterer willing to sleep anywhere, anytime.

The woman finally turned and left, furious that her evening had to include the likes of a malaya.

The street girl's name wasn't Malaya. Actually, that could become her name for the night if that's what her next customer wanted to call her. She'd go with any name. She'd been called plenty in her time on the streets. But not once, not one time with all the people she had slept with, had she ever been asked her real name. Then again, even if she had been asked she wouldn't have given it. She had to keep at least something for herself. She didn't want anyone to know that her real name was Nyathera.

She hated this job. Hated her life. Hated what she had become. If only there was a way out. If only there was hope of something better. But hope was out of reach for Nyathera. And as awful as this life was, she knew nothing better, and so she kept crawling back to it.

She waited in the cold. It worked its way through her skin and chilled her bones. She reached the point a person gets to when nothing they do can get them warm anymore. She was about to give up on this useless night when she turned and was startled to see an odd looking man with shifty eyes and a sweaty face staring at her. It was creepy. She normally kept a careful watch out to evaluate people as they were coming. Spot them from a distance and size them up to see if they would be worth the risk. But somehow he had managed to stay in the shadows, as if he didn't want anyone to know he was here.

He didn't say hello. Didn't ask her name either. Why would he? All he said was the price he was willing to pay. A waft of alcohol from his breath filled Nyathera's nose. She blinked as if doing so could get it out of her system. She thought about the number. It was a pathetic sum, really. That he was stone drunk didn't make his offer any more interesting. At her age she should be getting more. She began to shiver. It was the uncontrollable kind—like the way the body gets when it can't generate enough warmth and the involuntary reaction takes over to keep it from suffering real damage. But the cold was the least of her worries. The real challenge was facing the business decision of whether to let this opportunity go in the hopes of something better coming along and thereby risking a potential penniless night, or taking this shady character on and at least making some money this evening. In the end she figured that something was better than nothing so she agreed.

But the moment she said yes an incredible feeling of regret came over her.

He took her to a nearby rusted sheet metal shack. It was leaning over to one side. She noticed. He didn't. To drunkards everything crooked looks straight. He opened the door—it creaked—and went in first. When she entered she was greeted with a disgusting smell of stale booze. She breathed in through her mouth to control the stench. A single light bulb cast a dull haze over the messy one-room unit. Dirty, plastic bags were scattered around the dirt floor. A ripped mattress lay off to the corner.

The man turned to her. He was stronger than her. Quite a bit. Who wasn't? She didn't know what his face looked like. Didn't want to. She kept her eyes down. She knew the drill.

Over the years she had created an alter ego to escape to during times like this. It made coping with this easier. But after countless customers, her personalities all meshed together anyway. Exactly who was Nyathera now? Was she the girl who had once hoped of having a family? Was she the girl who stood on street corners begging to be delivered from this existence? Or was she now the sum total of all the depressing people she had met?

Either way, she went through with it, and when it was over she asked for her money.

And that's when everything went wrong.

He told her to get out. To his credit he used a polite tone. No sense in belittling the poor girl. Even immoral drunkards can be somewhat decent when they get what they want.

She should have gone. Just got up and walked out. There's no point in arguing with a drunkard. But she was tough, and pushing the customer sometimes got them to pay.

Other times, it got them violent.

She told him she wanted what was owed her. She stood her ground. It was courageous. But it was a mistake.

He thrust out his arm and pushed her against the wall. Her back rammed into the dead bolt on the door, sending a surge through her spine. She blinked as she winced in pain. But the instant she opened her eyes she saw his fist racing right towards her face. She tried to duck, but it caught her right in the forehead. Her head slammed back against the wall, cutting a gash on her scalp. She hit the ground and felt a sudden urge to throw up.

Bewildered, she screamed out for help. It was a passionate plea; she gave it her all, but deep down inside she knew it was useless. This was the slum, and no one was coming to her aid. She reached up for the dead bolt—she was willing to go without being paid now—but he grabbed her head and smashed her face against the wall. That sent a splitting headache through her brain, and she lost orientation.

This was all going from bad to worse. Usually it would be one hit. Maybe a few, and she would be able to escape her customers. But this one was getting serious, more serious than others, and it occurred to her that this might be the end of her right here in this forsaken place. He threw her down against the cold mud floor, the room spinning around her, with only the dizzying light bulb to give any indication that she wasn't dead yet, and screamed at her in his alcohol-laden breath. "You filthy malaya!" The politeness was gone. He was all alcoholic now. "You are a disgusting dog!"

He opened the door, clutched her by the throat and dragged her out. She wheezed, struggling against his grip, gasping for air. He lifted her up and punched her one last time, which sent her spiralling to the ground.

She heard the door close. That was good. He was gone. At least there was something positive she could work off of. She tried to stand, but like a boxer who tries to get up after crushing blow, she felt so disoriented from the beating that she fell back down.

She stayed there for an hour.

Not moving.

The shivering came back.

It took a couple of tries, but when she finally got up she managed to struggle down the street. *Just put one foot in front of the other. You'll get back. You'll get back.* People came out of restaurants, and when they saw her they quickly got out of the way. Most crossed over to the other side of the street. She didn't ask for help. That was pointless. Besides, it was Saturday. Some of them had to get to bed on time for church tomorrow.

She got as far as the police station. She pushed open the door.

Nyathera was still in a daze when an officer came to speak with her. She sat in a wooden chair, her eyes filled with horror as if she were reliving everything right now, and explained as best she could what happened.

"And what do you want me to do?" the officer asked. He was in his thirties. Dark uniform. Broad shoulders. Wedding ring. "It's your own problem because you are on the street. You should be in school or married, not on the street."

Thirteen? Married? Was this guy even listening?

They gave her a cell for the night. She sat down on the ground. Shaking. Her clothes and heart torn from the attack. The back of her head still bled. She felt bruises forming on her face. She wrapped her arms around herself, hoping that she could stop this uncontrollable shivering. She wasn't sure if it was because of the cold or the rank shock of what she had just lived through.

The officer came to her cell.

"Why don't you come with me?" he asked.

"Why?"

"This is no place for you."

She wanted out. She wanted some place better. So she went with him. He led her to the back of the station. And there, he raped her.

He dumped her back in the cell. She stayed in the corner, as far away as possible from the door. Not that it would help. Every sound of a chair moving, every voice that she heard caused instant panic in her that another attack was imminent.

She stayed awake the whole night.

Shaking.

The next morning the police opened her cell door and told her to leave. She left the cell, avoiding eye contact, and walked out of the building into the bright sunshine. It hurt her eyes to see it. She looked brutal. Dried blood on her scalp. Bruising on her face. Torn shirt. Her bottom lip was swollen.

The streets were busy. There were people all around her. Still, no one noticed her. It was as if everyone's subconscious alerted them to her presence, causing their minds to look elsewhere. Like they had all been trained to not see the grief.

She walked down the sidewalk. What to do now? Starve or work as a prostitute? Starve or work as a prostitute?

There were so many options.

"Are you all right?" a voice asked.

It wasn't addressed to her. Couldn't be. No one talks to prostitutes. Not in the morning anyway.

"Excuse me, are you all right?" the voice continued.

She stopped. She turned her eyes to the ground and out of the corner of her eye she managed to see a man. A little early for her first shift. But she wasn't one to argue. This time, however, it was going to be cash up front.

"Do you have money?" she asked.

"No."

She continued walking.

"Can I help you?" the man asked.

She stopped again. "Have you got food?" she asked.

The man pulled out a wrapped piece of bread and gave it to her. She began to eat. Fair enough. Money or food. Either way she would be ahead of the game with this one.

"I know what it is like not to have enough food to eat," he said. There was something different about his voice. He didn't sound like all the others. "I was abused and abandoned as a child. My name is Mulli. What is your name?"

Something inside her changed. Deep down. Like there was a part of her soul that she had only now come to know existed. She felt a strange desire to let her guard down.

"What do you want?"

"Only to love you."

"Why do you want to love me?"

"This is what God did for me."

"So you are a Christian?"

"Yes."

"Christians hate us," she said. "We are sinners."

"I am sorry that you have been hated by Christians," Mulli said. "I remember one time I was rescuing street children and the church kicked me out because of it."

"What do you do for street children?" Nyathera asked. Still no eye contact. What's ingrained is ingrained.

"The same as I want to do for you. I can give you a new home. A place that is safe, and you don't ever have to do this again."

"That's impossible." Her face became cold. She knew men. This was a ploy. She had no worth. And the only thing she was good at was going to cost him a lot more than empty promises.

"I felt that life was impossible, too. I was at the bottom. And that's where God reached me."

The wind blew against her, and she brushed the hair out of her face. Less than 12 hours ago Christians had ignored her, a man had beaten her and a police officer had used his influence to rape her.

That was enough contact with humanity for now.

Though if she had to admit it, the man in front of her *seemed* different.

"Goodbye," was all that she said.

And with that, Nyathera turned and left.

Nyathera and Mulli met often during the following weeks. He brought her food and offered to speak with her whenever she wanted. Slowly she began to open up to him about her horrors on the street. The beatings. The begging. The desperation. She wanted to believe him. Wanted to believe that a place like MCF was real. But the difference between her reality and Mulli's world seemed impossible to bridge.

Not once did he ask for anything from her. Not once did she feel that she was being set up for something. He consistently listened to her, which, in and of itself, was something completely new in her life.

Then, one day, she agreed to make the trip to MCF Yatta. No strings attached. If she didn't want to stay she could leave and come back. She had done enough homework on Mulli. She was satisfied that he was who he claimed to be. So she left the slum behind and for the first time felt what it was like to be free from her surroundings. When she got into the vehicle she met other people from MCF. They were happy. Welcoming. And best of all, when they looked at her they actually saw *her* and not her profession.

When she arrived she was brought to the MCF home department, where she received medical attention and was given new clothes. No tears on these clothes. She was shown her new bed and was given toiletries. She was introduced to a new friend who would be responsible for staying with her and helping her become accustomed to life at MCF. She was introduced to one of the counsellors, who would be responsible for her spiritual well-being and who explained her daily life of Bible study, prayers, meals, schooling and vocational programs.

She sat in the dining area, where someone was about to bring her a meal. She looked around. Was this a dream? Was she really here? Was she really out of that nightmare? The cook brought out a plate of beans and rice and told her she was welcome to seconds or even thirds. And it occurred to Nyathera that she would be able to eat until she was full.

"Are you getting enough to eat?" Mulli asked with a smile as he approached.

She nodded.

"May I join you?"

She nodded again. Mulli sat down opposite her.

"I am very glad you are here."

She put down her fork. She blinked once. The tears that began to form cleaned out the dust.

She glanced up and into his eyes. He was so genuine. Just the simple act of looking at him brought her so much peace. "Thank you," she whispered.

"Is there anything you wanted to talk about?" Mulli asked.

"You have time?"

Isn't Mister Mulli a busy man? Doesn't he look after hundreds and hundreds of other children? Doesn't he have to manage other MCF locations? If so, why is he spending all this time with me? He found time for me on the street, but now we are here. Doesn't he just want to move on to other people?

Doesn't he have anything better to do than spend time with me?

Yet as she looked at Mulli she realized he was willing to give her all the time in the world.

"Of course I have time," Mulli said.

Did she hear that right?

"You are sure?" she asked with all the insecurity and trepidation a girl has when all she has previously known is to be ignored.

Mulli smiled. "Of course. You are my daughter. I always have time for you."

She shared about what it meant for her to be here. The threat of being attacked was gone. The anxiety of having to wait for sunset in order to work the streets was gone. The worry of trying to get enough money, about whom to trust, about where to sleep…all of it was gone. There was something about this place. Something that freed her from the rusted armour she had to wear to protect herself from the world.

She talked about how this was far greater than she could ever have imagined and felt the incredible relief that comes when a person can share everything with someone who cares. She poured out her heart and for the first time in her life felt that someone had truly heard her. It was a new beginning, and instead of reliving the same dreadful existence on the street day after day, she felt she had turned a corner and now had a past that was fading away with every moment at MCF.

"You are already making great progress," Mulli said. "Can I encourage you with something?"

"Okay."

"You have had terrible things happen to you. I would like to challenge you to forgive those who have hurt you."

"Forgive them? " Her eyes focused on Mulli. She was trying to *forget* them. Forget everything. Just turn the page. Better yet, burn her whole life history book altogether. What was this? Why bring out the dark shadows of the past?

"There is fulfillment in forgiving," Mulli said. "Sometimes we think we can just ignore the past. But ignoring it only makes it worse. It can take time, but you can choose to do it right now. You can forgive and the Lord will heal you and help you to forget."

She sensed a small yet powerful energy rise up within her. She remembered the men who beat her. Remembered all of them. Remembered the police officer who used her.

"I'm not sure that I can."

"God will help you. To be truly free, you don't just need a new environment; you need to be new on the inside. You can release those who have wounded you."

It sounded good. Really it did. But the men she would forgive didn't even ask for forgiveness. They didn't even think what they had done was wrong. She exhaled. Maybe that was it. Maybe that was how she could deal with the past once and for all. She hated them. Felt embarrassed because of them. Humiliated, really.

"It is very difficult," Mulli said. "I had to forgive those who hurt me. Even my own father, who beat me. I forgave him. And it has made all the difference." Mulli waited as she wiped the tears from her eyes. "So," Mulli continued, "what do you say?"

CHAPTER 23

The incredible stars filled the night sky. They sparkled with such intensity that he thought he might be able to stretch out and touch one of them. It was breathtaking. Far more brilliant here than he could ever have imagined. He had seen stars back home in the West. But here at MCF, standing near the guest dorm, they seemed to be both brighter and far more in number.

As a child he had visited the local planetarium with his classmates and had marvelled at how the stars were portrayed in the man-made scientific exposition. When he got out of town, away from the city lights, he would look up late at night and see how much brighter the stars shone compared with being in the city. But neither there nor the planetarium came even remotely close to how awesome the Kenyan sky looked at night.

He had come to MCF to help, as so many volunteers from around the world had done. He considered MCF the most outlandish privilege he had ever been granted. It was bizarre, really. What did a white guy from suburbia have to contribute to the rescuing of street children in Kenya? Still, as a strange as it was, he had the uncanny feeling that being at MCF, on the other side of globe, felt like coming home.

After a full day of helping at MCF he would stand under the stars, looking up, smiling, mesmerized by the handiwork of God.

He heard someone approaching. He turned to see his friend.

"You like the stars?" Mulli asked.

"Unbelievable," the man said.

There was so much going on in Mulli's life, so much that demanded his attention, yet he displayed a constant peace, as if assured he was not ever given more than he could handle.

"Could I ask you a question?" the man said.

Mulli smiled. "Of course."

"I see how you've abandoned your own life for this incredible mission. What would you say is the biggest difference between a life that is pleasing to God and one that isn't?"

Mulli nodded. He glanced up as if the answer was already written in the stars.

"We have no mandate to control our lives," he said. "It is strange, but many people are afraid of God. They pray, but secretly they hope that God will not mess up their lives. They have it all planned out, and instead of giving themselves to God, they want him to approve of what they have already planned. And this leads to much frustration in people's lives. Release your life to God and he will do what he wants with you."

The man listened. Mulli's words reached deep into him. It wasn't just what he said, it was the spirit with which he was saying it that made his words not just interesting but compelling as well.

"We need to continually seek God," Mulli continued. "A strong relationship with him doesn't happen in a day. The big three are critical. Pray, read the Bible and serve Him. This will help you grow in faith and love. The key is not to try to do complicated things. The key is to do these simple things consistently. It is not complicated. It's easy. So easy that a child could understand it. And many do. Yet as adults we lose sight of these simple truths.

"This is not about our ability. It is not about whether you received five talents or two or one. It's about being obedient with what you have. God does love us, but he is not here to please us. It is about him and serving him. Not about God giving us what we want. And too many times we come to God and privately think that by serving him he will give us what we want. This is not correct.

"We serve because we love to serve. Serving is its own reward. Look around. Look at everything," Mulli said, indicating all of MCF around him. "This did not happen by bargaining with God."

The man didn't know what to say in reply. Like all brilliant orators, Mulli could say more in a few words than many could say in hours, or even a lifetime.

"Then what would you attribute this to?" the man asked. "Why does this work?"

"Of course we have many challenges here," Mulli said. "Many, many challenges. But what makes this work is wisdom."

The man would not have guessed that. It made sense, of course, as all things did right after Mulli said them.

"Wisdom is a gift from God. It enables you to make the right decision at the right time. You can discern spirits. You sense if it is right or wrong. It gives you a spirit of enduring. You can't endure if you are foolish. Wisdom gives you patience and prevents you from being led by anxiety."

"It seems so easy for you," the man said with a smile. "You come to the right answer so quickly. Even with the questions I ask. It's like you already know the answer before I've finished the question."

Mulli laughed again. Then he became quiet and returned to the depth of character that enabled him to both enjoy life and deal with its most pressing matters.

"I marvel at what has happened here," Mulli said. "I am amazed. It's like being in a dream world. But I am not special," he continued. "My Creator created me and I have great respect for him. The wisdom that God gives is so different from the knowledge that is acquired through education. Wisdom is God's divine direction, and the result of wisdom is the impact it has on the lives of people. You will know wisdom by her children. You will see the changes in the circumstances in a home, institution or country."

They both stood quietly, neither feeling the pressure to say something for the sake of keeping the conversation going. Both felt the comfort that comes with silence. Then, Mulli continued.

"Wisdom is a treasure, but it is not about money. It is about the benefit of others, unlike some people where wisdom and prosperity have themselves as the chief end. Wisdom has the chief end of others coming into knowledge of Christ and being benefited."

"Then how do you get wisdom?" the man asked.

"God gives it to some; other times you have to ask for it. And when you receive it, you will see that it makes a way for success. You will be able to know about many things. You can see things in advance. He gives you discernment.

"It is folly not to recognize God's anointment. People will listen and agree that it is right. They will put their faith in what is said. This needs to come from above. God will open things. Impossibilities will not be a problem."

Impossibilities will not a problem.

That line struck the man. It gripped him with such conviction that it opened his mind and heart to understand much more about what drove Mulli. Where others saw a desert, Mulli saw a community. Where others saw disaster, Mulli saw opportunity. What others saw as impossible, Mulli saw as possible. And for years to come, that simple truth consistently encouraged the man.

"And remember," Mulli said.

They made eye contact. The quiet night suddenly became more still. Like everything that had been said before was coming down to this moment. The man felt Mulli's words before he said them. "Wisdom is knowing when you are going into a problem—it will create something that will give you warning."

Those last words felt cryptic.

It was as if Mulli *was* being warned—that he was given advance notice right then and there of an impending danger.

And, as it turned out, that's exactly what it was.

CHAPTER 24

It should have happened by now.

The national election took place on December 27, and it normally took two days to count the votes. There weren't any natural disasters. No wars. No national breakdown in communication.

So why was it taking the electoral commission of Kenya so long to announce the winner?

The incumbent party was the Party for National Unity (PNU). They assumed it would be another victory for them and that they would be given a mandate to continue in power. But with only a few constituencies left to report, the voting results showed that the challenging party—the Orange Democratic Party (ODP)—was significantly ahead. Even though the uncounted constituencies were typical strongholds of the PNU, the opposition was still optimistic they would win because the total number of registered voters in the remaining constituencies was barely enough to make up the difference.

And perhaps most interesting was that the voting was split down tribal lines.

The allegiance to tribes in Kenya has a long and complex history. There are approximately 42 tribes in Kenya. The president, Mwai Kibaki, was part of the Kikuyu tribe, which had controlled much of the power in Kenya since independence. It was the Kikuyus who took over much of the fertile Rift Valley after the white settlers left. Historically, this land belonged to the Kalenjin tribe. But Kikuyus negotiated the land for themselves, and after independence, with the Kikuyus being in power and owning much of the best land, the Kalenjins felt marginalized.

Still, the two tribes had managed to live and work side by side. Kikuyu and Kalenjin seemed to have settled their differences. They seemed to have found a way to get along. They seemed to have gone on with life as if nothing had happened.

Seemed to have.

In a move that felt suspicious to everyone, the governing PNU pushed for a delay in counting the votes for the final province.

And that was when everything started to unravel into a chaotic nightmare.

The ODP moved ahead by more than one million votes. But the very next day, reports showed they were ahead by only one hundred thousand votes. Then with 90 percent of the votes counted, ODP clung to a lead of a mere thirty-eight thousand.

That in and of itself was not the biggest problem. Theoretically, it could be correct. The remaining areas *could* have returned votes overwhelmingly in PNU's favour. As unlikely as it would be to have such a high percentage for one party, it was possible.

But what did present a problem was when the electoral commissioner of Kenya discovered voting irregularities.

In one area, PNU received 105,000 votes. At first glance that was fair enough. But there were only 75,000 registered voters. In another area, the tally sheet was adjusted at the last minute to give PNU an additional 60,000 votes.

Nairobi, normally a city of incredible traffic, turned into a ghost town. Many people lived hand to mouth. But storekeepers couldn't open their shops, because everyone stayed inside glued to their television sets, anxious to hear the results. Some people had enough food for an extra day. Some could stretch it out for as long as two days. But by the third day, many people had been pushed to the limit. They had eaten whatever food they had left. Exhausted whatever savings they had. And when their hunger turned to desperation, crowds took to the street to demonstrate.

Some began looting to find food while others looted out of frustration due to the delayed election announcements, which an increasing number of people considered to be a sign of rigging. Reports came in of people tearing metal shacks apart with their bare hands. Windows were smashed, houses stoned, railway lines uprooted and car tires burned in the middle of the highway, blocking all traffic.

Then came the reports that people had been killed in the fighting.

Thick black smoke rose up from Nairobi as people set houses and vehicles on fire. Police in riot gear were dispatched throughout the city. The General Service Unit in full combat gear deployed to be ready for any type of onslaught.

On December 30, the electoral commission of Kenya announced victory for Kibaki and his PNU party. Some reports indicated that the probability of him winning was minuscule. In order for him to garner enough votes, the voter turnout in the final areas was reported to have had to be nearly 100 percent, with every single vote cast for Kibaki.

People took to the streets in a violent rampage. Police shot and killed attacking demonstrators. Some of those attacks were captured by news cameras, which provoked still more violence directed at police. During the first two days of unrest it was reported by the Kenyan media that 124 people had died across the country.

It was also reported that some Kalenjin youth aged 13 to 18 incited the worst of the rioting in the Rift Valley. They screamed at Kikuyu families to pack up and get out. Taking chalk they would mark on doors "VACATE YOUR PLACE TODAY OR YOU WILL BE KILLED."

They were ready to go to war. They were ready to fight, kill, burn, rape. It was eerie to believe that a powder keg of racism had been sitting dormant all these years, and that an apparently rigged election could be the fuse that would bring a nation to its knees.

A few days later, on January 3, Mulli, Esther, Grace, Ndondo, Kaleli and Dickson sat together on the veranda in Yatta, shocked by the news. Kenya? This was happening in Kenya? The country that often served as one of the brightest lights in all of Africa? How was this possible?

But reality sunk in fast, and the most pressing need was the safety of their children.

The rioting in Nairobi had begun to spread. If it continued, it would certainly reach them. And there was no telling the carnage that would result.

"Do we leave?" Mulli asked. It was more to express his thought than to ask the question out loud. It needed to be said. There wouldn't be time to protect all the children if the rioting reached them. They had members of nearly every tribe in Kenya. They took children regardless of age, religion, gender, health condition or tribe. Love your neighbour. Wasn't that the criteria? If others came with machetes to attack the children, what defence would an unarmed home like MCF have?

The family discussed the possibilities. Tanzania was the most likely alternative. Return to the land where that man had a demon cast out of him. To where they had the healing service and that woman had been instantly cured of her hip problem. But how do you move hundreds and hundreds of children? They would have to start now, right this very second, if they hoped to get them out.

But even then, would there be enough time?

For the first time in his life Mulli felt uncertainty. He was unsure of what would happen. Food came from the Rift Valley, and with that part of the country in turmoil it would be difficult to feed MCF. He felt a battle raging in his spirit and combatted it as best he could.

I've got you, Mulli. I told you I was planning something. And here it is.

Fear thou not for I am with you and be not dismayed for I am your God.
Oh, are you afraid, Mulli? The great Charles Mulli is afraid?
Do not fear those who can kill the body.
You are afraid of this? Mulli, you are an embarrassment. I haven't even begun.
If you are terrified now, what will you do when I really bring disaster on this land?
I'm just getting started, Mulli. It's my time now. I'm getting the machetes out. And
I'm coming for you, Mulli. I'm coming for you.

"If we go to Tanzania with the children, then we will be leaving friends and co-workers behind. What will happen to them?" Mulli asked.

They watched the update on TV. Children and adults had been hacked to death by machetes. Women had been raped. Buildings burned. Reports came from MCF in Eldoret that violence there was escalating.

Was this the beginning of the end for Kenya?

"This is what happened in Rwanda," Dickson said. "It was a tribal clash. Is this any different?"

"How much worse will it get?" Kaleli asked. "If it advances, what will happen?"

"Do we just stay and hope that things get better?" Ndondo asked. "And if they don't, what then?"

As intense as the conversation was, it revealed that they were more than just family. There was a unique cohesiveness about them. A singular purpose that bound them. There are bonds stronger than blood. The Mullis could tell you why.

"There are reports that mobs are burning buses," Grace said. "They stop the bus, ask the passengers for their identification, and if anyone is not part of their tribe they are taken off the bus and macheted to death."

That created an image in their minds that they would rather not have seen. Killing someone with a machete is no easy task. If the blades are even a little dull, it takes real effort and repeated strikes to kill a person. Esther closed her eyes a moment to absorb the impact.

"If we leave on the MCF bus we will have a problem," Grace began. "They will recognize the Mully name as a Kamba name, and they could…"

Mulli nodded. They knew what was at stake.

Even though the Kalenjins were targeting Kikuyus and not Kambas specifically, the Kambas had fielded a presidential candidate who was elected as vice president. And the impending danger was that the Kalenjins might attack Kambas as well. Given that a Kamba VP had been elected, it might result in some of the Kalenjins lumping the Kambas into the same bandwagon as the Kikuyus. And because some of the Kalenjins accused the Kikuyus of rigging the election, they could turn on the Kambas as well.

It would be guilt by association. Some of the Kalenjins wanted the Kikuyus out. And if they suspected the Kambas were part of the problem, then maybe the Kalenjins would go after the Kambas as well. It would not have been rational. But this, of course, was war. And being rational was not always a high priority.

"If we leave, are we abandoning everything we have ever worked for?" Grace continued.

Mulli felt the pressure of being the leader of the family. His right or wrong decision would either keep them safe or put them in harm's way. He exhaled. The solution wasn't there.

"Let's take a break," Mulli said.

Mulli walked down to the dam and the fish ponds. He prayed and thought through a solution. He didn't just need any solution. He needed God's solution. God's wisdom. And through his persistent prayer, the Almighty answered him.

He never took that for granted. A response from God was beyond description. To pray and have God hear from heaven is both a privilege and a confirmation that gives a person the affirmation of the connection between here and there.

Mulli laid out a plan to reach heads of state around the world with a concept of power-sharing between the two parties. Whether his emails and calls would be taken seriously, he did not know. But he was responsible for carrying out the vision he had received.

The fear left him. In an instant he had the unmatchable conviction that God had told him to stay in Kenya. He was reminded of the story of how Joshua was afraid to take over the leadership from Moses. Do not be afraid, God had told Joshua, and that was exactly what God was telling Mulli now.

Mulli felt a weight lift from his chest.

"I'm sorry, God," he said. "I'm sorry for being afraid. Forgive me for being discouraged. And grant me the courage that I may not fear, but that I will be able to move in boldness and not run away."

Mulli had no illusions about the risks ahead of him. Nearby Thika was not safe. And if the violence there escalated it could come to MCF Yatta or MCF Ndalani. If he stayed in Yatta or Ndalani he might be burned. If he decided instead to go to Eldoret he might be cut down by a machete. It felt like Israel staring at the Red Sea with the advancing Egyptian army behind. Going back meant facing their captors. Going forward meant drowning.

Or did it?

No matter.

Either way, Mulli was about to find out.

CHAPTER 25

When she heard the voices it was already too late. She was aware of the stories of violence. She knew the terror that was ravaging the other areas. But that was just it. It was the other areas that were affected. Not their area. She was safe.

That's what she presumed.

She was sitting at the table finishing supper with her two teenage sons when they heard the shouting. It was late in the evening. Pitch black. And the moment they heard the screams, a rip of panic tore through each of their bodies.

They took an instant to look each other in the eyes, both to confirm to one another that they had all heard it and, subconsciously, to say goodbye to each other if this did not go well. Being Kikuyu was normally a good thing. Today, it was the worst. There was such deception and bewilderment out there that it turned former friends against one another.

Blood is thicker than water. And racism is no exception. Unity through hatred forms an incredible bond, and the marauding youths took advantage of their license to murder. Within days an apparently latent passion within them was excited to such an extent that once law-abiding citizens turned without any coercion into field-burning, child-killing, woman-raping sociopaths.

The mother and her sons raced out of the door towards the treed path that led down to their field. They left everything in the house. Fleeing meant fleeing, and they ran out with only the clothes on their backs. The mother had just made it into the path through the bushes that led to the field with her sons right behind when a group of five thugs appeared out of nowhere.

The mob screamed and howled like drunkards, high on the thrill of feeling the evil freedom that came with having all restraints cast off of them. They didn't see the mother. She made it to the path. The violent youths cut off the escape path of the two boys, trapping them in the open area by their home.

The mother dropped to the ground and watched from behind a bush. Her name, Sikhudhani, means *a pleasant surprise* in Swahili, and her heart held out every hope that this would be all right. That they would make it through. Her mind fought against accepting that this was really happening, thinking that it would all soon go away.

But both her heart and her mind would soon prove to be misled.

With incredible speed, one of the thugs loaded an arrow in his bow and shot it at the older boy. The arrow made a hissing sound as it cut through the air. It struck the older one through the back, and the arrow did exactly what the shooter intended, which was not to simply hit the target but to pin him to the tree right in front of him.

The force was so strong that the arrowhead came out the other side of the tree. The older brother screamed in pain. The back of the shaft of the arrow stuck out from where it had entered his kidney.

"Nice shot!" one of the boys shouted.

The older brother struggled to free himself, but the trauma of trying to take an arrow out and the awkward angle of it made the whole thing an unlikely task. This wasn't going to end well for either of them. And, both fortunately and unfortunately, the younger brother would be spared having to live through much more of it.

Instinctively, the younger brother ran to help him. But as well-meaning as he was, there was no hope. As if on instinct a boy his age from the mob swung out his machete with such strength and accuracy that he sliced the younger brother right across the throat.

The shock of the slash stunned the younger brother so much that he stood motionless while his brain tried to catch up to what was happening. Blood spurted out as he clutched his hands around the gaping wound in a hopeless attempt at preventing the inevitable. He dropped to his knees and tried to suck in air. But the gash was so great that all it resulted in was a gurgling sound as blood seeped into his lungs. His eyes bulged out as he struggled for oxygen. The other boys laughed at him, mimicking the suffocating sound. The light in the younger brother's eyes grew faint and then shut off altogether. His body began to slump forward.

He was dead before he hit the ground.

The mother watched from the bushes. Her arms twitched uncontrollably, as if she was being electrocuted. She wanted to help. Wanted it to be her instead. Wanted to take the pain away from her children and put it on herself. And yet all she was able to do was to feel the tidal wave of disaster as it flooded her spirit with an indescribable sorrow that would never go away.

The boy who shot the arrow congratulated the other one on a good hit with his machete. The older brother attempted again to reach behind him to take the arrow out. But it wasn't working. The only other option was to pull his entire body back, and that might have worked if only the arrow had gone in at an angle level to the ground.

The archer took another arrow and lined up the brother in his sights. He waited, watching his prey struggling, getting an ungodly joy out of seeing him suffer. He shot the arrow, and it flew true and straight under the older brother's left collar bone. The team erupted in excitement on seeing the second success-ful hit. Arrows three, four and five came right after one another. He shot with such dexterity that the arrows flew into the brother, hitting him through the back every time.

It stopped hurting, and that's when the older brother knew it was almost over. He hung there, barely able to hear the laughter from the boys around him. He couldn't hear his younger brother anymore. Couldn't even turn around to see what had happened to him. As he faded out, his last thought as he left this world was what would become of his mother.

The mob jumped and cheered, which somehow gave the mother the moti-vation to turn and leave. She ran down the path, finding it nearly impossible to keep her balance. She hurried through the trees. It was a familiar route, but somehow it all looked brand new to her. Were they coming? Were they racing after her?

There were no tears. Tears come with grief. And shock is a long way from grief. Her body was in survival mode, and for a brief moment she hoped that whatever was keeping her going would never leave.

For if she had to process what she just saw, she feared it would be the end of her.

A man ran to Josephine's home to warn her and her family that youths from his tribe were coming to kill them. She never knew his name. Had never seen him before. But he was brave enough to break tribal lines and chose to side with humanity rather than fall into ethnic animosity.

"Our people are about to come, and they will kill you! You have to get out now!" he said.

She and her husband and their seven children ran out into the black night with the man. They met up with other families who were also fleeing the impending annihilation.

"Josephine!" her husband shouted. "Take her by the hand!" He pointed to their youngest daughter, a five-year-old. If they got lost now, in this madness, there would be no telling what would happen.

As she grabbed her daughter's hand she did a quick head count to seven to ensure they were all together. How many times had she done that? On trips to the market. On outings with their friends. On walks to church. One through seven. Yes, they were all there. And just as she counted to seven to confirm that they were all there she lost her balance. She fell to the ground and landed on her wrist, breaking it on impact.

The panicked crowd ran over her. Someone stepped on her back and cracked a rib. She winced in pain as her husband lifted her up. The family and the man ran to an empty house, out of breath, full of fear, and were about to debate their next move when they heard shouting outside. The man went to the door. There he saw a mob of ten youths with torches gathered outside.

It was horrifying enough to have them holding machetes and bows and arrows. But the flicker of the torches in the dark night illuminated parts of their faces, giving them a ghastly appearance, like they weren't human after all, and served as a final notice to each of them that the end was in sight.

"You are a traitor!" the tall, strong leader shouted at the man. "We are your brothers. Not these people. And now you will die with them!"

The leader threw his torch at the house. The others followed. The grass roof caught fire and filled the room with smoke. The mob chanted, "*Choma! Choma! Choma!*" meaning "Burn them!"

Part of the roof fell in and landed on the youngest one. She caught fire, and the father and mother beat the flames off. They coughed as the smoke became unbearable. There was no point in going out the front. They would be hacked to death. They couldn't stay inside; the smoke was already killing them. That left the back door. Which, really, didn't help anything, because the attackers would hunt them down. Still, as the alternatives went, it was the best option.

They hurried out the back door and rushed out into the field. The leader saw them and screamed for the others to join him. They took after them, their machetes in hand, and spread out to hunt them down.

Josephine clutched her daughter and looked left and right to see if the rest were with them. One, two, three, four...Panic gripped her. Four. That was all she got to. Everyone started fanning out around her. She ran as fast as she could, turning her head to see where the others were.

The shouts faded in the distance. She crept down and held her daughter close. She couldn't see the others. The mob grew quiet, which meant either they had given up the chase or...

Or they felt they had succeeded.

The house burned down and the field caught fire. It erupted into a bright red, sending thick smoke into the night air.

Disoriented and desperate, Josephine debated which direction she should run next. She wondered if it would lead her away from her attackers.

Or right back to them.

Makena had three things going against her.

First, she was born to the wrong tribe, and that defined her as the enemy. While the difference between tribes in physical appearance could be difficult for outsiders to distinguish, Kenyans were able to identify people from their various tribes with a high degree of certainty. Even in the night, even filled with the delusion that rage brings, the mobs were able to spot their enemy neighbours.

Second, in spite of what rank terror and grief can do to complexion, she was an attractive teenager.

And third, having been separated a few hours ago from her family in all the confusion of the attacks, she found herself walking down this road, alone, for miles, at night, hoping to find refuge in the next town.

And these three factors spelled doom for her when a mob of youths found her.

It was as if they had been waiting for her. They stepped out from bushes on the side of the road. At first she thought it was just one or two. But then more appeared. They were like shadows that materialized into people all around her.

She wasn't sure how many there were. Not that it mattered when the group got this large. What did matter though was that she wasn't able to find a way of escape. Her pulse pounded so hard in her throat that it made her feel all the more closed in. They shouted at her. Made gestures. Called her names. And started to form a ring around her.

She had seen others die in the attacks. Saw them cut down right before her eyes. She had been fortunate to have escaped all that.

At least up until now.

She had assumed that this meant a quick death. That's the way she would want to go if she had a say in any of this. At least there were some things she could still hope for. She bit her lip, raised her hands and moved backwards, hoping to keep them away. They cheered and laughed. And then to her surprise they dropped their machetes.

That should have been good news. Should have brought her relief that they weren't going to finish her off with blades of steel. But then she realized what was coming next. That disgusting look in their eyes said everything. And it sent such a shock of panic through her that all she could do was fight in vain against the rank fear that consumed her heart and mind.

One of them slapped her in the face. She hit the ground. And that's when it all started.

The next hour was a blur. She may have blacked out, or possibly discovered a coping mechanism to keep out everything that was happening. She lost track of the number of guys after five. Certainly there were more.

Oddly enough, when they were done, they left her lying there, on the road, by herself, in the cold evening. That was better than being killed. But not by much.

She dragged herself off the road, her body scraping against the ground. She shook from a combination of shock and cold as she managed to make it to a tree. Makena gathered together what she could of her torn clothes and put them on as best she could. She sat there, huddled against the trunk, afraid and unsure of what to do next.

Everything hurt. But sitting here was not the answer. When would the next group come by? Part of her wanted to stay and wait until help arrived. To find some kind of solace from this devastation. But the other part of her knew that there was no help coming. And as scared and in as much pain as she was, Makena forced herself to her feet. She continued her journey through the burned-out fields, down the road and past the scattered bloodied corpses on her way to the town.

And the greatest hope she had was that if she didn't find shelter first, if a group of boys got to her again, it would all be over quickly.

It was the fastest he had ever run. He raced through the field at incredible speed with all of the dexterity of a sprinter. His dark skin blended in against the black night, making him look like a sleek shadow racing across the land. He was alone. The rest of the village escaped, and he met them on the road as they were fleeing. They informed him that the mob came through on their rampage of terror.

He immediately began to run. It was illogical. One man against a mob was insanity.

But fathers do heroic things when their child's life is at stake.

His eyes narrowed. He clenched his fists. It didn't matter if there would be a thousand of them. Nothing would stop him from rescuing his son.

He turned down the road that led to his farm. His feet seemed to barely make contact with the ground as he bolted towards his home. He looked up, and at first it didn't register. He should have been there by now. Had he lost track of the distance? Was he in such a panic that he thought he was closer than he was?

Couldn't be. He just passed the turn on the road. That's where his farm was located. His house was supposed to be right here.

So where was it?

He ran farther down the road, and that's when the terror hit him. He *was* on the right property. The signpost confirmed it. And the house should be right there.

Only it wasn't. All that was left was the smouldering embers of the burned down structure.

His eyes scanned back and forth. He screamed out for his son. That wasn't smart. If any of the mob were still around they would hear and come back and finish him off, too. But passion and priority can do strange things to a man, so he called out again.

And that's when he saw the mess of a human body lying near the fire.

His mind immediately went into damage control. His body kicked out whatever chemicals it could to protect the core of him from the horror he was witnessing. Somehow it enabled him to walk closer without collapsing in utter despair.

The body was lying in an awkward position with its face towards the ground. He bent down to get a closer look.

And that was the problem.

Even at this close range, the body was so mangled and covered in blood that he still couldn't identify whether or not it was his son.

It was as if the attackers had tried to cut his head off with a dull machete but got tired with all the effort that was going to be required and quit halfway through. The father touched the charred, cold body and noticed a small birthmark on the severed arm that convinced him it was his son. And whatever the father's brain had done a few moments before to help him cope with the shock of what he was witnessing, it wasn't enough. The flood of grief that followed debilitated him to such an extent that all he could do was collapse to the ground beside his dead son and take in the putrid smell of smoke of his burned house.

He breathed in short bursts and clutched his head as if doing so could prevent it from exploding. It was so unthinkable. Was this really happening? Was his son really dead? He should have gotten up. Should have run to safety. But he couldn't leave his boy. Dead or alive, he had to stay by his side. As he lay on the ground it occurred to him that with everything he was suffering he could care less if the youths came back with their machetes and ended his time on earth, too.

And feeling an unbearable terror and grief, and being at a complete loss as to how life was supposed to go on, that result would have suited him just fine.

He thought about his wife, who had died last year. He could have used her beside him now. Some women have that incredible gift of setting the world right, no matter how difficult it has become, just by their presence. His wife was one of those women. Soft-spoken. Quiet. Hers was a gentle strength. You knew when she was there. Everyone did.

Most men need a woman. And he was no exception. Perhaps if she had survived her illness and joined him in his journey into town, she would be with him now. But he wouldn't have wanted her to go through this grief of finding their son this way. He wondered if it was better for one parent to have his heart torn to shreds rather than two. The only relative bonus in retrospect of her untimely passing was that she had been spared what the mob would have done to her. Still, if providence could have led a different way, if she could have been with him now, they could have helped each other through this unbearable atrocity. Leaned on each other. Felt the assurance of one another's presence. Was it wrong to wish that? Was it wrong to wish for her to be here? Probably. He wasn't sure.

He felt the pain his son must have gone through. He thought about what it must have been like the moment the mob came and the son realized that he would not be able to escape. He felt his son's anguish in those last moments of his life, when he must have wondered if his father would make it back in time to save him.

And it crushed him. It crushed him to know that he was not there for his boy.

He remained frozen in that position. Ruined. Unable to cry. Unable to scream. Unable to move his body. He felt like he was being injected with an immense pain to such an extent that his entire being was consumed by the onslaught of horror around him. As best he could, as much as his brain would comply, he prayed, begged, that somehow what his eyes were registering was wrong. That this wasn't really happening. That there was a different life waiting for him a blink away that could erase all of this.

But with every passing moment, reality began to seep in.

And the agony that followed was so impossible to bear that something in his mind switched. And he stayed there, suffering, paralyzed in a state of unimaginable devastation.

How long he stayed was anybody's guess. At some point he got up. Buried his son. And began the walk to...he wasn't sure. Down the road. By himself. Shocked. Everything he had known was gone. Just like that.

And it got so dark in his soul that the very notion of hope completely escaped him.

He was helpless. For the first time, he felt truly unable to do anything to change his situation. He felt at the mercy of anyone who would come to his aid. If that person even existed, he wondered who it could possibly be.

CHAPTER 26

"I'm going to Eldoret," Mulli said.

The Mullis were quiet. A reassuring stillness came over them. They had gathered back together on the veranda to hear what he had decided. In spite of the lack of clarity they had when they left for the break, and without talking with one another since then, they all arrived at the exact same conclusion.

"We're with you," Grace said.

As terrifying as it was to see their father going to Eldoret, directly into the place where the violent mob was on a rampage, they were in agreement.

A knock at the door. Mulli answered it. A worker with an intense expression on his face.

"The farmhouse and all of our storage buildings in Eldoret have been burned by arsonists," the man said. "We are completely out of food."

Eldoret served as an important location for transporting food throughout Kenya. The Rift Valley Province and Eldoret in particular were under terrible carnage as the violence spread faster than anyone could have predicted. This disrupted major transportation lines, making it impossible for people to move from Eldoret and other vital districts that served as the main sources of maize and wheat for the country. Not only did that spell disaster for MCF, but for the nation as a whole.

Mulli called all the children and workers together. There was something so powerful and humble about a leader bringing himself and his people before God. They all knew what was at stake. They understood. There was no food. The storage houses at MCF Ndalani had minimal capacity. Even a small family could only last a few days with the food in their storage facility. But a family like MCF with hundreds and hundreds of children and hundreds of workers and staff would soon be facing empty plates at mealtime.

"I am calling each one of us to stand together in prayer. We all come from different tribes in our country, but we are all one in Christ Jesus. The place you come from, your last name, your heritage—this is not what defines us. What defines us is the love of Jesus that makes us all brothers and sisters. We have given our lives to Christ and we are citizens of heaven. And we are here to have hope in God for peace in our land and for food supplies. We want to ask God to open doors so that we can have access to food."

Mulli paused. He looked out at the crowd of hundreds who stood before him. They were silent, waiting on his every word. Many of them had been there when they experienced the miracle of water. In spite of all the reports that confirmed there was no water at the Ndalani location, Mulli prayed and God showed him where to dig. And that's where they found a water source they called Jacob's Well. Others had been with him when he laid hands on sick children and they had been made perfectly well. Still others had been eyewitnesses to him praying for children who were possessed by demons to such an extent that they spoke in unholy languages and carried out superhuman activities. Yet Mulli prayed for them, and they were delivered.

But would it happen again? The water was in the ground, wasn't it? God just had to tell Mulli where it was. And the healing, that happened in the Bible, didn't it? So did demonic deliverance.

But could God actually provide food for hundreds?

He had done it before, hadn't he? For five thousand.

But was the God of the Bible still the same God today?

"It is always hard when you pray for something that you do not have, that you cannot see. It goes beyond our human understanding. There is violence and there is no food. This is serious for us. For our neighbours. For all of Kenya. And it can seem impossible. But the Lord reminds us, when you pray you must believe that you are going to have what you are praying for. Are we in agreement? Are we in agreement to trust God for the impossible?"

Mulli prayed in front of the group. For hours they prayed. They got down on their knees by the hundreds and pleaded for God to send help. It was a bold request.

But Mulli's faith drove him to do bold things.

Like what he was about to do next.

"This is absolutely crazy," Esther said.

She had a point. Not only was Mulli asking God for food, but the very little food he had left in the storehouse he was giving away to the community around him.

"It is crazy," Mulli agreed. "But it's right." He opened the storehouse doors. There it was. The last of their food. The very lifeblood of the organization before his eyes.

Esther was beside herself. She wouldn't disagree with him, not in public. But here, in private, was a different matter.

"Right? What's right? Taking food away from our children? These are the ones that are entrusted to us."

"In reality they are entrusted to God," Mulli said. "We are only here as his representatives."

"And are we representing him correctly by putting our children at risk?"

"We represent him correctly by being obedient to him," Mulli said. He turned to her. In his classic, congenial, yet confident tone he did his best to encourage her. "Esther, faith without action is not faith. If I give the food, the Lord will supply. Isn't he the one who told us to love our neighbour? And when do we love our neighbour? When it is easy and convenient? We love even in the difficult times. At times like this."

She sensed the conviction in his tone. She'd heard it countless times before. There would be no turning back for Mulli. Not after he had heard from God.

She took in a deep breath. How was this going to work out? "Okay," she said.

The MCF team took every bag of food out, much to shock of the workers. They distributed it to the desperate and poor throughout the community, giving them full stomachs.

And leaving MCF empty.

Mulli stood beside Esther. Their eyes connected. Standing on God's promises. Standing in faith. Together. This was it. The storehouse was empty. And tomorrow the children would be needing food.

A lot of it.

You are a fool, Mulli. What kind of a person misreads God like this? He never told you—

Mulli's cellphone rang.

"Hello."

"Charles Mulli?"

"Yes."

The businessman introduced himself. He was calling from Matuu, the nearest shopping centre to MCF Ndalani. "I made a large order of maize and beans from Tanzania just before the violence spread," he said. "The trucks have been stopped at the Kenyan-Tanzanian border because of all the fighting. However, I can have them delivered to your home as soon as the trucks are permitted to pass. Would this be of interest to you?"

As it turned out, yes. Yes, it was of interest to Mulli. Mulli confirmed the order and the man agreed to make contact with him as soon as the food was ready to be delivered.

Next was the little issue of getting the money to pay for it.

That evening Mulli sat down at a table near the kitchen in an open area with a sheet metal roof. He checked his emails and opened one from a friend in the West. His friend wanted to give a donation to purchase food for MCF.

Turned out the amount he was offering would be enough to feed all the children and workers at MCF for more than a month.

The next morning Mulli met the businessman in Matuu and delivered a cheque to him for the food. Mulli didn't have the money in the bank. Not yet. Writing a cheque that didn't cover the amount would not only ruin his name but would land him in jail. But none of that worried Mulli. He made the deal. And sure enough. the money came from his friend in the West.

Just as it was promised.

That evening Mulli packed his few belongings together. Even though the miracle of food should still have been fresh on his mind he was focused on his trip to Eldoret. And despite his faith, despite his assurance that this was the right move, he wondered, deep down, exactly how this was going to work out.

I told you I was coming for you, Mulli. And this is it.

I am following God. When God tells me to move, I move. That's how it works.

I'm glad you believe that, Mulli. Because you're not coming back here.

That got to Mulli. It was a distinct possibility. This wasn't a pray-and-it-all-goes-the-way-you-want ministry. Mulli was clear that he might go to Eldoret and die at the hands of people whom he was trying to help. But wasn't that what obedience was all about? Obeying even when it didn't suit?

The Lord says that his mercies never cease as long as we keep on trusting him and doing everything for his honour and glory.

And you believe that God will protect you? He never guaranteed that. And only a fool would go to Eldoret during the worst of the battle.

I am not interested in myself. I am only here to fulfill the calling of God on my life. For the sake of those in need. For those who have been denied their rights. For those who have been neglected and abused.

There's no guarantee he will let you escape. You're done, Mulli. Now comes the end.

My God is there as long as I keep calling on his name in earnest prayer.

Mulli left the room and hugged his wife and children goodbye. He got into the vehicle. As he drove off he looked back and waved at them.

And in his heart he did not know if he would ever see them again.

CHAPTER 27

Nduta's life continued its downward slide. She struggled every day to find enough food. She latched on to various men, all essentially the same type of men, who let her down. She found herself with three children, one of whom died of illness. It was bad enough that she had been tied down with ropes in the hospital. Bad enough that she had seen her stepmother kill her sister. Bad enough that she had been ready to drown herself and her baby in a well.

She had even tried to go to church. As depression prone as she was, she had become desperate and was willing to try anything. And the woman at the well who spoke about God seemed genuine enough, so Nduta figured she would give the man on the cross a shot. But as it turned out, slum girls weren't welcomed in that church. Especially not when she came with children but without a husband. She overheard women in the church referring to her as "that girl who only wants to come here because she needs help."

Fair enough. It was a crazy thought. Going to a church to get help. But didn't people come into a store because they needed to buy something? Didn't people come into a restaurant because they needed food? And didn't people come into a church because they recognized their need for help? Apparently not. Apparently people like Nduta who came to church because they needed help didn't understand a bizarre code that said they had to have their lives in order *before* they came in.

She didn't fit in with that church and made the assumption that this was what all churches must be like.

So she left.

Yet, in spite of her disappointment she had the distinct impression that there was a God out there who loved her. Exactly why he would love her in spite of all of her foul-ups she wasn't sure about. Why a God would care about her when clearly she had nothing to offer him in return was beyond her.

But he was out there. Somewhere. She had a conviction in her spirit about that. And she hoped that someone would help her find him.

In the meantime, she had the small matter of the need to survive on her mind. Out of options, she took to the streets of Eldoret. It was the usual. Feed her children during the day and find men to sleep with at night.

Not being able to read or write and having no marketable skills did not exactly make her competitive in the marketplace.

At least not in any marketplace besides the one she was used to.

She came home late one night after a decent shift. Her customers actually paid. She was about to go to sleep when she heard the screaming.

"They are coming! They are coming!"

What? Here? Now?

She scooped up her two children and burst through the door of her shack. She looked behind her and saw an inferno ripping through houses, heading in her direction. In the distance, hundreds of youth carrying machetes shouted and stomped up the street.

People raced out of their homes carrying what little possessions they could. The street was suddenly filled with panicked people running from the machete-wielding youth.

She had no place to go. There were no relatives and she had no friends. She looked behind and saw the group getting closer. She could make out their faces. Darker complexions. Taller. Narrower faces. It fit the attacking mob description perfectly.

She joined others in running to the chief's compound. It was a risky move because he was a member of the attacking tribe. But he was also a government representative. Perhaps he would see beyond his tribal lines.

Nduta knocked on the gate. She saw the youth getting closer. They screamed and waved their machetes in the air. She knocked harder. The chief came to the gate. He too was tall with a narrow face. Dark skin. He saw that neither she nor the others with her were part of his tribe.

"Please help us," Nduta pleaded.

He heard the shouting grow closer. He looked Nduta in the eye.

Nduta checked back again. This was it.

He looked closer. Looked down the street at the approaching mob.

He opened the gate.

"Quickly."

They hurried inside and the chief closed it behind her just as the youth arrived.

"Open the gate!" they screamed, machetes and torches in hand.

"These people have come to the government for help. Do not kill them," he said.

"You are part of our tribe and you are telling us what to do?! If they are here tomorrow we will burn your house down!"

The chief brought the news to the refugees. Nduta sat with her two children. Exactly where were they supposed to go next? Her children fell asleep beside her as she thought through what few options she had.

She didn't sleep that night.

When the sun rose the next morning she felt the clock ticking. In 12 hours it would be dark again and she would have to be gone. She heard others talking about finding a place to stay. She asked where they were planning on going.

One of them told her they were going to try for a church.

Great.

Church.

Again.

Nduta immediately began thinking of alternative locations. She had some money. But the roads and trains were all shut down. She couldn't leave. And who was going to take her in, even if she did have money?

They packed up and headed down the street. It felt strange. Had they been on this street the previous evening they wouldn't have survived. Strange how the sun seemed to bring a reprieve from the violence, if even just in this particular area.

They arrived at a church. The priest opened the door. He, too, was part of the tribe inciting violence.

He looked out at the group standing before him. They were exhausted. Terrified. At the end of their options.

"Come in," he said. "Please, come in."

Doesn't he know what I am? Nduta thought.

The church gave them each a tent to set up in the yard, which was protected by a fence. At night they could come into the church while the men would stay outside and protect them.

The mob made up of youths came the following night and threatened them, commanding the priest to bring out the enemy. But the priest refused. Even though the youth were infuriated at the priest's resilience, they would not torch the building. In spite of the trail of carnage they had left behind them, in spite of breaking the commandment of *Thou shall not kill,* they felt strangely obligated to obey a deeply held code of not harming a church. It was as if killing a person was no big deal, but burning down a church would surely bring down the wrath of the Almighty.

Rules were rules.

Nduta and her children came into the church for night. The nuns brought her food and helped take care of her young ones. They offered to pray for her. She accepted. That evening she fell asleep and felt the peace that came with knowing she was welcome in a place where people would not look down on her for her past mistakes.

Or because she needed help.

But it made her wonder how long this would last. As incredible as the church had been to her, this wasn't a long-term solution. How long before the violence would end and she would be back on the streets? Would she leave the church only to work as a prostitute again?

What other hope did an illiterate teenager with two children have?

CHAPTER 28

It was simply the best fun in the whole world.

The planet collectively refers to it as the Beautiful Game. Those in North America refer to it as soccer.

But the rest of the world calls it football.

Eight-year-old Michael stopped the makeshift football with his chest and dropped it perfectly on his foot. With lightning speed he took off down the field. He dribbled past an opponent and raced towards the goal. He faked like he was going to pass to the right midfielder beside him, causing the defender to move up and block the apparent pass. But in a move that can only be described as brilliant, Michael spun completely around the defender and ran still closer to the net.

Playing midfield rocked. You were always part of the play. If the ball was near your own goal, you helped out on defence. But on plays like this, you could join the attack and sprint towards the goal on a threatening two-on-one.

Michael glanced left. It was a classic tactic and proved to be all that was needed to look off the defender, who was now thinking more pass than shoot. The defender should have known better. Sure, Michael *could* pass. But when it came time to score, he wouldn't turn down the opportunity.

Michael lifted his left arm and watched the goalie out of the corner of his eye. He planted his left foot beside the ball, which was a combination of plastic bags tied together with yarn, and struck it with his right foot with such accuracy that it made the perfect *whoosh* sound as it blasted off through the air towards the net.

Goalies are taught to read and react. It's instinctive. Even when a shot seems like there is no chance, it's the goalie's job to jump anyway. You never know.

That feeling of impossibility is just a trick the goalie's brain plays on itself, and it's the goalie's responsibility to refuse that notion and jump all the same.

The instant the ball left Michael's foot the goalie had to make a judgment call about what the projection of the ball would be and where it would end up. If he waited until he was sure where it would go, the ball would certainly fly past him. If he guessed wrong he would jump too high or too low and miss it all the same. He had long arms, but instead of leaping with two hands to get the ball, he made that split second decision to jump full stretch with only one arm to make himself able to reach farther. He instantaneously discarded the idea of trying to catch the ball and went instead with a desperate attempt to deflect it.

Any object, such as a football, begins to slow down immediately after it is struck.

So why did it seem like the ball was speeding up?

Michael watched as the ball flew towards the top right corner. No way the goalie was going to get that. As tall as that kid between the posts was, he wasn't going to reach it.

Which is why Michael was so surprised when the goalie *did* reach it.

It deflected off the goalie's fingertips, off the crossbar and off the post. The ball bounced and then rolled right along the goal line. The defender was equal to the task. He raced towards the ball, slid on the dirt pitch and cleared the ball off the line, sending it sailing out to the field.

Great players don't go to where the ball is. They go to where the ball is going to be. And when Michael had seen the defender sliding in to kick it away, he started running to where he calculated the ball would end up. While others waited, Michael ran.

Michael estimated correctly. The ball was coming toward him, but the trajectory was such that the ball would go over his head and land past him.

No matter. If a goalie has to overcome impossibility, so does a player. And Michael changed his running pattern to set himself up for arguably the most coveted shot in all of football. The ball came down toward Michael, and all the players on the pitch turned their attention to him.

There are few things in sport that are as perfect as seeing a Kenyan boy in his faded red shorts and faded green shirt, worn to mimic his country's colours, jumping for a bicycle kick against the backdrop of the impeccable setting African sun.

He led with his left leg up in the air with his back pointed to the ground. He watched as the ball approached and waited until the exact moment to kick with his right leg in a motion that imitated riding a bicycle upside down in midair.

He made flawless contact with the ball. This time he directed it at the top left corner.

The other player stood in awe. When you're in the presence of greatness there isn't much else to do. It was crazy to try such a kick, let alone actually make contact with the ball.

Let alone get it to go toward the net.

The goalie picked himself up from the ground. He looked around for the ball and saw it sailing toward the other end.

Not again.

But he would not give up. The keeper was resilient. He charged to the opposite post against his brain's better calculation, which told him it was way past hopeless. He dove and realized that on this one, his brain was correct. All he could hope for now was that the ball would connect with the crossbar or the post, a goalie's best friend.

Michael hit the ground. He turned over and saw the ball fly into the top left corner. The perfect shot. It's like he could hear a stadium full of fans going crazy and the announcer shouting the infamous minute long "G-o-a-l!" A huge smile came over his face. His eyes lit up. He felt a rush of excitement fill him.

His team shouted in excitement. They ran to him and congratulated him with pats on the back and hugs. Scoring a goal is cool.

Scoring a goal when it's last-goal-wins in an all afternoon game is even better.

The goalie picked himself up off the dirt pitch. He was a good-natured kid who knew how to compete hard and how to take defeat well.

"That was a good shot, Michael," he said.

Michael turned around. "Nice first save."

The goalie laughed. "Best two out of three?"

Michael nodded. "Tomorrow. Game Two."

There's an unwritten rule around the world. Whether kids are playing football in Africa, hockey in Canada, baseball in the States, or cricket in India, when the sun goes down the kids go in for supper to fuel up for more of their activity.

So the boys headed off in different directions, already looking forward to tomorrow's rematch.

Michael had the longest walk back, and it was already dark when he turned up the road that led to his home. Sometimes at this place, if the wind was right, he could smell what his mother was cooking. The supper aroma would drift into the air and give him the feeling that a great meal was just down the road. But not today.

Today was different. Today there was an unmistakable smell of smoke in the air. Something wasn't cooking. Something was burning. And when he reached the top of the road he saw flames in the distance.

Entire fields were on fire. It was an inferno. Like a scene out of a battlefield where bombs had just been dropped. Thick black smoke rose, creating a general grey haze as far as he could see.

A man, whom Michael recognized as a farmer, ran toward the village screaming. At first Michael thought he was coming after him. But then he heard the chilling warning that he was shouting.

"They are coming! They are coming!"

Michael dropped the ball. That in and of itself was important. Business people don't just drop phone calls. Movers don't just drop expensive objects. And Kenyan boys don't just drop a football. Unless something truly important, or devastating, is about to happen.

People raced out of their huts. They saw the approaching fire and assumed correctly that the mob had in fact made it this far and were continuing their reign of violence.

Michael took off. He ran as fast as he could. Faster even than when he was on a breakaway. That smiling face on the football pitch was now replaced with a stone terror expression that seemed completely unfitting for any child. He turned off the road and down the path to their hut. But when he reached their property he saw that the attackers were already coming down the opposite path.

He hurried inside and saw his mother.

"They are here!" he screamed.

Her warm face changed instantaneously. They heard shouting outside. In a heartbeat her mind processed the situation and went from *How can this be? They aren't supposed to be here,* to *We have to get out!* to *I'm not getting out. They won't let women live. It's over for me,* to...

"Under the bed!"

Michael did as he was told. He hid under the frame his father had built when he was still alive. He heard his mother quoting Bible verses as she raced for the back door. The shouting came closer. Michael's attention turned to the entrance.

The youths kicked open the door. Six of them. Each of them had different builds but the same wicked intent written in the expressions on their faces. Their leader, a boy really, maybe 15, came in first. Strong muscles. Average height. Above average hatred in his brown eyes, which had a disgusting flood of yellow where the white should be.

"Well, well, well. A land stealer. A thief. You people steal our land and now you steal our election with your vote rigging,"."

It was strange. If it weren't for that crazed look in his eyes you'd almost make the mistake that he was sane. His tone was even. It was as if he were about to sit down and join them for dinner.

"No," she said and realized her mistake. There was no point in trying to fight with him. Disagreeing with him by saying *no* wasn't helping. "I am just living here."

"No? No? Is that all you people ever say to us?" His tone changed. It became deeper. Creepy. His eyes looked different. Worse, if that were even possible. Whatever rationality and humanity was left in him disappeared like a candle being snuffed out in the midnight dark. He was all evil now. And everyone knew it but him. "No, you can't have your land. No, you can't have your election. No? I will tell you what No is. No is what I say to you when you beg me to let you leave."

"Please!" she backed up. She saw the machete the leader was carrying. It's a strange state the brain goes into when the impending end is near. Panic can be overwhelming. But she was resilient. The knee-jerk reaction would have been to have one last look at her son. But even now, even with such a disastrous conclusion looming, she knew better and instead kept her eyes on that disgusting shade of yellow in those shells that no longer let any light through.

She saw the first swing coming and put up her arms. It caught her in the wrist. She was a frail women, and a machete with any kind of a sharpness to the blade would have taken her hand clean off. But it didn't. It just shattered a number of bones and sent a horrific shock through her body that made her want to vomit in pain. She determined that with such a dull blade this ordeal was going to get dragged on a lot longer than it should, and she was going to come to about as bad an end as anyone ever met.

She crumpled to the ground and begged for mercy. Both from them and from God. The group was determined. Once you cross the line and kill one, killing dozens becomes easier. And they raised their machetes, dull or not, and moved in for the kill.

Michael watched as the evil group attacked her. After the next hit Michael closed his eyes. That worked to keep him from seeing what was happening. Now if only there was a way to close his ears. Unfortunately, he heard his mother screaming and the sound of those blades whacking against her slight frame. Over and over again.

And then everything went quiet.

Until he heard a voice near him say, "Look at what we have here."

Michael opened his eyes. He would have seen the pool of red all over the floor had it not been for that putrid yellow staring right at him.

The leader pulled Michael out by his arm. He tried to stand, but his legs wouldn't allow him. His knee hit the ground. Right into the blood. He refused to look at his mother, but that football sense in him saw things out of the corner of his eyes, and what he saw changed him from a boy to a victim.

The mob stood in front of him. Their bodies covered with blood. Their machetes dripping red. The leader looked him over. Michael stopped breathing.

"You are young," the leader said. That was downright spooky. It was like he changed into what appeared to be a normal person. He spoke so matter of factly, like they were strangers who had bumped into each other on a busy street in a large city. "You are only a boy. We will not kill you, boy."

They laughed. How utterly bizarre that somehow they could dissociate themselves from what they had just done. Like they could compartmentalize their brains and switch back and forth between crazy and sort of human. But the scariest part about them was that they were so accustomed to killing and thinking nothing of it that it seemed they were just as likely to go out and kill another hundred people as they were to sit down with him and watch a football match.

They told Michael to leave the house with them. As they went, Michael resisted the urge to look back at his mother. He later regretted it, thinking that he had dishonoured her memory by not seeing the sacrifice of her mutilated body. But later still he felt comfort in believing he had done the right thing. He knew she wouldn't have wanted him to see her body that way.

It was only when they were near the door that Michael noticed the table was already set for supper and that she had made his favourite meal, ugali. He wanted to reach out and put his fingers in the now cold bowl. *Just one last touch of my mother's ugali. Just one last...*

Michael watched as the mob set fire to the house with his mother in it. He tried to remind himself that she was already gone. That this was just her body. But his brain wasn't doing such a good job. Ironically, the other guys' brains seemed to be doing just fine, depending on how you looked at it. As the place burned to the ground, the thugs talked about where they were going next on their murderous streak as nonchalantly as if they were discussing which friend to visit. When they were satisfied that everything was nicely reduced to ash and smoke, they left Michael to stand there, alone.

Wondering what he should do next.

This marked the end of everything he knew. Thoughts of someone helping him did not even enter his mind. Help was for the fortunate. And for the unfortunate sons of this world like him, the luxury of help was unthinkable.

Still, his heart cried out for someone to come to his aid. For someone to help his suffering mind through this unbearable disaster. For someone to wrap their arms around him.

For someone to comfort him.

For anyone.

CHAPTER 29

Eldoret had become a killing zone.

People of the victimized tribe fled for their lives. Bodies that had been hacked to death lay scattered on the streets. Houses had already been burned to the ground and their owners killed. Chalk markings found on doors of other houses served as warnings to those who would be killed next.

Some of the husbands told their wives and children to go the church in nearby Kiambaa. They would be safe there until the violence quieted down. While there would be no reasoning with the attackers, even in war there was some restraint, and even though the unspoken rule of not killing women and children had not been adhered to, the other unspoken rule of not attacking people in a church had been upheld.

The *matatu* taxis had stopped running, so everyone had to make the trek on foot. The plan was for the husbands to hide out in the bushes during the day, come to their families in the church at night, and wait until it would be safe. The men were the targets, and if the attacking tribe saw men from the opposing tribe taking shelter in the church there was no telling what would happen.

They arrived at the church property. No large fence. No gate to keep others out. Just a belief that they were on holy ground and were protected because they set foot on a church lot. The building itself looked small for the large number of people seeking refuge. Maybe it was as big as three large classrooms. Small windows. Metal roof. Wood trusses. Walls made of wood sticks filled with mud. The simple structure stood as a testament to simple living.

One of them knocked on the door of the church. The pastor, a kind young man with a concerned look on his face, introduced himself as Stephen and opened the door. He would have liked to have greeted each new person with a genuine smile and been more upbeat. He would have liked to have called his wife or his four children to come and meet the new visitors. He would have liked to have taken the time to shake every person's hand and ask them their names.

But his desire to serve outweighed his manners.

And given the circumstances, that was fine with everyone.

He did not ask their names. Did not ask their tribe. Did not ask their religion. He spoke one only word:"Come."

He opened the door wider to let them all in. But instead of looking each of them in the eye as they entered, he kept looking out in the distance for any sign of danger.

When the last person came in, he shut the door and locked it behind him.

It was crowded. There were far more people in here than there was room for. They began to settle into place as best they could. Some of them knew each other. Many were strangers soon to become friends. Collectively, their only crime was that they were born into the same tribe.

They introduced each other. And even though they made conversation about their husbands, their children and all the other things people talk about when they are trying to get to know each other, they were communicating involuntarily with the worried looks in their eyes, the anxious tone of their voices and their strained facial expressions.

Dalila, a twelve-year-old girl who under other circumstances would have had her trademark genuine smile, sat down on a wooden bench and took the series of scarves off her back that were used to hold her baby brother. She was quiet, never one to draw attention to herself. She rocked him gently in her arms as she sang a barely audible lullaby to him. Her mother, a slender woman with deep, compassionate eyes, kissed her baby boy and Dalila. Had the situation been different, she, too, would have smiled. But all she could manage was a look of desperation that she was trying hard to hide.

And as Dalila caught a glimpse into her mother's eyes, she saw her struggle to overcome the anxiety raging war inside of her. Even at such a young age, Dalila had taken on the responsibility of looking after her brother. She was never asked to do it. She just took on the role. Like she was designed for it.

She sat across from Philip, a fifteen-year-old who would normally have greeted her and asked her name. But people who have gone through trauma, and especially those for whom the threat of impending danger hasn't yet ended, are connected by a bond that needs no introduction. He nodded at her and gave a half smile. It was the best he could do under the circumstances. He thought to himself that there was something so natural, so endearing about the way she played with her baby brother.

It was nightfall when the first hint of trouble came. Most of the men had returned to hiding. Some of the men stayed with their families inside the church.

"They are gathering outside," one of the women said. And immediately people crowded around the small windows to look outside. And what they saw made them wish they had decided not to look.

Hundreds and hundreds of warriors surrounded the compound. Machetes, bows and arrows, spears and sticks in hand. Some held torches in their hands that gave them that eerie glow in the dark night.

People began to pray, calling on the name of God to rescue them.

Our God is our refuge and strength. An ever present help in the time of trouble.

Dalila bounced her brother on her knee to try to settle him down.

"It's going to be all right. Shhh. I'm right here. I'm right here." And she would have remained calm had it not been for the loud knock at the door that caused her to jolt and nearly drop her brother.

"Open the door!" the voice screamed. "All men out!"

People began to argue back and forth about what to do. One of the fathers whispered to the others around him. "Let's do it. All the men should get out. This is a church compound. What are they going to do to us here?"

But the rest disagreed. "Are you crazy?" another father replied. "You set one foot outside that door and they will cut you up!"

Philip didn't know on what side of the argument he stood. If staying here was endangering Dalila and the others, wouldn't it be better if they left? But if they did leave, wouldn't that just mean the others' deaths anyway? What if they just stayed? Just waited it out?

One of the women was brave enough to call out to the man at the door. "There are no men in here."

"I don't believe you."

"They are not here!"

"Then open the door and prove it to us!"

That wasn't going to happen. Opening the door to men drunk on murder, alcohol or both would not be of help to anyone.

So they waited in silence and watched out the window, looking for any hint as to what the attacking group was thinking.

Outside, the warriors became irritated. Some were ready for a fight. "We should burn them alive right now!" one of the men insisted. "Those filthy dogs should all die!" He gripped his machete tighter. He had sharpened it that morning. He had seen a lot of action. Killing that many people had dulled his blade. Hopefully it would stay sharp through this attack.

The self-appointed leader of the mob turned to him. He was taller than his machete-carrying tribesman. Taller than all of them. He had assumed the position of chief among them on the basis of the number of kills he had. "And kill people in a church?"

"Oh, what is that? If you weren't thinking of killing them, why are we here?"

"To get the men. Do you understand that? To kill the men responsible for beating down our people all these years."

"You and I both know that the only way to victory is to kill every one of them. Men, women, children. There they are!" he said, pointing down to the church. "Right in that building."

"I am not killing people in a church."

"Oh, and you are willing to kill people in their houses? What is the difference?"

That struck him. The leader had to admit to himself that the man had a point. What was it about keeping a church sacred? Did it represent the last place of holiness? Is that what it was? Even with killing all these people over the last few days, was there still a need to have a place of pureness, of God, in his life? As if to say, "In spite of all this evil, the sacred in life still exists"? He had murdered outside the walls of a church building. Was that a lot worse than murdering inside them? He thought about that warped question. Perhaps it gave him the last sense of dignity in his life to entertain at least a glimpse of morality.

But the worst part about him was that he was so far gone morally he was no longer able to distinguish between right and wrong.

It had all started for him the night after the election when the first suspicions of voter fraud took place. Something inside him called to him to grab his machete and take to the streets. Why? Why did he do that? What was it that drove him to feel the handle in his palm and desire the screams of victims as they felt the blade, his blade, slicing into them?

But that was just it. Nothing drove him to do it. He was simply presented with the opportunity. *This is your chance to get back at them for what they did to you and your father and your grandfather. Take up the blade and get even. Getting even will settle the anger in your heart. Getting them back will give you peace.*

And so he chose to do it. He believed it. And he went to the streets and killed so many people that he had lost track.

Within a few days it had driven him to such madness that he was now standing outside a church, late in the evening, with his machete in hand, debating whether it was all right to kill women and children.

In a church no less.

He knew some of the people he had killed. He worked together with them.

Laughed together with them. His children played in their homes. That all seemed like such a long time ago. And yet it was only one week. One week from being friends to wanting to kill them.

Something foreign had been creeping through his blood. Working its way through his system into his heart and mind. Like a poison that enters and slowly takes over. He had been a different person last week. Hadn't he? Or was he always this person who was only now being given the opportunity to do what his heart had always wanted? To get even. To get back. To kill. Is that who he really was all along?

He no longer knew.

But what he did know was that deep down inside, he was not the only person making choices for him. He had taken the bait on that first night when he grabbed his machete. He could have said no, couldn't he? He could have resisted. But he didn't. Instead, he went in and took part. And since then there had been someone else inside him. Directing him. Fuelling the fire. Taking the very worst of him and making him come alive (or dead) like never before.

He could stop. That much he still knew. There was enough of him left. The real him. That person who cared about the enemy tribe. *What makes them your enemy? Weren't you trained to love your enemy?* But instead of listening to that still, small voice, he chose to ignore it.

He gripped his machete all the tighter and debated whether or not to attack.

CHAPTER 30

Dalila woke up first. The initial signs of sunrise provided just enough light to see those sleeping around her. She was tired, but even at her age the instincts to look after her brother were strong, and she turned to see him sleeping beside her. She had woken up throughout the night. Every hour. It was impossible to sleep under threats of violence. She'd been here for three days, and it all felt like a blur.

Still, it was morning. And morning meant they had lived through another night without an attack. She felt cold and rubbed her shoulders. She yawned, rubbed her eyes, and hoped there would be enough food for today.

It was January 1, 2008. Happy New Year. For most people in the world it's a day of celebration. But for the few hundred gathered in the church and the surrounding compound, it marked another day that they had survived.

Pastor Stephen went out to the yard, where he spoke with elderly men about the violence in the area. Philip helped with cleaning the inside of the building while Dalila sat on a bench, rocking her brother. She tried to stay focused on humming a tune to him, but found herself wondering how much longer they would be here. The others felt the effects of staying in such a cramped place for so long. Life seemed like one long, unpredictable waiting game of desperation. And it would have stayed that way for quite some time had it not been for a tragic turn of events.

It was difficult to know exactly what prompted what happened next, why that particular time was chosen. Eleven a.m. Under a bright sunny sky. A quiet church outside of the city. It all seemed like the oddest possible setting. But whatever the case, that's when everything exploded.

Like a long fuse that finally reaches a powder keg and unleashes an unbearable blast, hundreds of warriors armed with spears, arrows, machetes and stones rushed the compound while chanting war songs. Pastor Stephen saw them coming. The blood drained from his face. He raced inside to warn the others. The elderly men were not fortunate to be as fast. The warriors reached them first and hacked seven old men to pieces. The renegade group formed a ring around the church and shouted at the people inside.

The ashen look on Pastor Stephen's face when he entered the church conveyed to the group that the worst was now upon them. Whatever hope they held out that violence could be avoided suddenly vanished and was replaced with a sense of urgency and panic that comes when life hangs in the balance.

People immediately began praying out loud. Dozens and dozens all at the same time. Children began crying. The church became a place of confusion. Dalila looked around in a panic, unable to find her mother. She picked up her brother, wrapped him in the scarves and tied him around her. As she did she began to pray.

God, please God. Please help me. Help all of us now. We need you. We need you right now. I ask for your protection and to take care of us and to save us from these people.

The mob outside poured gasoline on the building.

"You wanted to steal our land? You wanted to steal our election? Now we will show you what will happen to you!"

Some of the gasoline came in through the window and landed on the women and children inside. That prompted an immediate outcry for them to stop. But their pleas went unanswered. The train of evil had picked up so much speed that derailing it or getting it to slow down was going to take a miracle.

The mob torched the building. In an instant the place lit up and gave off an intense blast of heat under the bright sunshine. Women screamed for help. The temperature inside rose so fast that people raced to try to escape from the church. Pastor Stephen helped push children out of the windows. But the older ones could not fit through the tiny openings, and the panic for the door made it impossible for those near the back to get out.

Philip ran to one of the windows. He made it close to the front of the line. People pressed so hard against him, desperate for a way to get out, that he was nearly crushed from the impact. The roof began to burn and filled the building with smoke.

Dalila coughed as she struggled past the larger bodies for a way out. She was about to reach a window when she was thrust aside by adults delirious with fear and smoke inhalation. She pushed her way back towards the window with a fierceness that her gentle demeanour had never known as she clawed her way through the crowd.

Philip's pant leg caught fire. He kicked at it to put it out, but it only served to burn more of his clothes. He forced himself up to the window, feeling the flames burning his leg. He dropped out of the window and rolled over to stamp out the flames.

A warrior raced up to him. He raised his machete for the kill against the blinding glare of the blistering sun. Philip turned to see the crazed expression on the warrior's face. But when the man saw Philip's age he stopped and decided not to proceed.

Clearly there would be older, eligible targets nearby.

Dalila jumped and grabbed the bottom of the window ledge. She hung by her fingertips and strained to pull herself up. She gripped the wall with her feet to help push herself further. The flames burned all around her, enveloping her in a cloud of fire and smoke. *Please God. Please God, help me.*

She felt her grip slipping. The strength in her arms began to fail her. In a desperate move she lunged up and managed to get her right forearm on the sill. She coughed as smoke filled her lungs. She heard her brother screaming behind her. As she pushed with her arm she lifted her head up and could see freedom, if that's what it could be called, through the window. She caught a glimpse of a man being struck down with a machete. Out of the fire and into the killing field.

The flames began to burn her legs. And as she got her left arm through the window she felt the fire scorching her back. That terrified her. Because it could only mean one thing.

The scarves were burning.

And that was when Dalila's life changed.

With all the desperation that she could muster, she forced her left hand up through the window. But the flames burned right through the scarves and she felt the horrible sensation of the shift in weight as her baby brother fell off her back. She heard him screaming as he dropped down to the ground below. The crowd pushed at her to get out so others could have a chance at freedom. More and more people jammed at her body to get through. She heard her brother's screams become muffled as he coughed on smoke. She pushed against the crowd, wanting to go back into the fire to get her brother.

She looked behind her. And in all the panic and confusion, her baby brother was trampled to death. The screams stopped, his screams anyway, and her brain went into that strange place of deciding whether to accept what her eyes were telling her had just happened.

Getting out didn't mean much anymore. She fell out the window and down on the ground below. In a state of complete disbelief, she turned over so that she wouldn't be crushed by the next person coming out the window.

She lay on her forearms trying to absorb the impact of what she had just witnessed. Her little ears picked up the sound of people shouting as they were meeting their demise at the end of a dull machete. The logical choice right now was to get up and start running. Get out of here. Leave this awful place and find shelter somewhere. But the combination of shock and grief was so new and so intense that even the obvious became impossible to her.

The next wave of men that managed to escape the church met the same disastrous end when they reached the warriors. Many of them, still coughing from the fire, suddenly found themselves at the mercy of the attackers. Dalila saw machetes cutting into men. Arrows flying into their chests. And some even had stones smashed against their skulls.

Pastor Stephen was one of them. He collapsed to the ground. A warrior cheered and chanted his war song as he cracked a stone over Stephen's head, smashing it open. He fell unconscious, making his attackers think he was dead. Later he came to, blood pouring down his face, and tried to get back to his feet. Dalila turned around, hoping to see someone carrying out her brother. Hoping that someone could correct the horrific fate that had befallen him. Instead she heard a terrible cracking sound as the trusses failed. She watched as the entire roof came down, crushing the remaining people inside.

And for a split everything went quiet. The men in the yard had been slaughtered. The people inside were burned to death.

But all of this spelled victory for the attackers. And the bright, beautiful, horrible day was suddenly filled with the cheers at a job well done. Even the leader shouted for joy as they left for their next kill.

Murdering all these people, all these so-called enemies who apparently deserved it, should have brought him the greatest sense of satisfaction.

But all it did was shut him off completely to the needs of others and stamp out what little conscience he had remaining, leaving him at the mercy of the violence that had consumed him.

Dalila pulled herself away from the blazing church as best she could. She looked through the flames, trying to find her mother, and smelled the rotting flesh of burned corpses rise up from the ashes. Standing up, she negotiated through the dead bodies scattered throughout the compound, trying to identify if her mother was among them. When she made it to the street she looked back at the carnage before her.

Maybe her mother had gotten out. Maybe she had been spared from the fire.

So then why wasn't she here looking for her?

She had heard rumours of Internally Displaced Person camps (IDP) being set up near Eldoret. A refuge for people who had their homes burned, their loved ones killed, their lives ruined. People like her.

She felt confused. She felt abandoned. Where was God? Didn't she ask for his help? Didn't she plead? Exactly what would have been the outcome had she not prayed? Could this really have been any worse?

Everything she knew about God was suddenly pulled out from under her. A God of kindness. A God of goodness. A God of love.

Really?

Where?

But questions were for those who had the privilege of expecting answers. And Dalila had more important things on her mind. She wanted to pray. Really she did. But she wasn't sure anymore who that God was that she had been told about. Even though her baby brother was gone, his screams still echoed in her mind, bringing grief into her heart that she had never known could even be possible. She had to move on. Had to find help.

So under the sun that shone down on her burned clothing, charred skin and destroyed soul, Dalila began the journey, alone, back to Eldoret and wondered if somehow, someway, there would be someone out there who could help her put the pieces of her fragmented life back together.

CHAPTER 31

Mulli landed at the Eldoret airport early in the morning. Normally he would have driven, but given the unstable condition of the highways and the rank violence that ruled the streets, he took the prudent route of air travel. During the flight he had looked down onto the city. Even from high above the damage on what should have been a beautiful area was visible. He saw burned out houses and the smoke rising into the sky. If it was this bad at this elevation, how much worse would it be on the ground?

He hired a driver to take him into town. This was it. He was really doing this. He buckled his seat belt, and they drove off. On the side of the road Mulli saw corpses of people who had been slain the night before. No time for funerals. No respect for the dead. Some of the bodies were already attracting the attention of birds and animals.

That will be you soon, Mulli. That will be you.

I am with you always, even to the very end of the age.

Up ahead Mulli saw a group of warriors, armed with spears and machetes, form a line across the street as a roadblock. A row of rocks stretched across the road in front of them. That was odd. They were small rocks and certainly wouldn't be enough to deter a vehicle from racing through. Still, the machetes alone were discouragement enough from messing with these men.

The driver swallowed. Mulli noticed and wasn't sure why he'd be nervous. People of the same tribe didn't kill one another. The driver had nothing to worry about. It was Mulli who should have been scared. He was Kamba, a tribe that appeared to be spoilers as they mainly voted for a different presidential candidate and not one fielded by the two main parties. The current president, whom the mob believed had rigged the election, was Kikuyu. And the violence that resulted was by way of association. If they couldn't oust the president, they would lay the blame on his tribe and kill them. And possibly those who didn't vote for him. Sometimes not supporting someone can be considered the same as being against them. The challenging president, Raila Odinga, was also accused of vote rigging. Either way, one of them was responsible for inciting this mess.

And it served as a chilling reminder of how devastating an effect one person's sin could have on so many.

As they came closer to the roadblock two things happened. First, the driver began to sweat more and breathed in shorter bursts. Second, the objects on the road began to look less and less like rocks. It wasn't until they nearly came to a stop that Mulli saw them for what they were.

They weren't rocks at all. Instead, a series of cut-off heads formed a line across the road. Some had their eyes chopped out. Most still had the last frozen look of horror etched on their faces.

The driver was so nervous that when he went to roll down the window he got confused as to which way the handle was supposed to turn and actually pulled it tighter. He pulled harder and nearly broke the handle before he realized his mistake. His hand shook as if an electric current was zipping through it. Still he forced himself to turn the handle the other way.

When the window was down, a warrior looked into the vehicle. His face was tough and worn. He made such little expression that he could just as easily have passed for a creepy wood carving. The driver looked down. In his right hand the warrior held a machete stained with blood. Mulli looked straight ahead.

Here it comes.

"You are sweating," the warrior noticed, speaking in their tribal language.

"A hot day today," the driver replied, forcing out a smile. It wasn't hot out. It was just terrifying.

"Your identification."

"I'm sorry?" the driver said. Even at this close range he didn't hear him. He did everything he could to control the panic in his heart and mind, and it prevented him from hearing what the man inches from his face had said.

"Your identification," he repeated in a tone that was now lower and more sinister.

What do you think it would be like to get macheted to death in a car?

The driver pulled out his identification card. The warrior reviewed it. He looked at the driver and then at Mulli, who refused to look. Better not to make eye contact.

The driver stopped breathing. This was taking too long. What was the problem? *There's my identification; now let me through. Please.* It was downright spine-chilling to realize that a warrior with his strength could whip that machete into the vehicle and have the driver dead before he even knew what hit him.

The warrior turned to the other guards and made a comment that neither the driver nor Mulli heard.

"Okay," he said, giving the driver his card back. "Welcome."

Welcome? Welcome to what? Hell on earth?

It was strange. The warrior didn't ask for Mulli's identification.

One of the guards grabbed the severed heads and moved them off the road. The driver drove forward and gave a nod. When he had passed them he began to breathe again. Mulli turned around and saw the guard putting the heads back.

"Why are you so nervous?" Mulli asked.

The driver wiped the sweat from his forehead. He glanced behind him. He was well out of hearing range of the guards. But he checked back anyway as if somehow the warriors might be able to pick up what he was about to say or think. "I am Kikuyu," the driver said.

"What?" Mulli was taken aback. The man looked Kalenjin. He had all the physical characteristics.

"I am fortunate that I look like them," he said. "And even more fortunate that they believe my fake identification."

They drove to the MCF home in Eldoret, the original home that had been used to rescue street children when Mulli started this work some 18 years earlier. As a rags-to-riches multimillionaire, Mulli always had the plight of the street children on his heart. But when his car was stolen by street boys while doing business in Nairobi one day, he began to think more seriously about the priorities in his life and what he could do to help them. He was working at his office, running his vast business empire that he had built up from nothing, when he suddenly felt sick and left for the day. He thought he was driving home when he blacked out and found himself driving in the wrong direction. He stopped and got out at a bridge. A crossroads of his life. He told God he would do whatever he wanted. Convicted of his new course of direction, Mulli dedicated himself right there to selling everything he owned and helping street children. And the first ones came to his home in Eldoret.

When Mulli arrived he met briefly with the staff. He encouraged them in their work and commended them for their faithfulness.

The driver took him from there to the IDP camp. Various humanitarian organizations had been selected to set up the massive relief camp on the site of the showground's property. Mulli knew it well. It hosted an annual agriculture fair and stood empty the rest of the year. Mulli tried to imagine what it would look like now.

But when he arrived he found himself unprepared for the immeasurable desperation that lay before him.

A sea of white tents covered the landscape. A mass of exhausted people wearing dirty, damp clothes and hopeless expressions walked down the rain-soaked street. Some carried children who were crying from lack of food. Others carried laundry they had washed in the cleanest brown water they could find. But all of them carried hearts destroyed by loved ones murdered, houses burned and futures lost.

It was a land of suffering filled with devastated people who showed no indication that there was any reason to believe that anything would change for the better.

Mulli stepped onto the property. It felt different. There was something solemn about standing on land occupied by people undergoing such terrible suffering. He wore a suit and tie. It wasn't his normal attire. Far from it. But when people are living in grief and their surroundings are dirty and everything looks grim and grey, Mulli believed the visual help of them seeing a person dressed well gives them the respect they need to believe that someone values them in their situation.

He found the administration offices of the organizations set up at the camp. He inquired where he could find the leader, and the girl at the desk told him he was among the people in the tents. Mulli asked if he could go and see him, and she consented.

Mulli walked down narrow pathways between the tents that were filled with streams of people. The tents were small. Barely room for a smaller person to stand at the centre of the A-shaped structure. Children sat on the ground outside their tents looking up at him with eyes that were clouded with red and yellow where the white should have been. Women sat beside them, helpless with pale faces, holding screaming babies, with expectant eyes, hoping this stranger, whoever he was, would do something for them.

As he continued down the path he was overcome with the sorrow he saw in the people around him. The need stretched on and on and on. Like a never-ending line of misery. Their pain reached into Mulli. And the thought that gripped him was that there were still thousands upon thousands of others who were just as desperate.

Mulli cried.

Hearing the radio updates or watching the horrific developments on TV was one thing. But seeing it first-hand was different. More powerful and more devastating at the same time.

Not immediately finding the person he was looking for, Mulli stopped at the tents of various people to hear their stories and to learn how he might be of help to them. At one of the tents he saw a woman who looked so desperate that it was as if she was lost in a trance. She sat there. On the ground. Just inside her tent. Looking ahead as if staring at a television that wasn't there. And it made Mulli wonder what trauma she was going through to make her gaze at nothing like that, with such intensity.

"Hello," Mulli said. "May I sit down?"

She blinked. It was all she could manage.

"My name is Mulli," he continued. It would have been customary for her to respond by giving her name. But her pain was so deep that even simple cultural norms were escaping her.

"May I ask how you came to be here?"

She turned to look at him. What she saw seemed different to her. She hadn't seen that in a long time. Those eyes. What was it about his eyes that made him so genuine? All the same, it was hard to stay focused on him. She was seeing two things at once. She saw him, a man in a suit no less, sitting on the ground with her. That was different, too. But she also saw the images in her mind replaying over and over again. She saw her older son stuck against a tree, an arrow pierced through his back. She saw her younger son running to help him only to have his throat slashed. Then she saw the image of her younger son falling to the ground, and the other arrows flying into her older son's back.

She could leave her tent if she wanted. She could leave the presence of other people if she wanted to be alone. But no matter where she would go, no matter what she would think, she could not leave her memories.

She heard other people walking outside. People like her who had experienced similar atrocities. They were talking. She wondered how that was possible. How could someone who had suffered like her talk about it? Did that make her a weak person? Or do people deal with loss in different ways? Do people process death and unbearable sorrow differently? She was used to being active. Used to being helpful. Used to focusing on the needs of others. Yet here she was. So incapacitated that she might as well have been a paralytic. It was like an unbearable tidal wave had crushed her spirit. And even the simplest tasks now became impossible.

The sadness was so overwhelming that it debilitated her. She found it strange and unwelcome how similar grief felt to fear. She wasn't just experiencing loss. She was experiencing what it means to be perpetually scared. She was afraid of absolutely everything. The past. The present. The future. People. Isolation. Daytime. Nighttime. She hadn't expected that. Hadn't expected to be so overcome with dread that it could freeze her in this state of never-ending hopelessness.

But the impact of grief is impossible to predict, and she spent her days in uncontrollable anguish, unable to recall what life was like before it all went so terribly wrong.

They stayed there. In the silence. Together. Sometimes a person's presence is enough to start the healing process. And that's what Mulli did for her without saying anything.

She started slowly. Just a few words at first. Most of them disjointed. Pain this deep doesn't just come out in perfect sentences. She wanted to tell. *Needed* to tell. But not to just anyone. Which is why it was so odd that she opened up to Mulli, a complete stranger. What was it about him? He sat there with 100 percent of his attention devoted to her. Despite all the demands on his time he listened to her from beginning to end.

She told Mulli what happened. It had only been a week ago, which didn't seem very long. But when she thought back to the week before the atrocities, when she was laughing, playing games with her family at the kitchen table…back when she was herself, it felt like many, many lifetimes ago.

She stopped often and cried. This was the first time she could tell someone her story. She presumed he was a busy man. Clearly he wasn't here just for her. But he showed no signs of impatience. No hint of looking at his watch, no glance to the side to see how many more people he had to visit on this trip. She felt loved and respected by his patience and attentiveness.

And she felt the incredible relief that came with being able to share her pain with someone who was willing to listen to all of it, beginning to end.

She shared about the attack on her two boys with the machete and the arrows, and how her husband was missing. She had no idea where he was. Perhaps he was among the bodies lying in the streets. When she was done, Mulli waited in silence just to make sure she was finished.

"What is your name?" Mulli asked.

"Sikhudhani."

"That is a very nice name."

"Thank you," she whispered.

"Sikhudhani, thank you for sharing your story. I am very sorry to hear what has happened," Mulli said.

She nodded. Then she went back to looking out at nothing, deep in thought. Deep in misery. "Is this all?" she asked, glancing at the muddy waters that had seeped into her entire tent with the last rain. "Is this all I will have left?"

"In a moment like this, when the skies are so dark, there is a vacuum that can only be filled with hope from Jesus."

"Hope?" she asked. "Hope in what? What…what do I hope for?…How will I ever get hope when everything I have is gone?"

Her face became angry, her tone bitter. Others who heard came to stand around and listen. Everyone had their own problems. Serious problems. While they all had a need to share their own grief, they had little capacity to absorb any of the grief of others. So when there was someone willing to listen, it drew the attention of others.

"Through forgiveness," Mulli said.

Everyone became quiet.

"When we forgive others we will have a stable heart," he continued. "What those people did was terrible. It was completely awful. And I encourage you to come to the cross of Jesus and forgive them."

She closed her eyes, wanting to clear her mind of seeing her sons dying. But instead of seeing her sons this time, she saw the attackers. Machetes in hand. Laughing. Laughing at what they were doing.

"They are not asking for forgiveness," Sikhudhani said.

"I am sorry that they have not seen the evil they have done. Even if they are not asking for forgiveness for taking away your sons' lives, I encourage you to forgive. To release them from having to make up for what they did. When we forgive it seems like we lose the right to revenge. We want to hold our pain close to us. But when we release it into God's hands, he can heal us."

She closed her eyes again as tears streamed down her face. She saw the attackers smiling and congratulating each other over their accurate shooting and machete cutting. No, no, they weren't at her tent pleading forgiveness. They were out there, maybe doing more of it. The thought of forgiving them felt like disowning her own sons. She felt that forgiving the attackers was the same as condoning it and allowing her boys to die in vain.

But she could not go on like this. Maybe the strong could hang on to bitterness and unforgiveness. But didn't the strongest One of all forgive? When he was nailed to the cross, didn't he forgive?

In spite of how much it went against her logic, she saw past her boys, past the laughing attackers, and sensed in her spirit the relief that would be hers if she would forgive. She sensed all the grief that came with wondering how good life could have been had things just gone differently. If the attackers had not picked their home, if she had lived in a different location, if she had been able to discern the warnings, then maybe, just maybe, this could all have been averted and everything could have been the way it was supposed to be.

But the dream of the life she had always hoped and prayed for was now gone. And she felt the sting that came with having to let go, not just of what she had, but of what she could have had in the future.

She bowed her head. She wanted to pray, but the words weren't there.

Exactly what do you say about the attackers who had killed your sons? She didn't actually care about her own grief. She was a mother, and she was wise enough to know that life was not about her.

"May I pray for you?"

She leaned forward. Her eyes were red with pain. Her mind tired of agony. She nodded.

Mulli placed his hand on her shoulder.

"Father, we come before you. We put our trust in you. We keep on trusting even now. Father, you see Sikhudhani. You see her terrible suffering. Lord, she wants to forgive. She wants to release these men from what they did to her sons." Mulli leaned closer to her and whispered. "Would you like to forgive them?"

She bit her lip, nodded, and through her tears she managed three words. "I forgive them."

Mulli took his hand away. She opened her eyes. Were they in the same place? It looked different a moment ago. Didn't it? The same tents were here. The same people were here. Everything looked like it was in the same place. But it *felt* different.

It was as if a weight had been lifted from her. Relief. Peace.

There was a new future now. It was as if she had been travelling on a train that was heading in one direction when the track suddenly shifted and the train headed in a different direction. She resisted the urge of wishing to return to the original line of her old life with her two boys. There would be no going back. No transfer station that could take her to that line.

She had to make the decision to let go. To forgive. To accept the new direction. The new line. No easy task. She fought the notion that her life from here on in would be second best. That it could never be as good as what she could have had if the attacks had never happened, if she would have been allowed to stay on that original track with her two sons still alive.

But for her, forgiveness meant letting go of everything. God was with her. He was leading her. Did she need more than that? He led her through disaster and brought her to this point of forgiveness. That in and of itself was previously an unthinkable task. Now she had the conviction that he was going to stay with her the entire length of the journey.

It made her wonder if there would be more track shifts still be coming down the line. And if there were, she resolved to follow him in spite of them.

"Thank you," she said. She looked different. Like there had been a cleansing of her soul. Like the devastation had dug out a part of her that now was filled even deeper with God, making her that much more compelling and deep than before. "When will you come back?"

"Soon," Mulli replied.

She reached out her hand and touched him. That felt good to her. It felt good to connect again.

It felt good to want contact with another person.

As Mulli stood up he looked out over the incredible sea of people waiting for help.

And the unbelievable burden of need was so heavy on his heart that all he could ask was for the Lord to prepare people in MCF who would be able to withstand the challenge of ministering to the masses.

It was one thing for MCF children to be rescued and to work toward rehabilitation. That was stage one. But the next stage was to help others.

And this would prove to be their greatest test yet.

CHAPTER 32

The Red Cross assisted Mulli in becoming an authorized relief organization at the IDP camp. It was no simple task. This was a chaotic time, and people had to be careful about who was allowed to help.

Mulli met with the Kenyan government in the central business district area of Eldoret, where he would receive final approval. He sat down opposite a manager in the district children's office under the Ministry of National Heritage and Children's Services. The man was young, energetic, and had a sharp mind that kept up with Mulli.

"So you are originally from Eldoret. You operate a home for street children here, also in Yatta, in Ndalani, in Mombasa, and on and on." The man grinned. "Impressive."

"Thank you."

"And what do you want to do at the IDP camp?"

"I want to provide food for the children. Also we will provide teachers for the students. We will bring school supplies, and we will also provide counselling for the families."

The young man leaned forward. He was an optimist. He had to be to believe the situation would turn out for the better. But what Mulli was proposing was past optimism.

It was unrealistic.

"I am impressed, really I am. But, can you really do all that?"

"It is a lot, but I can tell in my heart that it is the right thing to do."

"Well, for example, can you tell me where you will get the food?"

It was Mulli's turn to lean forward. "Me, I don't know where."

"You propose to bring food to thousands of people, yet you have no food to offer? Where do you suppose it will come from?"

"The Lord will provide."

Mulli wasn't just saying that. For this to work, God alone would actually *have* to come through. Again. There was no recourse. MCF didn't have remotely enough money. There was only three thousand dollars left in the general account, and even that was not enough for looking after the hundreds of MCF children, let alone carrying on an additional feeding program like this at the IDP camp.

It was like five loaves and two fish to feed the multitude.

Only they didn't have the five loaves and two fish.

"All right," the young man said. "If you manage, it will be a miracle."

Mulli stood up and shook the man's hand. "I agree."

Mulli returned to the IDP camp that afternoon at 4:30 to show the approval to the Red Cross personnel, who looked forward to seeing him. He then got on the 6:00 p.m. flight and headed back to Nairobi. His mind was full of what he had seen and heard, all in less than a day. It felt like he was coming in from a battle. As he flew back he laid out a plan for how he would carry out the vision.

Mulli met with his family in Yatta. Only days earlier they had been here discussing what, if anything, could be done about the violence. Now here they were implementing a plan.

"I have made a decision," Mulli began. "It's a decision that will affect us as a family."

They'd been here before. Twenty years before, Mulli announced he would sell everything and begin this rescue ministry for children. It was a surprise to all of them. Yet, here they were, all these years later, and look what had been accomplished.

And it made them realize how the family's obedience to an incredible call of God two decades before had made an incalculable impact on thousands of children in Kenya.

"We will take a step of faith and help people in the IDP. We will need to train people from MCF and encourage them how to counsel people and how to be effective workers with the refugees. And then there is the small matter of money," he said with his trademark laugh. It lightened the mood.

"Are we ready?"

Mulli called workers from Mombasa, Kangundo, Ndalani and Yatta— approximately 65 people in total. They were made up of grade 12 graduates, department heads and pastors. They were people with a good record who were also hard workers.

It was a new challenge. Up until then Kenya did not have a refugee problem. They had been spared that.

But they were not spared this time.

Nor would they be spared again in the near future.

Mulli gathered everyone together in Yatta at the start of their training and prayed over them.

"Lord, give us the compassion, commitment and understanding to minister to the people in the IDP camp. Lord, provide all that is needed. And help us to trust you and not ourselves. Help us, Lord, to be your servants, and we thank you from the bottom of our hearts that we can be used of you in this mighty way. We commit the whole program to you to supply according to your riches in glory so that we will not lack at all."

The team learned how to help people who are in trauma, how to give first aid, and how to stay close to God and to each other during the immense trials that would follow so as not to become discouraged and not to burn out.

"We need to stay faithful in prayer," Mulli said. "Prayer is powerful, and we need to have endurance. Sometimes things don't happen right away. But the Lord always responds. You have to be patient, and God will move in time."

The team was connecting well. They each had a combination of humbleness and eagerness.

"Remember the story of Elijah. There was a famine in Israel. A widow had a son. She had very little left to eat. Elijah prophesied famine for three years. The widow said she didn't have much, only a little bit left, and when she had cooked that she would die. Elijah told her to cook it, and she did. God used it to change everything in her life because she gave all that she had. The bottle of oil continued to be filled. We are giving God all we have, even our little bit of money, and God can use it to make it full," Mulli said.

"Also Moses. God spoke to him through the burning bush. Moses said he could not speak well and wouldn't be able to lead the people. God asked Moses, 'What do you have in your hand?' Moses had a staff. God told him to throw it on the ground, and when he did it became a snake. And when he picked it up again it was a staff. God showed him his power. And like us, we should not be afraid about where our supplies will come from. We move with boldness and courage, and then with our own eyes we will see the Lord."

The team fasted for two days straight. Mulli believed going without food made a significant difference in their prayers. By going without food, the body and soul found joy and comfort only in the Lord. And it prepared them for the challenges ahead.

"You will be meeting people who have gone through terrible suffering," he said to the team. "So we need to discuss how to reach people. How to help them in dealing with trauma. The first is to make sure you are dressed well and introduce yourself. 'My name is so and so and I am from Mully Children's Family. I'm here to listen to you and help you through this situation. May I come in?' And in this way you have shown respect to the person, and they can choose to receive you or not.

"It is important to be like them. If they are sitting on the ground, then you sit on the ground. Even if it is dirty. And be sure to face the person and look in their eyes. Don't worry about anything else. Just entrust to God anything else that comes to your mind. You are there for that person or that family in the tent at that time. No one else.

"Start by asking the person to share. You want to understand the history of that person. You want to listen to everything they have gone through. This is not the time to suggest any solutions. Be sure you have truly heard the person, because everyone is unique. When you begin to think 'Oh, this is just like the other person's story I heard.' No. That is not true. Everyone is special.

"Then, when someone has told you something, paraphrase or repeat back a summary of what they have told you. It shows you have truly understood what they are saying, and by doing so you are building trust and you will stay active while you are listening.

"Of course the whole time you are praying and asking the Lord for wisdom. So when someone has finished sharing, resist the urge to give solutions. Telling someone what to do is not helpful. The better strategy is to ask questions. 'How do you feel about this situation? Do you think that forgiveness is the right thing to do?' When they have expressed their emotions, whether it is sadness or anger, then you can encourage them to think through their situation.

"And the hardest part—this is one where people will really feel a lot of pain—is to have them come to the point of accepting the situation for what it is. Very bad things have happened. Maybe you, too, have had difficult things in your life and you wonder, Why did this happen? Why didn't God intervene? Will I ever be happy now that this has happened? How can I trust a God who lets this happen? But we cannot change the past. And we will not get answers to all of our questions. We can help people make great progress by challenging them to think through their solutions and bringing them to a place where they accept what has happened. Then and only then can they move on.

"But the most important thing is that this is not about simply bringing people through trauma. We are here to help, and we are here to help anyone in need regardless of their religion or background. We are not just giving food or giving an education. We are here because we believe in Jesus Christ and that he alone can make a person whole. He made me whole and he made you whole. If someone gets enough to eat but doesn't have Christ, what good is that? If someone gets an education but does not know the Lord, what good is that? We help regardless of whether they accept Christ or not. It is not our job to discriminate against people who choose not to believe. No. But it is our job to share the love of Jesus."

He looked out at the team. They were determined. They were excellent. And they were ready.

Which was good.

Because they needed to be.

They boarded the Mully Children's Family bus and drove from Yatta to Eldoret under Kenyan military escort. Kenyan police officers rode inside the bus with them. There were roadblocks and gangs the entire way, and Kenyan military was prepared to use lethal force against any attackers. Thankfully, the team arrived in Eldoret without major incident.

When they reached the MCF home in Eldoret one of the staff members who had been to market that day expressed that there was a lot of fear in the community. They learned there was a plan to attack the area they were in.

The team had devotions that evening. Mulli reminded them about how the apostle Paul had been persecuted and that they should not fear. "Psalm 91 reminds us that we are covered. The Lord will take care of us," he said.

They all went to bed that night grateful that they had made it this far. Mueni and Ndondo stayed in an upstairs room together. The impending task weighed heavy upon them. Neither of them could fall asleep. It was three a.m. when they heard screaming outside. They both hurried to the window.

The home was surrounded by a fence. A black steel gate was the only access to the property for vehicles. They watched the road for any sign of danger.

They heard more screaming as people uttered threats to each other.

The shouting grew closer.

And then they saw a person's hand reaching over the gate. Mueni's and Ndondo's heartbeats raced. Then another hand. Another person climbed up the gate. And another. Three people managed to get their arms over the gate. One lifted himself up to reveal an angry and crazed expression on his face.

A voice shouted in the distance. "Stop! Get down from there immediately!"

A gunshot pierced through the night. The screaming stopped. Another gunshot. Then another. The hands disappeared from over the gate. Mueni and Ndondo heard footsteps running down the street.

And then everything was quiet. They stayed focused on the gate. Their eyes searched for any hint of movement. When it seemed like the immediate danger was over they left the window.

Exactly how they were supposed to sleep after that they weren't sure. But they sat down on their beds all the same, tried to calm down, and only then realized how fast their pulses were actually racing.

And it left them wondering if this was a sign of things to come.

CHAPTER 33

Mulli led the team to the IDP camp early the next morning. They weren't sure what to expect on their first trip here. They had an idea of what the camp would be like. But sometimes seeing is believing, and the team had the same reaction to the camp that he did. Seeing pictures was one thing. But being here in person was completely different.

They had prayed. They had trained. They had organized. Still, seeing such a great many people in such terrible suffering was so overwhelming that it arrested each of them. Normally when people see something out of the ordinary they comment to express what they are experiencing, to feel the sense of sharing life with the person or group they are with. But there are other things people see that are in a category that goes beyond words. Words almost seem an injustice because they can't describe what is really going on. And all the team could do was stand there in a grave moment of silence.

They walked past tents and countless desperate faces. Men. Women. Children. These weren't just a mass of people. They were a large group made up of individuals. People with as many hopes and dreams as they had. People who didn't want to be here. People who at their core were just like them. Remembering what they had been taught about building trust, they tried to give compassionate and understanding smiles to the people, almost as much for themselves as for others. They saw the expectation in people's eyes. A look of desperation that pleaded for them to offer the solution to their misery. They felt enormous pressure to help people.

They reached the area they had been assigned. They set up their command location, the schools and the food distribution centre, and began cooking food for lunch. With the last of their money in the general account they had purchased what they could of maize, beans and rice. They had just begun and already they were out of funds. Not exactly the way a person would normally start a project of this size. They had put their foot forward. Somehow, someway, God would have to provide for the rest. Not only did they not have enough to pay for future meals at the IDP, but they did not have enough to pay for the meals and expenses for the hundreds of rescued street children at the MCF homes.

When Mulli saw that the food team and the education team had everything in control, he went to do what he loved to do best—talk with people in need.

He organized the counselling team into groups, prayed for them and strategically sent them into the camps to bring hope to those who were in a place past desperation.

Mulli and Esther approached a tent. The linen sheets at the entrance were pulled back, allowing him to bend down and look in.

He saw a mother in her early thirties next to her twelve-year-old daughter. They sat on makeshift stools that barely kept them off the rain-soaked floor.

"Hello," Mulli said.

They made no reply. Pleasantries were normally reserved for those who had the currency of hope.

The mother did make eye contact, though. And in Africa, that can mean as much as a hug.

"My name is Charles Mulli. This is my wife, Esther. We are with Mully Children's Family, and we would like to hear your situation and help you. Is it all right if we come in and speak with you?"

The mother nodded. Mulli and Esther sat down on similar stools at the entrance. The opening was large enough for a passersby to look in. The sun shone in just enough to illuminate the mother's anguished face. Mulli's left foot was in a puddle. If he noticed, he didn't give any indication that he cared.

"Thank you. Thank you for inviting us into your tent. We are very happy to be with you and to meet you."

Still the daughter did not look up. There's a difference between shyness and shame, and everything Mulli saw in her body language told him this girl was not just feeling the horrors of war, but also the guilt of some past event for which she felt irreversibly responsible.

"I would like to know your names and to hear your story," Mulli said. "To hear how you came to be here."

The mother closed her eyes. She began to cry. Tears streamed down her face. The daughter held back as long as she could, but the tidal wave of a memory is inescapable, and she leaned forward, started to cry and tried to find someway to cope with this disaster.

The mother gave her name and began to share her story. Mulli listened and felt her sorrow. Pain connects. And those who have suffered understand each other. She stopped halfway through and turned to her daughter. She hugged her and told her over and over again, "It's okay. It's okay. It's okay."

The mother then turned to Mulli and spoke with all of the grace that is apparent in people whose lives have been formed in the kiln of suffering. It felt to Mulli as she was speaking that the violence that resulted from the election was just another link in the chain of anguish in her life.

"My husband was killed by madmen. My son is gone. I am not going to ask God why. But please. Please, I beg you. If you can do anything, I do not want my daughter to suffer because of this."

They all remained silent until Mulli offered to pray for them. They agreed.

"Father, I pray right now in Jesus' name that you will come into this tent and touch these suffering people, to let them know that you love them and that you are their helper."

Mulli opened his eyes. He waited patiently for the girl. And finally, she spoke.

"My name," she began in a soft voice and then wiped her eyes. "My name is Dalila," she said. "My father has been killed and my brother…" She spoke so quietly that Mulli had to read her lips to confirm what she was saying. "And my baby brother died in the church fire at Kiambaa."

The commotion around them grew dim. It was as if the outside world had disappeared altogether and all that remained was the four of them. For the first time since arriving at the camp, Dalila spoke about how she had tried to climb through the window of the burning church. How the scarves had burned. And how her brother had fallen to his death.

She had replayed the scene in her mind every waking second of the days since the event. Even the night did not provide her with any comfort. Her subconscious desperately needed to process and reprocess and reprocess what happened. Whenever she reached the part with the scarves burning and felt the shift in weight off her back, she would reach behind to grab him, and that's when she would wake up to discover she was a girl in a tent living in an inescapable torment of despair in not being able to rescue him.

Grief exhausted her.

"I am so sorry that this happened," Mulli said. "You are very sad because of what these people did to you and what happened to your baby brother."

Dalila couldn't hear him. Not entirely. Her mind refused to let her rest. A part of her wanted to believe that she could be freed from this. But another part of her stayed trapped in the endless cycle of wondering what could have been had she made other choices.

It's my fault. It's all my fault. I should have wrapped the scarves better. Why didn't I wrap them tighter? Why wasn't I more careful? He was my responsibility. I was the one who was supposed to look after him. Why didn't I take better care of him? I should have ran faster to the window. And I should have climbed faster. Why didn't I climb faster? If I had climbed faster I would have been able to get out before the scarves burned.

"You may be thinking to yourself that it is your fault," Mulli said.

That was true. That was exactly how she felt. And even as it comforted her to know that he understood part of what was bothering her, it also amazed her that he could discover it so quickly.

"I would like to ask you a question. Is that okay?" Mulli asked.

She nodded.

"Your baby brother was very young and you probably like to sing to him, yes?"

She nodded.

"And you know, I am sure that he liked that. I am sure that he liked to hear you sing to him. Could I ask you, where do you think your brother is right now?"

She wiped more tears from her eyes. They didn't stop. A steady stream that came as fast as she could clear them away. It was a good question. She hadn't thought about that yet. "He is in heaven," she replied.

"That is right. And he has all kinds of people singing around him right now. He is okay now. He is actually doing really great."

That helped. She sensed a rush of water flow through her.

"How do you think you should respond to the people who did this to you?" Esther asked.

Dalila thought about her response. She hadn't been here before. Hadn't considered the people who had done this. She had been so overcome with the passing of her father and brother that the layer of bitterness against the attackers had not even surfaced yet. She knew the answer to Esther's question. That wasn't the problem. The trouble was that now that she was in this situation, she didn't like the answer very much.

"I should pray for them," she said.

And immediately she realized that would not only be difficult, but likely impossible. She remembered the last sounds of the attackers; she recalled them cheering as they watched the roof collapse. They were the filthiest, most vile people she could ever imagine, and it disgusted her to think that she would allow them to occupy space in her mind in order to pray for them.

Isn't the whole point to forget them?

"That is not easy," Mulli said. "But I agree with you. When we pray for our attackers, God helps us to forgive them, and he will use our prayers to heal the very people who hurt us so much."

The daughter folded her hands. Her mother put an arm around her. They waited in silence until Dalila spoke in her signature quiet tone.

"Dear Father God in heaven." She stopped. Was she actually going to do this? It seemed so wrong. *These people don't even think they have done anything wrong. They don't deserve to be prayed for. Or maybe this is exactly it. Maybe praying will help them understand what they have done. But how could a person not know that they have done evil? How could they not be aware?*

She didn't have those answers. And as much as it grieved her to even think of them, she pushed herself to pray for them. And she would have, had a voice not tried to prevent her from doing so.

Why pray for them? That's giving in. How can you give in to people who have done this to you?

It's not giving in. It's giving them the chance to know God.

Why bother? God wasn't there for your brother in that fire. He wasn't there for your father. Why should God be there for them?

They are lost.

And they don't deserve to be found.

Am I any different?

Any different? Of course. You are Dalila. You are an excellent girl. Those filthy pigs who did this, they are not like you. They are animals. You have nothing in common with them.

But if people had not prayed for me, where would I have ended up?

You wouldn't have been like them. They are enemies. Enemies!

I have been taught to pray for my enemies.

Does that make sense? Tell me, does it? You are an intelligent girl. What is the use in praying for your enemies?

I don't know. And I am not supposed to know everything. Sometimes it is more important to just obey.

Obeying doesn't help.

You're one to talk.

Dalila exhaled. It was like the burden of confusion and pain and everything else was just too much. She heard it all over again. The laughing of the warriors at the church burning. The sound of her brother crying. The crash of the roof as it came down. It was all so much. And yet, she pushed forward. She didn't want to do this. Yet somehow, deep down, she sensed it was the right thing to do. To release them. To release them from having to pay back and make right what they never could anyway. To release them from punishment, not that she could really punish them externally. But she could punish them with her thoughts. Though that wouldn't really work, would it? Wouldn't unforgiveness just mostly hurt her? It all got so confusing for her. She didn't want to have this occupying her head anymore. She wanted to be free. Free from anguish. Free from pain.

"Father," she said. It took her a long time to get the next words out. But she waited. Hoping for a good moment that never came. So she continued. "I pray for the attackers. That you would help them. That you would show them what they did was wrong. And that they need you...I forgive them for what they did."

She opened her eyes. It didn't look any different. No earth-shattering moment of truth. But it *felt* different. Suddenly there was distance between her and that tragic event. She thought back to the fire and could recall everything that happened in perfect detail. But now, somehow, she was free from the guilt. It was like the empty ocean of her life was suddenly filled with water. She felt as if a protective cocoon had formed around her as she mentally walked back into the church, climbed out through the window and walked onto the field. She could remember and not feel shame. She could recall and not feel remorse. She could walk through the fire and not be burned.

The whole thing was still clear in her mind, yet it did not have the same power over her as it once did.

"We love you," Mulli said.

That felt good. That felt really good. And without even meaning to, she gave a slight smile. It sent off the slightest glimmer of hope that change had begun.

"Can we come back and visit you?" he asked.

She smiled again and nodded.

"Tell me," Esther said, "do you like to play games?" She nodded again. "And school? Would you like to go to school?"

"Yes."

"Well, that is good, because this afternoon you can go with your mother to the Mully Children's Family area, and we will help you get settled."

"Thank you."

"You are most welcome," Esther said.

"Goodbye, and thank you for letting us talk to you," Mulli said as he and Esther got up.

As Dalila watched them leave, she felt the amazement of how their visit had sparked a journey of change within her. She had experienced the presence of God because of them.

And it made her wonder if perhaps someday God could use her to do the same for others.

CHAPTER 34

They shouldn't have been able to accomplish this much.

MCF managed to provide a care program at the IDP camp that was staggering in scope relative to the smaller size of their organization. In addition to the care they were providing at their homes, MCF provided aid to approximately 3,500 children at the IDP who were displaced due to the violence. This involved a daily food program, education, sports and games, counselling, tent-to-tent outreach, food supplements and clothing for new and expecting mothers, group therapy and medical care. Resources permitted only one meal per child per day, resulting in long lineups of children crying so loudly before mealtime that it filled the entire compound. MCF also set up weekly Sunday morning church services where a thousand people attended. Mulli updated his supporters around the world, and they responded by giving financial resources that enabled MCF to continue its work at the IDP camp.

This IDP camp in particular provided shelter to over 18,000 people. But it represented only a fraction of the overall problem in Kenya. Initial figures estimated the total number of displaced persons to be between 350,000 and 500,000.

Inflation rose to approximately 20 percent, bankrupting thousands and forcing additional people to come to the IDP in the hopes of surviving. This placed an even greater burden on the schools, with some of the classes having over 300 students.

Even so, camp life was still better than being on the streets. At least for most people. For some, however, the trauma was too much. One man committed suicide. The desperation for food caused some girls to resort to prostitution. And it became possible for women with unwanted pregnancies to undergo a risky abortion procedure on IDP camp property.

Mulli helped scoop a combination of beans and maize into the plates of the three thousand children who stood in line. After mealtime, Mulli looked up and saw a girl sitting on the ground by herself near the edge of camp while the others were playing a game organized by MCF. She had her arms wrapped around her stomach like she was suffering from an illness. She pressed her back up against the only tree, a small one at that, left in this area of the compound. It was rare to see a tree, because all the other ones had been cut down and used as supports for the linen sheets of the thousands of tents around them. The tree was on slightly higher ground to keep her from the dampness around her.

"Hello," Mulli said as he approached her.

She glanced up and then returned to looking at nothing in particular.

"May I sit and join you?"

She looked back. She had seen him before. The man with the hat. She raised her eyebrows as a sign of agreement, and Mulli sat down on the ground. He introduced himself, confirmed that she had gotten enough to eat and asked what had happened to bring her to this place.

The girl hesitated. She clenched her teeth and debated about whether to divulge what had happened to her. The odd thing was that she wanted to tell someone. She wanted to talk about it. But no one had asked, and so she had become accustomed to holding it all inside. And here was her chance to finally share what had been troubling her, and to do so, she had to unlearn her coping mechanism of believing that no one cared about her.

She was so overcome with grief that all she could manage was to say it in a cold monotone. She told her story of how her family had been killed in the fighting. As she was walking to the next town to find refuge a group of thugs found her and gang-raped her. She introduced herself as Makena.

She was relaying the information. Technically, she was correct in all the details. But she had separated herself from the emotional attachment of it. It was as if there were two of her—one who would say the right things and do what it took to survive, and the other one who had been hurt so much that she stayed safely hidden away to ensure it would not happen again.

At least not to her.

Mulli felt her pain. And as he spoke to her he sensed there was something else bothering her. As if the rape itself wasn't enough, there was a worry, a fear in her eyes that conveyed she wasn't yet out of whatever happened.

"I am sorry to hear of what you went through."

"You? You are sorry? Really? Tell me, why are you here?"

"To help," Mulli replied.

"Are you from Rift Valley?"

"No."

"Were you here in December?"

"No."

"Then you should keep quiet. You have seen nothing. You know nothing."

She glared at Mulli with eyes that were full of anger. He had seen this look many times before. Girls who had grown up dreaming of giving themselves to a husband, raising children and having a life, only to see it all shattered and have the realization settle in that no matter what they did they would not be able to go back to the hope they once had.

"I can see you have really reached the end," Mulli said. "Can you tell me, is there anything else that is bothering you?"

Yes. Yes, as a matter of fact there was something bothering her. It never ended with Makena. The pain seemed to go on forever. As awful as the atrocities were, the raping and killing were over and a person could try to move on. But with Makena there was still more. Grief can only stay locked up for so long. And her mind was so confused that the thought of just saying the words gave her the optimism that perhaps something good might come of it.

"I'm pregnant," she said.

It flooded her with emotion. That cold stare melted, and her shoulders began to shake as she sobbed. She was completely overcome with finally getting it out. All those childhood and teenage hopes had vanished. All that looking forward to a future clean start with a man of her dreams was gone. Instead, it was replaced with—how many boys were there again?—maybe ten boys whom she would never see again, and no clue who the father was.

"I am very sorry to hear about this," Mulli said. Even though he had heard this kind of story many times before, each time it was like hearing it for the first time. "You have been raped and are carrying a child and you are here at the camp. How can I be of help to you?"

"I don't need help."

"How will you care for your child?"

She turned back to her cold stare into the distance. Mulli waited for her; then he gently repeated the question. She didn't respond. Not at first. Finally, she said, "I am going to abort the baby."

Those words crushed Mulli. Even at a time when there was so much despair around him, the thought of ending a life struck him to his heart. He loved her.

And instead of reprimanding her, he challenged her thinking in the hopes of demonstrating his compassion.

"That is a very serious decision," Mulli said. "Do you think it is the right one?"

"Is this what I'm supposed to live with the rest of my life? It wasn't bad enough to see my family killed? It wasn't bad enough to be raped? Now I am supposed to have a child and whenever I see this child it will remind me of what happened? No."

"I know this is very difficult for you. Tell me what you think. Do you think that on top of all that has happened, killing a life will help? These men who did this to you, in addition to the rape, they will now be causing you to kill. How do you feel about them doing still more harm to you?"

She hadn't thought of that. The furthest she got was her desperate need to be out of this mess.

"I don't know," she said.

"Abortion can leave you childless in the future. Is this a risk you are prepared to take?"

There was so much growing up she had to do in such a short time. How did this happen? Just a couple of months ago everything was different. Life was proceeding the way it should.

It was normal.

"I am not sure," she said. "I am not sure it even is a child."

She was working hard to convince herself of that. She knew better. But if she could just get her conscience around to believing that the baby was subhuman or not human at all, it would make this all so much easier to end.

"What is your opinion? Do you think that God believes it is a child?"

She hadn't asked herself that question yet. Deep down, she didn't want to. She didn't want to have God involved in this equation. And why should he be? Wasn't God the one who she believed had sat idly by and watched all the horror unfold around her?

And if he had been that distant from her in her darkest hour, exactly what hope did she have of moving forward with him now?

"Yes," she said.

"When God created man, it was not for him to suffer. But through people's wrong attitudes and choices we cause each other to suffer. Someone I don't know can make a choice that causes a problem for me. Or I can make a bad decision and create my own problems. I create another problem when I end a child's life. God loves you. God's Word is a weapon that you can stand on. Ours is to wait on the Lord. The Lord knows all our suffering and knows all we are going through."

She closed her eyes and leaned her head back. It sounded good. Really, it did. But it didn't help. At least not with her greatest fear of all.

"Do you have any idea what will happen?"

She exhaled and leaned forward. She shook her head. This problem had so many complexities to it that whenever she felt she got one part of it solved, ten more would take its place.

"Everyone is going to hate me," she said. "When they find out that I am pregnant they will point a thousand fingers at me. It does not matter that I was raped. I will become the filthy woman who had a child without a husband. They will chase me away, and I will have to resort to anything I can in order to survive."

She closed her eyes to absorb the impact. She was trapped, and she knew it.

"What if I offered to help you?"

"And what are you going to do? You are doing all you can. You will sit there and ask me a hundred questions and convince me that it is wrong to kill. Then you will leave, and I will be in this same situation."

"What if I went to prepare a place for you so that you could have a new home? We have many, many children, and we have young women like you who have babies and they do not know who the fathers are. What if you could have a new home there? What do you think about that?"

That was an option she hadn't considered. And why would she have? It was outlandish to even have it on the table. There were so many good things she heard in Mulli's brief words, but the one that stuck out for her the most was the word *new*. Was that really possible? Could he make all things new for her?

Another tear began to form, and her stone-cold heart began to recall what it meant to feel compassion. She ran her fingers through her unkempt hair.

"When I was a little girl, my favourite thing was to go out in the fields and look at the flowers and crops. I would stand and feel the warm sun on my face and the wind as it blew past me. I felt so at peace then. I dreamed that one day I would have a family and we would walk together in a field. Now I wonder if there will be anything for me at all."

"I will help you, and I will be with you. You will have a new family. You will learn a trade like sewing or hairdressing, or you can learn microfinance. Whatever you like. And you will be able to get a job. You can be a mother, and when you see your child you will not have to think about what happened, but you can think about how God can take something that was so bad and can make it into something really great. And who knows what your child will become. We don't know yet. But you will see. Yes, you will be able to see it."

She closed her eyes and squished out the tears. There was something so reassuring in the tone of his voice. She felt more relaxed. Had she heard him right?

Was that actually correct? She sensed in her heart that he was telling the truth, and she marvelled that only a few minutes earlier she had all but made up her mind to end the child's life.

She did wonder about what the child, her child, would become. Boy? Girl? Outgoing or soft-spoken? Makena looked over at Mulli.

"Thank you," she said.

She and Mulli got up, and he walked back to the class that was about to start. He told her that MCF would continue to visit her each day over the next few weeks while they made things ready for her at her new home.

She sat down in class. And even though the sun was high in the sky and the heat made for unbearable learning conditions, she wrapped her arms around her stomach, looked out at the incredible number of students sitting in front of her, and imagined that one day her child would be in school, too.

CHAPTER 35

The MCF team met together each evening at their home in Eldoret to share about what they had seen, heard and felt that day. They crowded together into the large living room, sensing the solidarity that came with being with others who faced similar issues. Mulli led them in a prayer and a Scripture reading. Then they began to share what they had experienced that day.

The team found it difficult to hear the victims' stories. The murders, the rapes, the missing children. It was not possible to hear them without having it affect them. In the same way that sharing helped those in the IDP camp overcome grief, so sharing helped the counsellors overcome their grief. Mulli organized these sessions so that they would be able to bear one another's burdens.

One of the members of the team shared how she had visited with Josephine—the mother who had scrambled with her seven children away from the attacks and discovered as they were fleeing that only four had made it safely away.

Fridah, another one of the counsellors, shared about her day. She had a deep, genuine smile that put anyone who met her at instant ease. "We fed over three thousand children at lunch today. It was very hectic," she said. "We had to really call on the name of the Lord." She laughed, and, for the moment, the mood in the room brightened. "May I share a story?" she asked.

The group agreed.

"You are sure? I don't want to take too much time."

"Please," Mulli said.

She was a great listener and heard people right from their hearts. Yet as the days wore on she found it increasingly difficult to sleep. The stories she heard during the day kept revolving around in her mind at night, and being able to have others hear helped her to believe that she didn't have to keep it all to herself.

"I have visited parents in the tents who said there were some pastors preaching to the congregations in local Christian churches who knew all that was planned. They had believers who did not belong to their tribe in their church and knew that they were going to be killed. Yet the pastors said nothing and maintained their loyalty to the tribe instead of to Christ." Fridah shook her head. "I cannot understand that. I cannot imagine telling someone that God loves them, knowing they are going to be murdered, and not doing anything about it. That is not easy. I have heard that some of our MCF people have gone to these churches of those particular pastors. Some have recognized that they did something wrong and have repented."

"Fridah," Mulli began, "you have shared that you have trusted the Lord to give you wisdom and strength as you speak with people. What would you say you have learned so far in your time here?"

That turned things around for her. She led group therapy sessions with as many as 50 children at a time at the IDP camp. There, the children shared. It was different for her here when she needed to share.

"I have learned that I should live with a passenger attitude. When you enter a bus there will come a time when you have to step off because you have reached your destination. And for the time that I am here I am invited by the conductor to sit down. I am part of a public vehicle, and I get to share life with whomever I have beside me. I want to care for whomever I am sitting beside as if it were my brother or sister. I only have this short time here. I am just a passenger. I ask myself, who am I impacting, who am I serving while I am here? And I have this opportunity to be here at the IDP to help these people whom I have been placed with to help."

People continued sharing their stories. Mulli encouraged them, especially when it came to speaking with people who were angry or who did not want help. "Just keep praying for them, even if at first they show no signs of improvement. You never know what the Lord is doing."

Which was good advice.

Because he was going to need it.

They found him sitting in his tent, preoccupied with the dirtied white linen wall ahead of him. He hadn't eaten in two days, and the neighbours hadn't heard from him. Not that they were expressly looking for him. Each person at the IDP had enough trouble of their own.

Mulli approached the tent with an MCF co-worker—a young man whose initial trepidation about this mission had been replaced with courage since the moment he decided to ignore his fears about being here. Mulli called from the partially closed entrance to the tent to ask if they could come in. Daylight was slipping away. In moments the light would be gone altogether. They pulled back the tent cover and looked inside.

They saw him staring ahead as if in a trance.

No movement. Not even the blink of an eye. His face was tough. Like it was chiselled out of rock. It was eerie how a person could sit that still to make others think he was nothing more than a well-crafted statue.

Mulli and the co-worker introduced themselves and asked if they could sit down. They waited, wondering if the man would respond. Finally, he did. It wasn't much. A slight grunt. But that in and of itself was reassuring. His grief was so deep that he had gotten lost in his own world, and the very ability to recognize people from this world was already a sign of hope.

"I would like to hear your story," Mulli said. He and the co-worker sat down. They waited, hoping that the simple courtesy of sitting with him in silence would be enough to encourage him to know that people cared.

Time seemed to stand still under the approaching darkness. When nothing is happening during the day it can feel like productive time is slipping away. But here, with the approaching darkness, it felt like time could go on forever.

"I was running," he began in a voice that was just above a whisper.

He spoke in slow, measured sentences, as if he were reading lines etched on the linen tent in front of him. It seemed he had repeated this thousands of times to himself, and yet only now for the first time out loud. He told the story of how he had run back home as fast as he could. In the distance he saw that his house had been burned. That didn't concern him. What *did* concern him was the well-being of his son. With the threat of the attacks he had gotten down to his absolutely-must-have list, and all that was on it was his boy. Not the house. Not the possessions. Not the farm. He was willing to part with all of it. But when he reached the smouldering ruins he saw a body lying face down, cut up, on the ground.

He stopped talking at that point. Mulli thought it was odd how there were tears streaming down the man's face, yet there was no change in his tone as he recalled what it was like to approach the body. He wasn't able to determine whether or not it was his son until he concluded from a birthmark that it was him.

"My heart goes out to you," Mulli said. The man said nothing. He went back to staring at the linen sheets. His face grew colder, his eyes narrower, and Mulli had the distinct impression that the man would stay there forever without some kind of outside intervention.

"What do you think would be of help to you?" Mulli asked.

The man breathed in. He reached up to wipe the tears off his face as if he only now realized that he had been crying.

"I was active in church," the man started. "Whenever God asked me to do something, I did it. When a neighbour was in trouble I gave food or money. Whatever was needed. I would travel long distances to help relatives. I would work late into the evening for anyone who needed something. I prayed every day. Read my Bible. And then came the attacks. As I was running to my house I thought to myself, This is when I actually need him to come through for me. I need him right now to protect my son. And what did he do?"

The man turned to Mulli. "What did God do for me? When it was time to rely on my God whom I have served, when it was time to have him show that he is for me, what happened?" He turned back to the linen tent. It was hard to tell if he was really staring at that sheet or just using it as a pretense for looking into the past and reliving everything over and over again.

"This is who God is," the man continued. "It is all fine and good for me to serve him, to give my life to him, to do whatever he asks. But there is no guarantee that God will help in return. It was my fault, really. All of this is. I presumed that I could count on God. That I could follow him and he would look after me and my family. And I am sure there are others who still think this way. They think they can trust God to work everything out for them. But they are wrong.

"All of us are vulnerable before God. We think he is our protector. That he will come to our aid when we are in trouble. But he is like a game warden who is miles away, and we are left in the jungle, alone, with a dozen ravenous lions ready to tear us apart. God is so far away from us that not only does he not come to our aid, but he doesn't even hear our cry for help."

He looked back at Mulli. "Whether we like it or not, this is who God is. We say that he is looking out for us, but this is not true. And it would be easier to believe that God has abandoned us, because I am no longer interested in a God who sits by and watches destruction. I should have known better. I should have known when my wife died. But still, there was something inside me that wanted to believe in a God who would take care of me."

Mulli waited, trying to absorb what the man had told him. "You have suffered a lot."

"Have I?" the man asked. "Tell me, if God is willing to allow this much evil—my own son butchered—then God is capable of allowing any evil in life." The man's face grew intense. It was as if his entire being turned into a furnace of rage. And then, just like that, he went back to his cold, calculated stare. "There is no God out there to help us," he said. "We just think there is."

It was not easy for Mulli to hear how this man had pleaded for God's help only to be denied the request. He felt the man's despondency, his disappointment in having placed his entire confidence in a God who appeared not to be in control anymore.

"Sometimes we wish we could change the past," Mulli said. "Now that everything has happened, we cannot reverse it. We would like to. But we cannot. So the question is, What is the path forward?"

The man turned to Mulli and studied him. He clenched his jaw ever so slightly, as if he were a man trained not to lose his temper. But Mulli saw it and felt the seething anger even in the man's quiet voice.

"The path forward? The path forward is realizing that there is no point in truly trusting God. Sure, you can trust God for the sun to rise. But for the things that really matter in life there is no guarantee. Our pastor would always encourage us to 'take God at his word.' Fine. Go ahead. But it is only a matter of time before you realize it does not work."

"It is difficult when God does not act the way that we think he should act."

"My life is over, do you understand me? My family is finished. Whatever happens now will just be a cheap imitation of what could have been." He looked around and found a cup beside him. He drank the last bit of water in it. "We were caught unaware, you know? But we will never be caught unaware again. We stayed with these people as if we were all brothers. In every election from now on we will have guns. We will protect ourselves. Just like the other tribe organized themselves, we will organize ourselves. We will be ready the next time. And when they attack, we will kill them all."

Mulli waited a moment to let the man's anger subside.

"It is not easy."

In an instant the man's anger flared. "Oh, and what do you know? What could you possibly know?"

"As a child I was beaten terribly by my father."

"You see! That is what I mean. Did you kill him for it?"

"I nearly did."

"You should have done it. It's your own fault that you were weak."

"May I encourage you? Do you know the story of Job? He lost everything, and God gave him back twice what he had."

The man's expression turned briefly to astonishment, and then he did everything he could to prevent himself from becoming enraged.

"You are talking of God paying us back? Where was this God during the violence? Where was he? I don't want to hear about the Bible. And if I am to listen, come here with that God now and tell him to answer why he was so weak and useless."

"It is difficult when we wonder 'Why does God not intervene?'"

"I went to church every Sunday. I gave food to people when they had nothing and almost caused my own family to starve. I gave money to people who had nothing. I prayed. I trusted God. I taught my son from the Bible."

Mulli paused, thinking it best to allow the man to continue expressing his anger rather than debate him in this moment.

"Psalm 91: 'No evil shall befall you.' Psalm 46: 'Our God is our refuge and strength, an ever present help in the time of trouble.' Oh really? Please. I beg you. If you really want to help me, then give God back his Bible and tell him to come down to earth with a book that I can actually use. Because the verses I memorized from that book do not work."

"It is true that God does not always do things the way we want them."

The man covered his face with his hands. He was tired of being angry, yet he didn't know how else to feel.

"Why did God allow this?"

Mulli waited. There was something healing in the silence. "God is not a foolish man," Mulli said. "What is your opinion—can we wait and see what God will do? God is watching. It is only that you can't see him."

"If I cannot trust God with the lives of my wife and my son, then what can I trust him with? If he is not able or willing to help me when I really need him, then what confidence can I have in him moving forward?"

"One thing I have learned is that the more you suffer, the nearer God is to you."

The man became quiet. He rubbed his forehead as an indication of great agony. "But why this? This is the worst thing imaginable."

"I do not know. If you permit me, may I quote a verse from the Bible? I do not mean to offend you; it is just that this is a verse that may help."

The man nodded.

"'There is no wisdom or understanding or counsel against the LORD.' We do not know why. And it can hurt that such a big God seems to abandon us in our time of need. There is wisdom about this, and God alone has it. When Job was suffering he never forgot God, even when his wife told him to curse God, whom she thought was making him suffer. Job was there to endure and come to the victory of his sufferings."

"Those people who attacked us must die."

"Do you think this is the right answer? What do you hope this will achieve?"

"You are telling us not to take revenge. But the Bible tells us so many times of God leading his people. Maybe God is waiting for us to take revenge against these people. We've been quiet for so long. My house has been burned down four times. My son survived the first three, but now he is gone and my wife is gone. Enough is enough."

Mulli waited. He let the man feel everything that was on his heart before he spoke.

"It is very difficult to accept the situation you are in. And you think, how do I move forward? How do I go on from here? Do you think that forgiveness would help?"

He raised his hands palms up in a gesture of bewilderment. "What do you mean by forgiveness? Should I forget these people? The ones who killed my son? Is that what you mean?"

"Forgiving others not only helps them, but it helps us to overcome what has happened. We release the power people have over us. It helps clear our mind of the hatred we have for them. When we pray for our enemies, which is very, very hard to do, then by God's grace we escape bitterness."

"And so they continue killing and we sit here? That is useless."

"It does seem that way. Yet, we do not deny vengeance; we only turn it completely over to God. He will act in whatever way he wants. He carries it out the best."

"Does he? We begged for God to send a calamity and wipe them all out. But he did nothing. So it falls to us now to do something. This will never come out of my heart. We will destroy them."

"If you continue with revenge, what is the result? How does God really feel about killing?"

The man dropped his head. His tent was dirty. He had no change of clothes. Once a married man with a family, job and home, he was now reduced to a displaced person in a tent too small for him to stand up in.

"I don't even know the last time that I prayed," he said. "If God can't kill these people himself, then what is the point of following him?"

"Do you think God is giving them a chance to repent?"

"Why should he?" the man asked. "If God is too lazy to carry out justice, then I will do it."

"If you kill, would that be considered a sin against God? What do you think of the Ten Commandments?"

"This is impossible. So I should let them kill us, but we can't kill them?"

"It doesn't seem fair from our perspective, does it?"

"No," the man agreed. His face relaxed. Was God really still in control?

He wasn't sure. But he was sure that Mulli had helped him get closer to God in this conversation than he had been since before the attacks. "I am suffering because of my vote. Members of Parliament are all enjoying their life while we are suffering here. It is not right."

"Our only hope is to pray and to trust God with the past and the future."

The man closed his eyes in pain as if a memory had just flooded his mind and brought with it a torrent of guilt.

"Have you ever made a mistake?" the man asked.

"Of course," Mulli said.

"If I had been home with my son, I might have been able to stop it. And I think to myself—If only I had been there. If only I had seen the signs of impending danger. I feel like a fool for not being smarter. For not being more wise. And at the same time I am disappointed and angry with God for not giving me the guidance that would have saved him. How do I love a God who allows me to suffer so much?"

"This is the great test of faith in life," Mulli said. "Jesus was beaten and crucified. God could have helped, but he didn't. Why not? There was something greater. Jesus did so many miracles, yet people saw them and never accepted him as the Son of Man. They killed him. God himself knew that Jesus would be killed by people, the people that God created. God could have prevented his Son from going through this. Even Jesus asked, 'Father, can you remove this cup?' God didn't. God waited until they crucified him. Then God raised him up. It shows that God is still powerful.

"I want to encourage you; as long as you are living, you have hope because you don't know what God has in store for you. When Jesus died he killed death. I don't know what will become of this, but it is in God's hands. All we can do is put all of our past in God's hands and move forward. Somehow, life has to continue," Mulli said. "What do you say, would you like to give your past to God and forgive the people who did this?"

His head said yes, it was the logical choice, but his heart said no. Forgiving felt like he was giving up the fight. Like he was losing. And in a sense, he realized he *was* losing. He was losing his right to revenge. His right to blame God. His right to feel justified in being angry. They had destroyed his life, and now he would lose even more by releasing them from having to pay back what they took.

"How do I forgive such brutal, merciless, barbarians?"

"This only comes when we realize we did not bring ourselves into the world. We have no authority over our lives. By releasing them, you allow God's peace into your heart."

It made sense to the man. For the first time he felt that a solution to this never-ending nightmare might actually be within reach. But that was the big issue. He wasn't there yet. He hadn't forgiven. Why was it so easy to understand what Mulli was saying, yet so difficult to let go and follow through on what he was saying?

He couldn't go on this way. He didn't have all the answers and had come to the realization that he might never have them. Not down here, anyway. And, as far as he was concerned, when he got up to heaven, who knew? Maybe the answers then wouldn't seem as crucial as they did down here.

Either way, living with revenge wasn't working for him anymore. Deep down he knew that. What he didn't know was what it meant to live by forgiving the ones who destroyed his son.

But he was willing to find out.

A tear rolled down his cheek. "You have really changed my mind about this. I think you are right."

"I am glad to be here with you," Mulli said, "but please remember, this is not about me being right. It is about you being in a right relationship with God. And that is only possible through forgiveness."

"I have lost everything. But only by forgiving and forgetting the anger is there hope. Because if I keep remembering in anger, I am sure that I will go mad."

"Can we pray?" Mulli asked.

The man looked at Mulli. His eyes seemed different. Still exhausted, but there was a peace in them that Mulli did not see before.

"Yes," the man replied.

Mulli prayed with the man. It would be a long journey to forgiveness. Grieving over the past and living with an uncertain future would test the man's resolve to trust in God. But as Mulli left the tent, as he said goodbye to the man, he thanked God for the opportunity to share peace with him when at first it looked totally pointless to try.

As he walked back to the MCF headquarters at the IDP camp he stopped and looked out at the massive group of tents. Yes, he was a passenger. He was God's passenger. And a few months earlier he would never have guessed he would be here today.

Which made him wonder what God had in store for him tomorrow.

CHAPTER 36

She had had enough and wanted to leave.

She had been rescued from the church and brought to the IDP camp. She received a tent, cooking wares and food. What started out as an optimistic change in her life turned into disappointment. Whenever it rained the water came into the tent, making it impossible to sleep. Camp life was safe, but difficult. It was supposed to be a temporary measure. The organizations at the IDP worked incredible hours to help everyone as best they could, yet through forces outside of their control it became apparent that the IDP camp was going to be a long-term solution.

It was while waiting in the food line that Nduta met a woman named Waruguru. She was taller than Nduta, had long braided extensions and wore the same exhausted expression as she did.

"We're going to be here forever," Waruguru commented.

"They say we will be provided homes soon."

"When was the last time that a promise to build housing for the poor was actually fulfilled?"

They inched their way closer in the food distribution lineup. It was the highlight of their day. The rest of it would be spent doing nothing.

"When the rain comes in, it ruins our tent," Nduta said. "My children are constantly sick, and no one is able to help them."

"I have the same problem. Everyone does."

"I'm tired of being here," Nduta said as she inched forward in the lineup. "I hate this place."

That was strong language considering the alternative. Even though IDP life wasn't bliss, it was a far cry better than risking being killed in the slums. But boredom can sometimes cloud logic, and the girls wanted adventure.

"Then why don't we leave?"

"The camp? And do what?"

"Sell our tents and rent a small hut in Eldoret. We'll sleep with men to get money, and we'll have our own lives back."

It was such a terrible idea that in retrospect she would later feel embarrassed for even entertaining it. The IDP camp wasn't bliss, but it had perks. Food. Shelter. Even if she hated it, at the very least, it was still the best option for her children. But the old life had pull. And when she felt the call to go back to the street, she answered it, even though part of her knew it was a mistake.

Why exactly was she doing this? She felt a conflict within her. But it didn't last long, and soon the two mothers were taking their tents and their children and leaving the camp. It was odd seeing two women and their kids carrying their tents off the property. But people were too worried about their own survival to spend energy thinking about the actions of others.

They sold their tents for a paltry 300 Kenya shillings. They could have gotten at least double that amount, but they were looking for quick money. They used it to find a dingy place in nearby Langas. Mud floor. Stick frame walls filled with mud. Metal roof over their head, which kept out at least some of the rain. They stayed with their children and took turns heading out into town to find work. Nduta took the first shift on the street.

She found a man who was interested, remembered the lesson she had learned previously, and this time agreed on a price with him before going back to his place. When they were done she asked for payment. He refused.

She asked again, and he told her to take off. Then she demanded it, and things got ugly.

The man stood to his feet and was about to hit her when he got the surprise of his life. Even though Nduta was considerably shorter, she was tough, a natural by-product of life on the street. She pulled back, and he missed her completely. She wasn't going to do him the courtesy of a slap. Instead she formed her hand into a fist and with lightning fast reflexes drilled him right in the face.

He wasn't expecting that. He wasn't expecting any kind of resistance. Certainly not from a small prostitute like Nduta. He stumbled back, shocked, and suddenly felt inferior in the fight. He prepared himself for another counterattack, but Nduta was not interested in an exchange of punches.

She was interested in giving them all herself.

She whaled away on the guy. Two solid rights, and he was backed up against the wall. She unloaded a flurry of rights and lefts that landed solidly on his face, cracking his head back and sending him crashing to the floor.

"I didn't leave two kids in the slum tonight to come here for free! So where is your money?"

She screamed a slew of expletives at him, threatening to pummel him into oblivion.

He believed her. Nduta could fight. His bleeding nose and cut lip were evidence of that. He told her he didn't have any money.

Nduta dropped her shoulders. She looked around the room for something to steal. There was nothing. A disgusting mattress. A small table. Some toiletries. Nothing worth value. She swore at him again, already feeling the futility of what she was doing. She needed money to pay for medicine for her kids. Needed food. Needing everything, really. And she wasn't going to get any help from the bloodied wannabe boxer down for the count on the ground.

She left and went back to the hut. The two women, each with two children, went to bed in their small one-room place. Nduta stayed awake. She listened to the rain, watched whether it would seep onto the floor, and hoped her knuckles would stop aching soon.

No one likes to make mistakes, and when Nduta got up the next morning she decided a life at the IDP would be better than this. It was a sign of retreat. There was no telling what the guy she beat up last night was capable of. Word would have spread, and a guy getting whaled on by a girl was not going to go over well.

She grabbed her kids and walked back to the IDP, checking behind her frequently to see if he was coming after her.

When she arrived at the camp she saw the big Mully Children's Family bus arriving. People with bright smiles and team shirts stepped off to greet them.

Nduta asked a person she had known previously at the camp who these people were.

"This is them," her friend said. "The ones who feed us and who give a home to children and their mothers. You should go and see them."

People who give a home to people like me?

As if.

She watched from a distance. It took her the entire morning to gather courage to see them. Finally, she approached the MCF tent. She explained her case history to a girl named Kituku.

Nduta had made it this far. She expected to be rejected. She had a number of strikes against her, and whatever the criteria for acceptance, she was sure to fail them. A prostitute. No education. No skills. No money. Two children. A history of mental illness. Had been suicidal.

Not exactly a great candidate.

But Kituku encouraged her and told her that her case would be sent to MCF Nairobi for processing.

Nduta stood there. Shocked. Did she hear that right? Kituku noticed and smiled. She assured Nduta that Nairobi would review everything.

Surprised by kindness, Nduta stood there in silence. It felt awkward for her. She'd never met people like this before. She managed a brief thank you. She wanted to say more. But it was all she could manage.

When she left to go back to her tent she should have looked content. She should have been happy or even excited.

But she didn't show any of these emotions.

She was in too much shock to believe that someone would go to these lengths to help her when clearly she would never be able to return the favour.

CHAPTER 37

Everyone else had gone back inside. Even the diehards.

But Michael stayed out, alone, with his makeshift football, dribbling under the stars on a small patch of dirt. It gave him comfort. Connected him back to a time when life was still okay. He played football as often as he could. Even at night when he could barely see the ball.

Farther away, Mulli came to the end of a row of tents. It had been a long day of counselling, but in spite of diabetes Mulli showed no signs of slowing down. He was about to turn and head down the next row when he looked out and saw him standing there. That a boy was out late was not a concern for Mulli. But what did get to him was that there was no one else with him. So Mulli changed his mind and went to see why this boy was there all alone.

"Ooh-aye," Mulli said. It was a classic greeting that was known throughout the camp as the way MCFers greeted the children.

Michael stopped. He turned and tried to recognize who it was. One of his teachers? Hard to say. He did have a male teacher. But he sat near the back, and there were over a hundred students in class, so it'd be tough to pick him out, especially in the dark.

"You are still playing football. You must have very good eyes," Mulli said with a deep laugh. "How are you?"

It wasn't meant simply as a greeting, and Michael understood that. When Mulli asked how someone was doing, he really wanted to know. Still, Michael didn't respond.

"My name is Charles Mulli. What is your name?"

Mulli. As in *the* Mulli? Michael was in a class run by Mully Children's Family. The children who still had parents said Mulli was the nicest man ever and went to talk to their dads and moms to help them.

"Michael."

"That's a very good name. Like the strong angel in the Bible. You know?"

Yes, he knew. His mother had told him why she had given him the name. Which was odd now, considering that the mighty Michael seemed to be strangely missing in action when the mob butchered her in front of his eyes.

"Let me try to receive a pass from you in the dark," Mulli said. He backed up. Michael kicked him the ball. Mulli stopped it and passed it back to him.

Back and forth they went under the stars, barely able to see the ball, going as much by sound as by sight.

"I can see you are a good football player," Mulli said. "Yes. You have very good control of the ball. Is it your favourite sport?"

Michael nodded.

"I like football, too. I have many, many children, and they organize football tournaments and the whole school plays. Do you play on a team?"

Again Michael nodded.

"I can see that. I wonder, which position do you play?"

Michael accepted the pass from Mulli. He dribbled it to his left, then passed it back.

"Number eight."

Football players sometimes referred to their positions by number. Each of the positions from goalie to striker was assigned a number of one through eleven. Midfield was eight.

"A lot of running in midfield. What do you like better? Playing back or playing forward?" Mulli one-timed the ball back to him.

"I like to score goals." Michael kicked the ball back to him.

"That is good," Mulli said, stretching out to contain the pass before sending it back. "Tell me, before you came to the camp, when was the last time you scored a goal?"

Michael trapped the ball. He was about to kick it back when he held the ball and waited. "It was on the day of the attack," he said. Michael passed the ball back, but it was such a light kick that Mulli had to step forward to get it.

"That was a very sad day," Mulli said. "Would you like to talk about it? I would like to hear your story."

Michael considered. Mulli passed him the ball. Michael felt it hit his foot. He debated kicking it back, but then picked it up. "All right."

They sat down at a table. Mulli brought them each a glass of water. Michael told his story starting from when he scored the winning goal with a bicycle kick and then arrived back home. He shared about how he had hidden under the bed and watched his mother die and how the attackers had let him go because he was too young to kill.

"I don't know what will happen now," Michael said. "I don't know where I will go."

The camp became quiet at night. Most people stayed inside their tents. Small groups here and there gathered together to speculate how many more days, weeks or months they would be here. For most, the prospect of leaving was dreadful because there was nowhere to go. And staying meant the continued frustration of having to be cared for instead of the satisfaction of working to provide for their families.

"I am organizing more places to sleep at our home, and they will be ready in about two weeks' time. I would like to invite you to come and live with me," Mulli said. "I would be your new father. You would have many, many brothers and sisters. You would go to school, and you could play football, too. What do you think?"

The legend was real. The man the other kids talked about in class existed. Michael felt a whole new world open up for him. Like the endless maze of an uncertain future at the IDP suddenly had an exit point.

He was soft-spoken everywhere but on the football field, so the quietness of his reaction wasn't meant to be indicative of how he felt. Mulli had met thousands of children—the extroverts like Mara and the introverts like Michael. He saw the new optimism in the boy's eyes. There was life there again. The anticipation that something good was waiting for him down the tracks.

"That would be great."

"I would like to share something else with you, if that is all right?"

"Okay."

"I am preparing a home for you because I love you. And there is God in heaven, who would like to give you a home."

"What kind of a home?"

"This would be a home that you would have forever and ever."

"Forever? That is a long time," Michael said. "I wonder how something can go on forever."

"It is a long time, for sure. Some things, we cannot understand how they work. We know that God will be there. And so we trust and have confidence that it will be okay." Mulli took a drink of his water. "God would like you to come to this home. And even now, he would like to make a home inside your heart and fill it completely. All the memories that you have and the sadness, God wants to take that away and to give you a heart full of joy, so much joy that you really wonder—wow, God has made me really, really happy. The kind of happiness that is not on the outside, but one on the inside. One that never goes away."

Michael processed everything he was hearing. He remembered what it was like to be happy. Scoring that bicycle kick. That's what it meant to be happy.

At least that's what he *thought* it meant to be happy.

Now, looking back on it, it felt different. Not quite happy. It was a shadow of being happy—as much as he knew at the time. Now, hearing about a God who wanted to know him and care about him made the exuberance of that goal seem less fulfilling than it did at that time.

"Why would God want to do that?"

"Because God loves you."

That spoke right into Michael. Love. When was the last time he heard that word? He knew. It had been a while. But he knew. He knew the exact date. His mother was soft-spoken, too, and every night she would come to his bed and tell him that she loved him.

I love you, Michael.

He could hear it in his mind. He could recall the tone of her voice. The peace of her presence. The gentleness of her lips when she kissed him. Now she was gone. But was Mulli saying that he could have that again? That he could hear someone, every night, even though he was alone, telling him that he was loved?

"How do you know?"

"Because the Bible tells us. It says, 'For the Father Himself loves you.' It also says, 'For God so loved the world that he gave his one and only Son, that whoever believes in him shall not perish but have eternal life.'"

"Live forever," Michael said.

"That is right. And the Bible tells us who is allowed into heaven. It says, 'But as many as received Him, to them He gave the right to become children of God, to those who believe in His name.' That is the most important position a person could ever have. To be a child of God.

"But, we have something that keeps us from getting to heaven," Mulli continued. "It is like when you play football and there are not eleven defenders on the other team but a thousand, and they block you and you can't get to the goal. In our life we have bad things that we have done. We have sinned. We feel the effect that sin has on our life. There are people who do evil things to us. You have experienced a terrible tragedy. And all of us, we do bad things as well. They may not be as bad as what other people do, but they are still bad. Sometimes we think, 'Oh, I have been as good as I can possibly be.' But it is not enough. None of us can reach the goal. We are even born with sin. The Bible tells us that all have sinned and we don't reach the goal that God has set."

Michael gripped the football in his hand. He felt the impact of the sins he had committed. He had lied. He had stolen. He hadn't listened to his mother when she asked him to do things.

"But the good news," Mulli continued, "is that Jesus died in our place for our sins. He came down to the earth and died on the cross. And we think, 'How is that helping? The man is dead.' The Bible says he took our sins in his body to the cross 'so that we might die to sin and live for righteousness,' for 'by his wounds we are healed.' The good news is that Jesus did not stay dead. The Bible says, 'If the Spirit of him who raised Jesus from the dead is living in you, he who raised Christ from the dead will also give life to your mortal bodies through his Spirit, who lives in you.' Whether we have nothing and are at the bottom, or we have everything and think we are on our way to the top, all of us need him. There is no exception. This is who Jesus is. He is the one who gives hope for the hopeless."

Michael looked up at Mulli. Their eyes connected. He felt something changing inside of him.

"What do you think, Michael? Would you like a new start? Would you like to be born again so that you are totally new on the inside? To give your life to Jesus and have Jesus' life in you?"

Michael felt the pain of losing his mother. Felt the trauma of everything he had been through. Yet somehow, he saw it differently. It wasn't that it all suddenly made sense—how could it?—but despite the horrors, there was the promise of peace on the horizon. A new peace. It was as if all the confusing threads representing everything he had experienced were converging right to this question that Mulli was asking him.

"Yes," Michael said. "What do I have to do?"

"I will pray with you, and you can invite the Lord Jesus into your heart. How does that sound?"

Michael nodded. They folded their hands, bowed their heads. A concentrated and focused intensity came upon Mulli as he prayed. Michael repeated the words quietly beside him.

"Father God, thank you that you love me. Thank you, Jesus, that you died on the cross for my sins and that you rose again from the grave and that you are alive today. You have seen everything that has happened in my life. I give it all to you right now. I ask you to forgive all my sins. And I ask you to make me your child and to help me to follow you. I thank you that I am now your child. In Jesus' name, amen."

They opened their eyes.

"Thank you, Mister Mulli."

Mulli hugged him. "Can I make you a deal?"

"Okay."

"You can call me Daddy Mulli. How does that sound to you?"

"It is good," Michael said.

Mulli smiled.

They got up from the table and headed towards the camp. As they walked back, Michael looked up at the stars.

He wondered what it would be like to travel to each one of them someday.

CHAPTER 38

Nduta watched through the window of the white passenger van as it travelled down the road. She passed pineapple farms and roadside markets where people would rush to the van with bananas and drinks and other goods in the hopes of making a sale. She had come from Eldoret that morning and was on her way to MCF Yatta. She kept trying to convince herself that this was happening. That she was actually getting a brand new start at life. She glanced at her children sitting beside her. Behind her sat other rescued street girls, who stared out in anticipation. It was all so surreal for Nduta. Girls like her shouldn't be getting breaks like this.

Or should they?

Before meeting Mulli her future was predictable and bleak. She would work as a prostitute by night and try to be a mother by day. But that had all changed, and today was the day of promise. The day when she would be given a new start.

She wondered what it would look like. Wondered about the people she would meet. Wondered if reality would match her imagination. And when the van turned right off the road onto the Yatta property, what she saw was far beyond anything she could dream of.

Tall, massive greenhouses stretched out to her left. A large water tank stood high on a platform to her right. Dormitories dotted the landscape ahead on the left. She saw little children playing on swings.

The van stopped. She and her children stepped out and put their feet on MCF soil.

Even though she had never been here, even though she had never thought a place like this could even exist, the moment she set foot on the property it felt like she was meant to be here.

The MCF driver took their luggage. Other girls came to the van, introduced themselves and welcomed them. They were given a tour of the area and shown their new accommodations and the classrooms where they would have the opportunity to choose a new vocation. Nduta felt the sting of tears forming in her eyes when she saw that there were beds for her children. There was one for her, too, but that was bonus beyond bonus. She hadn't envisioned a future where her children wouldn't have to sleep on the floor any longer. And it amazed her that people who didn't know her were giving this to her.

One of the pastors introduced himself. He was young and energetic; more importantly, he was kind and welcoming. Best of all, when he looked at her, right into her eyes, she felt no condemnation. She struggled to maintain eye contact. She wasn't used to that. Not from a man. How was it exactly that someone she had never met would treat her this well?

Dinner would be served soon. Nduta took the opportunity to bathe her children. They splashed and played games the way children are supposed to when they're in water. One of them touched her wet hand onto Nduta's nose. Another held water in her hand and beckoned her mother to come closer. The children giggled as they reached above Nduta's head and poured a small amount of water over her.

Nduta laughed.

They sat down at the table with others. They ate until they were full. There would be three meals a day. Three. Her children would go to the MCF school on the property while she would attend the vocational school for dressmaking, hairdressing and catering.

She sat together with 30 other women who were all in the same situation that she was. The pastor led the group in singing. She noticed how happy everyone was. They were not forced to do this. They were singing from their hearts. Nduta hadn't seen this before. Hadn't seen people who were genuinely content right to the core.

It made her wonder if that might be possible for her.

She met Mulli for the first time in Yatta. First impressions are lasting, and this was no different. He was kind. Humble. Caring. He put her at instant ease. He sat down with her on the veranda overlooking the fish farms and asked about her story.

Where to begin?

She told him everything. Right from as far back as she could remember. The beatings. The mental breakdowns. The suicidal thoughts. The prostitution. The post-election violence in Eldoret.

Mulli listened.

And when she was finished she felt that she had been heard. Sharing facts was one thing. Anyone could sit there and listen to that. But Mulli didn't just hear her words. He didn't just pick up information. He heard her. The real her.

"I am willing and ready to help you in every way I can. I will continue to support you as long as you need, even until you get your feet on the ground," Mulli said. "I want to encourage you that Jesus will never leave you nor forsake you. You can count on him to be with you at all times and in all your trials and also all your good times as well."

She thanked him.

And for the first time she felt what it was like to have a father who cared about her.

It was getting close to suppertime at the Ndalani property when Mulli met with Michael. Even though there were hundreds of students, Mulli could pick out any child who needed attention. Michael was doing well in school. He was part of numerous activity groups. He worked hard at his chores. He seemed like a model case of a child who was being transformed.

But like all good fathers, Mulli saw past the exterior.

"Can you tell me, Michael, have you made many friends here?"

They stood outside near the kitchen. The staff cooked supper. In the distance they heard one of the choirs practicing.

"Yes. Especially on our football team."

"And how is your team doing?" Mulli asked.

"We are doing well. We have won more games than we have lost."

"And are you scoring goals?"

"Yes."

"That is good."

A big smile came to Michael's face. He had a new home. A new start. And already he was beginning to put the past behind him. But his smile was going to fade when he heard what Mulli would say next.

"Michael, can you tell me, do you have any Kalenjin friends?"

Michael looked to the side. A clear indication he didn't want to answer. The word *Kalenjin* was enough to take the smile away from any Kikuyu boy.

"I am glad to hear that you are doing very well here," Mulli continued. "And as you can see, we are a very big family. We have many different tribes here. Not only one. We have many. What do you think, is it important to be able to be friends with everyone here? With all of your brothers and sisters?"

That wasn't going to happen. Michael wasn't going to be friends with a Kalenjin. No way. Not with the enemy. Granted, if you wanted to get really technical, the Kalenjin children here at MCF didn't directly take part in the violence in Eldoret. They didn't specifically hold machetes or spears or bows and arrows. But they were guilty by association. When any part of the tribe does something, then the whole tribe becomes accountable for it.

At least that seemed reasonable to Michael. That way he could stay justified in being angry.

"I do not want to be friends with them."

"Can you tell me why?"

He couldn't. When he was challenged to think about it, the irrational basis for his position because apparent. But he would give it a try all the same.

"The Kalenjin killed my mother."

"That is very sad," Mulli said. "I am very, very sorry about what happened to your mother." Mulli waited. Sometimes there is healing in silence. "Do you think it helps you and them if you stay angry?"

"No."

"Why does it not help?"

Michael looked to the side again. But Mulli waited.

"Because they are not to blame," Michael said. "And the anger creates problems."

"When we have been hurt, it is important to forgive the whole group. We are not sure who the bad ones are. We don't know where they went or what happened to them. So in this case we choose to forgive them all. Why do you think forgiveness would help?"

"Because then I won't have anger inside my heart."

"The Lord will help you with this. Forgiveness can be a decision, but it is also something we have to put into action."

It was Michael's turn to wait. This all sounded good. The part about forgiving. He was on board with that. But he knew what was coming now. That part about putting forgiveness into action? That didn't sit so well with him.

"There is a goalie here," Mulli continued. "He is about your age. Do you know him?"

Sure. Michael knew him. Tall. Dark face.

A Kalenjin.

"Yes."

"Would you like to put your forgiveness into action by asking him to play football with you?"

"We have supper soon."

Good comeback. That was quick thinking. Mulli would understand that. Michael needed to eat, and that superseded forgiving the enemy.

"I think you still have half an hour. It might be a good start. Do you think it would help you and the MCF family if you did?"

He didn't want to admit it.

But Mulli's logic was tough to argue against.

Michael gave a half-hearted search around the property for the goalie. He was supposed to look for him. But he hoped he wouldn't find him. Besides, it was getting late. The sun would be setting soon. He had chores to do. He had to study. He had to do just about anything besides find the enemy and make peace.

Thankfully his search didn't produce any results. He was about to stop looking when suddenly he did see him. He had his heart so set on not finding him that when he did see him his heart rate sped up. Sure enough. There he was. Walking across the small bridge towards the schools. The goalie saw Michael, too, but he didn't wave.

They had an understanding.

Michael watched as he crossed over. This was the perfect range to call out to him. But Michael didn't. He waited. He wasn't exactly sure why. Maybe it was because he didn't want to actually do this. Maybe he was afraid of venturing into the unknown world of forgiving. Or maybe the indecision of calling out to him came from realizing he would have to sacrifice the anger he felt against him.

The goalie continued walking. He was just about out of shouting distance when Michael called out to him.

He turned around. Their eyes met.

"Want to go to the football pitch for some free kicks before supper?"

The goalie's mind raced. He too tried to think of a million reasons why he couldn't. Supper was soon. Chores. Studying. Yeah, you know you've hit rock bottom when you're using studying as an excuse not to play.

But even if he could have found a good reason, he wasn't sure he would have used it.

Football is very tempting.

Even when it is with the enemy.

He thought a moment. He was Kalenjin. Michael was Kikuyu. Oddly enough, when he first came to MCF he felt no distinction in the classes. But ever since the attacks, he sure felt it. They all did. The goalie felt terrible about what his tribe had done. Felt so guilty whenever he saw a Kikuyu boy or girl.

"Well, are we playing football or not?" Michael asked.

"That's too close," the goalie said.

"It's not too close. It's already past the 18-yard line," Michael argued. They were the only ones on the football pitch. Two nets, a dirt field and a makeshift ball.

"But you are a good shooter."

"And you are a good goalie, so what is the difference?"

"You are sure it is past the 18-yard line?"

"Well, I am guessing. I don't have a ruler."

"Fine."

"Fine."

Michael took two steps back from the ball. He eyed the goalie and tried to judge if he was standing slightly to the right or left so as to concede any kind of advantage. It didn't seem that way. He looked to be dead centre.

The sun began to set behind them. It cast a perfect orange light around them, just enough so that both of them could see the ball.

Michael debated. Top right or top left.

"I think you are scared," the goalie jeered.

"I am not scared."

"I think you are. You are worried that I will stop your shot."

"For a goalie you do a lot of talking."

"That is what goalies do."

"And we midfielders—we do a lot of scoring."

"You do a lot of waiting."

"Get ready. And no crying when it goes in."

"If I cry it will be because I am too old to move by the time you get around to shooting."

Top right. Definitely. When in doubt, pick top right.

No, no, not top right. Bottom right. This guy was big. He could stretch, and most goalies will tell you that down and away is harder to stop than up and away.

Michael started his run towards the ball. The goalie focused his eyes, waiting for that all important first instant of when the ball leaves the foot and begins its path to the net.

Michael planted his left foot beside the ball and leaned forward to keep the ball from blasting too high. He struck the ball as best he ever did.

The goalie reacted well. Either he had incredible hand-eye coordination or he was a good guesser. Either way, he went the right direction. He took one step and then lunged. He didn't reach with two hands. Just one. Two hands would have meant less distance. With one hand he'd be able to deflect it.

And that's exactly what happened.

He made contact with the ball; it bounced off the post and came right to him.

Michael exhaled in defeat. Clearly he was farther than the 18-yard line. Next time he was bringing something to measure this out.

Someone called out that it was suppertime.

"That was a good save."

"Thank you. I am a good goalie."

"Best two out of three?" Michael asked.

"It is suppertime."

"I understand. You only have one good save in you and you just made it. So now you would like to go for supper so that I don't score on you."

"I just proved that you can't score."

"Then prove it again."

"All right. All right. But no crying when you miss again."

The goalie rolled the ball back. Michael set it up. The goalie took his place. Dead centre. Again. Michael stepped forward and in an ingenious move, he stutter-stepped, and the goalie froze. Michael carried through and blasted the ball low and right again and clear into the net.

"That was a dirty trick."

"It was a trick, but it was not dirty. Unless you don't want to count it. I would understand."

"Come. One last one. We will see who is better."

It was tough for both of them. They should have been concentrating harder, but they both started laughing.

"This is serious," the goalie said, trying to contain himself from smiling. "Serious business. This best-of-three championship is second only to the World Cup for popularity in the world."

Michael placed the ball. The supper bell rang. He stepped forward, no stutter this time, and blasted it against his better judgment to his favourite place. High and right. It took off. The goalie read it well. He took one step and stretched out for it. It deflected off his finger, went up and hit the bottom of the crossbar and dropped down.

The goalie got up and grabbed the ball.

"Did you see it?" Michael asked. "Did it go in?"

"If I had to tell you what I thought I would say no. But if I had to tell the truth I would say maybe."

"Maybe? How does a ball maybe go in?"

"I do not have my ruler. I could not tell."

Michael burst out laughing. They met at the penalty marker. They slapped each other on the back.

"I would say it probably went in, Michael."

"Tomorrow we will try again."

They ran, together, from the football pitch to the dining area just as the sun began to set behind them. They talked about their favourite football players and who they thought would win the next World Cup. They congratulated each other on being good players.

Michael figured the goalie would be a good fit for his team.

Makena arrived pregnant at MCF Yatta. Arriving anywhere pregnant at her age without a husband should have been prime cause for stigma. For finger-pointing. For those all-condemning looks, or worse, those accusatory attitudes that people convey without even having to say anything. But she didn't get those at MCF. Imagine that. You walk off a bus, close to giving birth, and there is zero condemnation. Instead of the guilt treatment, what she received was a warm welcome from the team, who then went on to help prepare her for being a new mother.

When she gave birth, MCF supported her with everything she needed to care for her new daughter. They enabled her to continue with her education by looking after her baby while she was in class.

Whenever she held her new baby girl, she marvelled at the miracle in her hands. During one of the breaks from class she took her baby into the field to show her the trees. She stopped and closed her eyes. In that moment she felt the warmth of the sun on her face, the breathing of her daughter as she lay quietly in her arms, and the peace that came with moving on from events in her past. Ironically, she didn't give that group of five or ten or however many there were that night any thought. That terrible evening on the road back when she was attacked by all those guys faded from her memory. It wasn't gone. Maybe it would never be gone completely. Exactly how was it supposed to disappear? But it took on new meaning. Somehow holding her daughter did that for her. And all her fears about how the presence of her daughter would remind her of the atrocities of her past did not materialize. She had hope. She had a future.

It was a new path. She hadn't anticipated this. And yet Mulli had chosen her in spite of what had happened. She breathed in the warm summer air and pointed out to her daughter a new branch that was just beginning to grow on a nearby tree.

Everything was going to be all right.

Makena sat down at the supper table with the others. The number of women in MCF Yatta continued to grow each day. What started out as a few dozen increased to over a hundred and kept on expanding. Across the table from her she saw another young expectant mother with her children.

"Hello. My name is Makena."

The other woman stretched out her hand and smiled. "I'm Nduta."Nduta introduced her children. Makena greeted them.

"How much longer for you?" Makena asked.

"One month to go."

"Really? I have a daughter. She was just born."

"Congratulations. Then my son or daughter already has a friend."

As they began to eat they talked about their lives and realized they had both been at the same IDP camp at the same time. They shared stories about the rain coming into their tents. About standing in line for what felt like forever to get food. About wondering what would happen to them. They remembered the night they had first arrived at the IDP and had settled into their new surroundings.

It all felt like such a lifetime ago.

Dalila came to MCF Ndalani and fell in love with everything. For some, education, clothing, family and a future are expectations. But for others, like Dalila, they were a privilege beyond comprehension. She loved being in class. Loved the mealtimes with her friends. Loved swimming and playing sports. Loved singing in the choir. And she absolutely loved being in the dormitory. Talking with her friends at night. Sharing life. Sharing the future.

But what she loved most at MCF was when she held the young babies of the new mothers like Makena and Nduta and felt the joy that came with being able to see the future in the present.

Yes, she had lost her baby brother in the fire. The trauma she had suffered from that was unspeakable. Some suffer out loud. Others, like Dalila, suffer in quiet desperation. But she had walked with God through the pain. She had desired to be able to turn the clock back and redo things. But God had helped her leave the past in the past. And she had begun those difficult steps of moving forward. Her brother was gone. But he was all right. He was in heaven. And now she had hundreds of siblings to share her life with. She had a future where she could grow and become someone who in turn could be used to help others. Starting with the babies that she loved to babysit.

Dalila felt the same way Mulli did about MCF.

It was like a dreamland.

CHAPTER 39

Mulli had seen it all. He had lived through enough terrifying events to fill ten lives. When he was a child his father would come home late at night drunk and beat him, his mother and his siblings senseless. During his business years he had gone to settle a dispute with unruly tenants who refused to pay their rent. They formed a ring around him and threatened to burn him alive right then and there. He prayed, and miraculously the crowd dispersed. In his ministry he had seen demon-possessed children exhibiting horrifying unnatural abilities. Yet he led a team in prayer and cast the demons out. He had also faithfully gone into Eldoret during the post-election violence—a complete death zone—to help people in IDP camps.

Mulli had been victorious over so much in his life.

So why had he become this afraid during a unique and strange three-day period while on one of his trips to the West?

The fear came at the most unsuspecting time. He had taught all his children never to be afraid when facing evil spirits. "Never show fear," he told them. And while it may have initially seemed counterintuitive not to be scared when people are possessed, it was actually logical to have faith. There was no reason to be afraid. God was bigger than whatever they were facing.

While there were always pressures in running a home for hundreds of rescued street children, even while he was away, there was nothing specifically out of the ordinary this day. Which is why the feeling of dread was so hard to place.

He walked down the stairs to his room. His steps felt awkward. Unsure. Like he was being led to a place he didn't want to go. It was as if all the power in his life had been sapped out of him. That he had been injected with a poison that made him feel overcome with dread. His normally clear mind now felt engulfed in a never-ending storm of black clouds. Like he was flying a small plane through lightning and thunder and all the instrumentation had gone haywire.

Mulli couldn't explain the sensation. Couldn't put his finger on what was happening. He knelt down at his bed. That was the normal place he went when things got rough. He hoped everything would return to normal. That at least a ray of sunshine would appear in the distance.

But instead, it became more difficult.

At first it felt similar to when that rush of sickness came over him while at his office all those years ago. It had served as a catalyst to change course and rescue street children. But now, on his knees where things were supposed to get better, the feeling grew worse, and by the time he started praying he sensed a terrible fear in his spirit that he had never known before.

I told you, Mulli. I'm coming for you. You are slippery, you know that? You escaped death while being beaten by your father. You escaped the tenants who were going to burn you. You escaped all the demons. You even escaped being killed in Eldoret during the post-election violence. But it can't last forever, Mulli. I will get you.

He who dwells in the shelter of the Most High abides in the Shadow of the Almighty.

I'm planning it out, Mulli. I see how you are getting away from these attacks. But no more. You will not make it much longer. And isn't that too bad? You will die without really accomplishing much of anything.

That is not true. I have been used of the Lord to rescue children.

That's just great, Mulli. Give yourself a great big pat on the back if you think you deserve it. You believe you have done a good job? Maybe, but only by comparison. You see others around you who have not done as much and you see what you have done and that makes you feel that you are better.

That is false. I have never looked down on anyone. This is all God's doing. I have never claimed anything was my doing. It is only because God worked through me. And what has been done is good.

Sure, what you have done is good. But it is nothing compared to what you could have done. Stop looking at what has happened and look at what should have happened. I mean, really. The sum total of your life is a few small settlements in the middle of nowhere. Not exactly impressive.

It is not what I accomplish but the faithfulness with which I carry out my calling.

You keep telling yourself that, Mulli. But you and I both know you fell way short of what you were called to do. You go ahead and affirm yourself with the smiles of the children you have rescued. It's all you'll be able to do to hide the truth that behind

each one of those rescued children are another ten thousand who have not been res-
cued. That isn't much of a testimony, Mulli.

The fear gripped Mulli to such an extent that he thought he was going to
die. He wondered if his heart would stop right then and there while on his
knees. That this would all come to a crashing halt. He clutched his hands
together even tighter. The room suddenly felt full of evil. Like those storm
clouds had entered and erased any thought of hope. He remembered his best
friend. Remembered how he had struggled. He needed that story now. So he
turned in his Bible to Luke 22:44, to read about Jesus in Gethsemane. He read
the words over and over again. "And being in anguish, he prayed more earnestly,
and his sweat was like drops of blood falling to the ground."

Are you afraid to die, Mulli? That's it, isn't it? You are afraid.

I am not afraid. It is that I am not ready to die. I have so much left to accomplish.

*Why bother? What is your work really doing? A few children here and there. But
in the grand scheme, what is it really?*

*It is a testimony. I want MCF to be a good example of what followers of Jesus
can do for God when they surrender and give themselves in total commitment to God
for his glory. I want good things for MCF so that it will be a help to many people.*

*The ministry won't accomplish this. You won't either. You're coming to an end
and it will all crash. Get ready for the collapse. You might even be privileged enough
to see everything fall apart right before your eyes.*

I want it here to impact future generations.

*Sure you do. That's understandable. But you won't complete your mission,
Mulli. You're finished. And this is hopeless.*

It is not hopeless.

But it is.

Mulli turned to Psalm 34:19. He wiped the tears out of his eyes and read
the words out loud. "A righteous man may have many troubles, but the LORD
delivers him from them all."

He felt comfort in knowing that no one was spared in this world from trouble. Every person, himself included, had their point where they could be
tempted.

*There is no one to continue this work once you are gone. It will fade away like
the grass.*

*I am working on a succession plan. I am working on transferring to the next
generation.*

But it won't happen in time. How does it feel to be irresponsible?

*Greater is he who is in me than he that is in the world. How does it feel to know
that you are finished?*

I am not finished. Not with you. I'm only getting started with you, Mulli.
You are finished.

Mulli prayed for hours that evening. But the feeling did not leave him. Either way, he would not be deterred. He understood what it meant to be faithful in prayer. Understood that it takes unwavering commitment. Understood that even when Christ seems miles away he is still the friend who sticks closer than a brother. Yet for three days he had the most intense struggle of faith and fear that he had ever known.

He carried on with his activities as best he could. But life is different when you are under constant attack. And when he was alone he read and reread passages in the Bible, confirming in his mind and in his spirit the difference between the truth he was reading and the fear he was sensing.

He stayed faithful in prayer. Especially when it seemed like nothing was happening. His own advice worked. Whatever it was in life—raising hundreds of children, believing God for food and water, confronting attacks of the evil one—it didn't come down to doing complicated things. It came down to doing simple things consistently. Praying. Reading the Bible. Serving.

It wasn't about Mulli. He had long since come to the end of himself. That precious place that defines true followers of Christ. Not that he had totally arrived. But it was settled in his mind that nothing was about him. It wasn't about his reputation. His future. His security. It was about Christ.

And this conviction gave him an incredible freedom to not care about his own life.

He continued to trust. Continued to believe. And like a fog that lifts to allow the sunlight through, Mulli felt the relief that comes when temptation leaves. The thunder and lightning stopped. The storm clouds dissipated. He picked up his Bible and turned to Matthew 28:20. That always felt so good. Somehow life was just better with a Bible in his hands.

"I am with you always, to the very end of the age."

He continued to read from his Bible and prepared for his next challenge.

I'm only getting started with you, Mulli.

I am not afraid.

Why would you not be afraid?

Because I will press forward in faith, Mulli replied. *I will not give in. Not to you. Not to anything.* He clutched his hands around his Bible. Closed his eyes in earnest prayer. His mind was so focused that nothing else got in. Nothing else mattered. *And God will work his miracles as per usual.*

CHAPTER 40

The unbearable humiliation beat down on her as relentlessly as the African sun. The looks. The whispering. The comments. It all sat like an impossible weight on her fragile shoulders. Being poor was bad enough. But there was no shame in poverty, because everyone in her slum was poor. Being uneducated was the second strike against her. But even that was no cause for embarrassment, because no one around her could afford the unimaginable luxury of school either.

But being a pregnant teenager was the death knell that spelled disaster for her. She was already a financial burden on the family, but now she had become a burden to them morally as well. And with a child on the way she would soon be adding yet another mouth to feed.

No one in the slum came out and said anything to her. There were no direct accusations. No finger-pointing or insults. That would actually have been easier to deal with. Better to get things out in the open than to keep them concealed. But she saw and, more importantly, she felt the stares of people all around her. It's the unspoken attitudes that condemn the most. They didn't have to come out and tell her. She knew what was going on in their hearts.

You are not wanted.

She gave birth to a baby girl and named her Charity, which, ironically, was exactly what she could have used in her own life. Becoming a mother is supposed to be exhilarating. Fulfilling. An absolute thrill of bringing life into the world. But not for a single teenage girl in Africa. And instead of feeling joy, the moment she became a mother it occurred to her that the best possible solution for her and everyone else would be for Charity to die.

Then she would finally fit in again. No more stares. No more looks. No more of any of it. Instead, she could experience again the most coveted of all human emotions.

Acceptance.

Even with getting rid of Charity there still wouldn't be enough food. It wouldn't solve the problem entirely. But at least there wouldn't be one more draw on the meagre family meals. She could do it. She could find a way to end this whole mess. Then she could make it back to the deplorable existence that she had come to know as life.

There would be the stigma of murdering a child to deal with. So she would have to find a way to do it quietly. Just get rid of the child somehow. Still, people might suspect. People might wonder. But, big deal. People have short memories. And the risk of suffering the agony of future ongoing suspicion was worth it. Better to go through with killing her daughter than to live in the perpetual shame of being looked at as the one who had a child out of wedlock.

She took her daughter and left the hut. She didn't say goodbye to anyone. Didn't say where she was going. It didn't matter how long she would be gone.

She wouldn't be missed.

She walked down to the river. It was quiet. Only the faint sound of the knee-deep water rushing past her. That would be deep enough. She swallowed and sat down. This was it. This was her chance to finally put the shame behind her. And she would have done it right then and there, but a curious emotion came over her.

She suddenly wasn't entirely sure who this person was who was sitting here on the rock. Was this really her? She remembered the person who used to come and play here as a child. Dirty water and all. She would laugh. What was that like again? What did it feel like to be happy? Who knew? She used to come here to play with her friends. Life was poor, but life was manageable, even if there was no future. But then came the evening. That fateful evening. And nine and a half months later Charity was born. That's when something in her mind switched and all she could think about was doing whatever she could to get back what she once had.

She left Charity on the rocks. Better this way than to see her actually drown in water. She walked back, no last looks, no goodbyes, and put her daughter out of her mind.

But as she returned to her hut the relief she expected to feel did not materialize. And ridding herself of her child only served to sink her into a deeper despair. Strong as she was, she forced herself to continue. She would not go back. She would find a way to deal with the guilt of murder. And she would finally be set free from the stares and shame of those around her. If carrying the burden of murder was the price she would have to pay in order to be released from condemnation, then so be it.

It was later the next day as she was lying down in the hut trying to cope with the onslaught of guilt when someone came running down the dirt road shouting that they had found Charity. The poor child was so emaciated it was hard to comprehend how she could still be alive. And at the words of her daughter being alive, Charity's mother's heart sank in frustration that she had not had the courage to finish her off.

She was reprimanded by her family. Despite their overall disappointment with their daughter, the parents disapproved with even stronger vehemence that the child was not cared for.

No matter. If at first you don't succeed…

When the next opportunity presented itself she took Charity and decided this would finally be the end of her humiliation and despair. She checked around her to make sure no one was looking. Then she clasped her hands around Charity's neck and began to strangle her. Charity coughed once and then went completely still. It would only be seconds now. And she would have died had it not been for the neighbour who saw what was happening and intervened.

The neighbour shouted at her as she ran towards her. She broke Charity loose from her mother's fateful grip and hurried to bring Charity to safety.

Charity's mother slumped down. Her mind was a mess of confusion. Whatever moral code was left in her was scrambled with mismatched messages. She looked up against the blinding sun and saw Charity disappearing in the distance. And part of her, that slim small part that still connected reason with sanity, felt relief that Charity was free from a woman like her.

The elders from the village contacted MCF with a desperate plea to rescue Charity. Mulli brought Charity into his home, where she would experience what it was like to grow up without fear of harm—a benefit that only very few in Kenya would be able to experience.

There's a fine line between being courageous and being crazy. Canadian Arvid Loewen might get as close to that line as a person can get. Arvid began ultra-marathon cycling at 37, covering distances that can only be described as staggering. During events on solo rides he would push four hundred kilometres a day. But as amazing as his ability was, his compassion for the underprivileged was even more compelling. He had been planning to use his cycling ability as a platform to raise awareness for a children's rescue ministry and was hoping to connect with the right mission.

Sometimes the most amazing adventures begin with the simplest of conversations. And while waiting for a Sunday school class to start at his home church in Winnipeg, Arvid sat next to a friend of his and asked what his friend's son was up to these days. His friend replied that his son was going to serve at Mully Children's Family in Kenya. That sparked a chain reaction of events that eventually saw Arvid tackle his first MCF project, where he cycled on a tandem bike with a rotating group of three of MCF children in the back non-pedalling seat. Arvid transported them over two hundred kilometres a day to make the cross-Canada trek of over 6,000 kilometres to raise funds for MCF. And he did this without ever having been to MCF.

Blessed are those who believe and have not seen.

What he did see, however, were pictures of children at MCF. He carried a picture of one girl in particular on a special non-drinking water bottle that was filled half with water from Vancouver on the west coast of Canada and then the remaining half with water from the east coast of Canada after his trip was finished. He carried this girl's picture as a symbol of all the MCF children he was riding for.

The girl in the picture was Charity.

The following year, Arvid and his wife, Ruth, travelled to MCF to see the ministry first-hand. In one of the evening programs they sat near the back, and a little girl of about three jumped into his arms. She began to play with Arvid's wedding ring, smiling the way children do when the world is at ease for them. The young girl was Charity. And as Arvid held her in his arms she changed from being a picture he had carried across Canada to a real living person with a need for love and a relationship with God. Seeing Charity in person clarified in his spirit that his efforts were having an impact. That lasting change was coming to children.

That it was possible to make a true difference.

That same year Arvid resigned from his position as a manager in a furniture manufacturing plant to pursue his goal of creating awareness and raising funds for MCF full-time. With a generous severance he was able to do so for some 29 months. After that he had exhausted all his resources. At the age of 50 he found himself living off of his RRSPs. His financial advisor told him there was no plan possible to make this work in the long term.

That wasn't easy for Arvid and Ruth.

But it was all right with them.

Their vision for their next venture for MCF was to break the Guinness world record for fastest cyclist across Canada. The existing record was 13 days, 9 hours, and 6 minutes, which meant Arvid would have to finish this solo ride at an average of 453 kilometres per day. At an estimated average speed of 23 km/hour, that would mean Arvid would have to cycle 20 hours a day.

If you're going to dream, dream big.

But if the 6,000 km coast-to-coast distance across Canada wasn't enough of a challenge, Arvid's health condition added an extra obstacle. Arvid suffered from osteoarthritis in his hip, making him walk with a limp. During a training expedition he got off his bike at a restaurant and was in such anguish that he couldn't even make it to the counter. He grimaced in agony at the door and waited until the pain subsided.

His right thigh was in good shape. That wasn't the problem. But his left thigh was 2 inches smaller in diameter, and his left leg about 1. 5 inches shorter than his right.

"You have the right thigh of thirty-five-year-old elite cyclist," his doctor said in the pre-event checkup, which made Arvid feel good. "But you have the left thigh of a fourteen-year-old girl."

What's a race without difficulties?

The doctor cleared him all the same. And the race was on.

Arvid got off to a blistering start. His pace from Vancouver through the first 2,000 kilometres put him an incomprehensible 20 hours ahead of the pace of the previous record. It all looked great. But it was when he hit the provincial border between Manitoba and Saskatchewan that he entered the dreaded middle third—that part of the race where he was too far into it to change his mind, yet too far away from the finish line to envision that this crazy idea was even possible to fulfill.

And as if that wasn't enough, this was also the time when his legs began to swell. It started out as discomfort. Something he figured he could push through. But it continued to grow in intensity as his body reacted against him cycling an average of 545 kilometres per day and sleeping a paltry two hours a night. The battle began to shift from being physical to being both physical and mental.

What were you thinking? At your age, trying to beat the Guinness record?

I am not quitting.

It doesn't matter what you want. You're going to quit because you're not in good enough shape to do this.

I will press on.

All the way to Halifax? The other side of the country? You overestimated your abilities.

I don't need to finish the whole race in one day. One step at a time.

You're a logical man. Think it through. It's not possible. You're not even halfway and you're exhausted. You're already slowing down.

That was a good point. He *only* needed to average 453 kilometres per day to break the record. But he was fading fast. And his legs had swollen to such an extent that it felt like he was pedalling under water.

To make matters even worse, exhaustion began to play tricks on his mind. Late in the evening, around Lake Superior in Ontario, the moon shone down and he saw a sprinkler oscillating back and forth. *What is a sprinkler doing all the way out here on the TransCanada Highway in the middle of nowhere?* It seemed so strange. So bizarre. When he got closer he saw that it wasn't a sprinkler after all, but it was actually the tall grass at the side of the road blowing in the wind.

Farther ahead he was shocked to see a woman wearing a red and yellow jacket lying down on her back with her feet up. Arvid blinked to make sure what he was seeing was correct. Sure enough. Someone was in serious trouble. He was about to turn around to warn his support crew when he noticed that it was just a road construction sign that had been turned over.

Time for a rest.

So Arvid stopped, and after a two-hour sleep he was up and at it again. During the first seven days the two hours a night seemed enough. Now, it felt like nothing. He'd lie down and get up and wonder if he had taken a break at all.

He got back on his bike and took off. But as soon as he did, the immense feeling of impossibility crept in again. A hundred metres seemed like a hundred kilometres. The finish line felt like forever away. It was dark, it was late—or early, depending on how you looked at it—and he was so exhausted that all he felt was the enormity of a task he now felt was impossible to complete.

He stopped by himself at 2:30 in the morning for a break on the side of highway. And that's when it hit him.

Do you see it?

See what?

Down below. Look carefully.

Arvid looked. A deep ravine stretched out beneath him. Craggy rocks. A stream ran through it.

It's just a ravine.

It's much more than a ravine, Arvid. Do you know what it is?

No.

It's your escape. You're not going to make this race. We both know that now. Quitting is too embarrassing. There's a better way.

I can still make it.

I admire your fortitude. Really, I do. But it's time to pack it in. There is no shame in stopping before you do some real damage to yourself.

People have quit on those starving children in Kenya. They don't need another person jamming out on them.

So now it's up to you to do the impossible to make things happen? Is this what God asks?

Arvid exhaled in exhaustion.

I can't let those children down. I can't use a little discomfort as an excuse—

An excuse? Who's blaming you? You've done great. Look back, Arvid. Look at how far you've come.

What good does looking back do? I'm looking to the finish line. That's where I'm going.

Listen to yourself. You're speaking words you don't even believe.

I believe what I'm saying. It's just...

It's just what?

I'm...I'm exhausted. I am so exhausted.

It's okay. I understand. Let's call it a day.

I don't see the light at the end of the tunnel.

And you won't. It's over. But take heart. You've done your best.

Have I? How can anyone ever really say they've done their best? I don't see any relevance to what I'm doing.

Then call it off, Arvid. If God were really in this, he would give you courage and strength. Isn't that was God does?

Arvid dug down deep. He tried as best he could to recall his goal, his vision, his reason for being here in the first place. But it was all as fleeting as his breath on this chilly morning, which showed up for a brief moment and then vanished altogether.

I'm not sure what I'm doing here. I'm supposed to be helping the kids in Kenya.

But are the kids really your responsibility?

...I'm not sure.

They aren't. Let someone else look after them. What does a Westerner have to do with Africans anyway? It's not your continent. They aren't your people.

I don't know what I was thinking in doing this. I just...I just can't do it.

All you have to do is take your bike and give it a little nudge.

Arvid looked down at the ravine. That felt good. The relief of knowing it could finally all be over. Just one little push.

What do you say, Arvid? Everyone believes in accidents. Just toss your bike down and you can go home and relax.

Just as Arvid glanced down again, the support vehicle arrived. The bright headlights pierced through the thick darkness. On the back of the vehicle he saw his spare bike. One bike going down into a ravine is understandable. But a second bike biting the dust? Might be a bit tough to explain away.

Arvid got back on his bike and cycled to the ironically named town of Marathon. The team booked him into a comfortable motel. A shower. A warm bed. It was all so inviting.

So much so that Arvid declined.

Instead of taking the room, Arvid went to the motorhome, where he stood in a two foot by two foot shower and slept in its tiny mosquito-ridden bed. As beat as he was, his logic was sound. If he took the bed in the motel, he might not get out. It would be too easy to cave in under the comfort. And so he thought it better to plant a hedge and take his lumps by spending the night in less comfortable surroundings.

As he went to bed that night he prayed to God. It was different this time. Up until now he had prayed, "God, help me to do this." But that prayer seemed beyond wishful thinking now. Instead, tonight, Arvid prayed, "God, I cannot do this, but I will continue to do my best. I surrender the outcome of this event to you."

There is something special that happens when a person comes to the end of himself. And for Arvid Loewen that was exactly the case. But it was not an instant, dramatic difference.

Unfortunately, things got worse.

He got up the next morning, and his cycling was harder than ever. His daily output had dropped to 400 km/day. Still superhuman by any standard, but at this level, it wasn't enough. Not only was Arvid in danger of not setting a new record, he was in danger of not finishing.

His previous lead of 20 hours ahead of the record had now dwindled to 12. The road conditions were brutal. He felt increasingly discouraged. And the once energetic attitude he had was now replaced with solitude. Just a man, his God, his bike and a whole lot of emotional turmoil.

It was in the town of Mattawa, some 4,300 kilometres into the journey and more than 1, 700 to go, that everything came to a halt. Arvid had been crawling along. His legs were so swollen that the progress he was making was insignificant. The compression stockings he had on to contain the extent of swelling seemed to be doing nothing. Everything he had tried was not working.

Arvid was finished.

The logic went like this: the record was out of the question. He was clocking in at 52 km a day *less* than what he needed to break the record. Worse yet, he was declining each day. The rational choice was to take a break. A real break. To relax completely and hope for a miracle beyond miracles, that God would do something.

After all, there was a big, fat cheque waiting for him at the finish line if he did beat the record.

Arvid contacted Mulli to keep him updated and to share his struggle about his desire to quit. Mulli had flown to Canada and had planned to be part of the support crew for the final third of the journey. It all looked so hopeful.

Now it seemed Mulli's journey would be in vain.

Arvid headed into the motel. He didn't need any encouraging speeches. They wouldn't have worked anyway. There comes a time where there are no words.

"Ruth, I'm done," Arvid said. "I can't comprehend what I'm doing."

Ruth was the usual tower for Arvid when he was at his weakest. She had the precious possession of quiet strength. A prudent wife is from the Lord, and her wisdom was far beyond the "you can do it" truisms that others might have resorted to. She knew the exhaustion had to run its course.

He was committed to getting back on his bike. But the record was now out of reach. He got into bed and should have felt relief. But instead he felt an ongoing onslaught.

You failure. How can you quit? All those children dying in Africa and you take a break?

I just can't go on.

Oh, you can't go on? How nice for you. Nice bed for you. Nice roof over your head. How about all the starving children in Kenya? You are spitting in their faces, Arvid. You're pathetic.

I'm not even sure what I'm doing out here.

Wonderful. That's just great, Arvid. You get up in front of all those media and call all those people to pray and you reward them with quitting?

I'm going to get back on my bike.

Oh please! You are getting back on your bike when? In ten hours? Twenty? How many children will die between now and then? Go have a nice rest, Arvid. Sleep tight. But do me a favour, will you? Give at least some thought to those starving kids, will you? Think about all the Charitys out there who will be strangled to death all because you couldn't tough out a little trip on your bike.

That's not fair.

But it is completely accurate, and you and I both know it.

Am I really justified to quit?

No! No, you are not. What kind of a champion quits?

Are my problems really that big to warrant being in a motel as opposed to riding?

No!...Wait. What did you say? Did you say your "problems"? Is that what you said? Your "problems"? How about being beaten in a slum? How about being a twelve-year-old forced to prostitute herself to make enough money for food? How about sleeping in the pouring rain and eating out of garbage bins? Those are problems, Arvid. Not your little bike-o-rama through scenic Canada with a little-bitty fluid in your legs. Bite me. Bite me with your so-called problems. You know nothing about problems. Do me another favour. Go back to Africa and find a girl in a slum and tell her all about your problems. I'm sure she would love to hear about how a man with medical coverage and a roof over his head and food to eat has problems compared with what she has to endure. Oh, that's right. It's not your problem. Because you're too busy sleeping off your "problems." Please.

There comes a time in a person's life when they can't accomplish anything more for themselves. They hit the limit. And for Arvid, he didn't even know what to pray or think or how to defend himself against the ongoing attacks. And that's where Arvid was fortunate to have his soulmate, Ruth, at his side. Seldom did she pray for Arvid to have strength. But she did pray for him to be at peace.

And as he went to bed, the burden of failure lifted from him. A person can only do so much. A wall is a wall. Still, he had total peace. "I will do my best," he whispered to God. "That's the best I can do."

But God had more than that in store. It was as if Arvid reaching the absolute end, sensing his inability to succeed, became the catalyst for greater things.

And what would happen next would be nothing short of amazing.

CHAPTER 41

Arvid got on his bike 17 hours later. If he had an uphill climb ahead of him when he started this break, he had a mountain ahead of him now. To beat the record would require him to blast through the next 1,700 kilometres at an unthinkable pace of 485 km/day.

Hundreds across Canada were following Arvid's progress online, receiving regular updates. The record that seemed in the bag during the first third of the journey now looked perilously in danger. He was five hours off the pace. But the record was only that. A record. There was far more at stake. What weighed on the hearts and minds of his friends and family around the world was the anguish they knew he was going through in an effort to bring hope to abandoned children.

About 120 kilometres west of Ottawa, Arvid looked ahead and saw his friend waiting for him on the side of the highway. He was expecting to see him at some point. But nothing could prepare Arvid for actually making eye contact with him. He saw the familiar smile. Saw the familiar love exuding from him. Saw the man whose mission had become his own.

Arvid stopped on the side of road.

"Arvid!" the man said.

And it was at the sound of Mulli's voice that Arvid began to cry.

Mulli hugged Arvid. And in that instant, as difficult as everything was, for a moment the world seemed to be put right. The calming effect of Mulli's presence washed over him.

There wasn't much Arvid could say. Words aren't always necessary when deep friends are together.

Mulli felt Arvid's struggle. That made sense. As an abused and abandoned child, Mulli was keenly aware of what it meant to hurt. God had used the pain from Mulli's past to help thousands of people. And this time the empathy he had for Arvid connected the two together, giving Arvid a renewed encouragement to face the final third of his journey.

Mulli put his arm around Arvid.

"I am so proud of you," Mulli said. "You have done what men cannot do. But with God all things are possible. We are promised in Isaiah 40 that the young men will get weary, but they that trust in the Lord will never get weary. And this today is the manifestation of the Lord. God is showing his power in you. You do great things. And you are going to finish it in the name of the Lord."

They closed their eyes, and Mulli prayed with the confidence that comes with walking close with God.

"Father, we thank you so much. We come before you with thanksgiving. I want to pray for my dear brother. We are in the wilderness. We are on the way, O Lord, to victory. I pray that, God, you will grant unto him victory in Jesus' name. That, Father, the world will know that you live and you can raise those who are weak to become strong. And, Father, for the cause of the children in Africa, for the cause of the children at MCF, God, we thank you and we pray that you may use this son of yours, the man you made, the man you created, the man whom you called upon. He has sacrificed his body, soul and spirit because of your name. Thank you, Jesus. Amen."

The prayer was powerful. Odd how something with such impact could happen on the side of the road with only the few crew members to witness it. And yet, Arvid found it difficult to understand Mulli's faith in claiming victory on his behalf. Not just victory to make it to the finish line in Halifax, but victory in beating the record. It seemed too much to grasp. Exactly how does someone have faith for someone *else* to achieve something?

"When you phoned me," Mulli said, "and told me about the very difficult struggles you were having, I called Esther in Kenya. I asked her to take the older children out of school to fast and pray for you, Arvid. Six hundred children are praying for you. And together with the many people here in Canada we are standing strong in the Lord to believe him."

They hugged. Arvid wiped the tears from his eyes. He rode off. Mulli joined the support vehicle for the final leg of the journey. And as Arvid cycled down the highway he sensed a confidence that if he did his best, God would grant victory.

Whenever Arvid took his five-minute breaks, Mulli would always be the first out of the motorhome to serve him with whatever he needed. He was riding well again. The swelling in his legs was virtually gone. To help him get back on track Arvid cut his normal 120 minutes of sleep per night down to 90 minutes. The crew read emails to Arvid as he was riding as a means of encouragement. Dave, a friend of Arvid's, coordinated media attention, which exploded with excellent coverage as it became apparent that the grandfather of three might actually beat the record. Donations poured in from all over.

At 1:00 a.m. Arvid stopped for his 90-minute rest.

"This is going to be our last night," Arvid told his crew. "After this we're going to go forty hours straight through to the finish line."

When he got back on the bike he was greeted with strong headwinds. But Arvid was determined to make it work. With only minimal 5-minute stops for water and food, Arvid pushed through. With 90 kilometres to go Arvid finally got a tailwind and hammered it to Halifax at a rocking pace of 40 km/hr.

It was expected to go well all the way to the finish when his pastor, who was on the crew team, indicated that Halifax was gridlocked because of a heavy metal concert about to take place. They made it to a bridge outside of the city. The finish line of the Halifax city hall was within reach.

The crew urged Arvid to continue on and that they would catch up with him. But Arvid declined. He could have gone on ahead. A bike has an easier time in traffic than a motorhome. But he wasn't going to finish without his wife and his crew at his side.

Traffic started to move. Arvid raced into Halifax. Up ahead he saw city hall come into view. This was it. Thirteen days of exhaustion, perseverance and faith culminating in this moment.

The support crew watched as he closed in on the title. Ruth saw her man gunning it for the end and felt the conviction wives feel when they are united in purpose with their husbands. Mulli saw his friend who had sacrificed everything to help MCF race towards the goal he had believed he would reach. Mulli's faith that this moment would happen when he met Arvid on the side of the road, when things looked so bleak, almost made it seem that Mulli already saw this day back when he prayed. And now, Arvid was here.

Of course he would be.

Back in Winnipeg many of his church family watched the live feed that Melissa from the crew was transferring through her cellphone.

Arvid gripped the handlebars and gave it one last burst. He blasted through the final turn and made it to Halifax city hall.

He posted a finishing time of 13 days, 6 hours and 13 minutes. A new record by 2 hours, 53 minutes. His average distance per day was 457 kilometres.

Arvid felt the relief that came with finally arriving. It was pure joy. He had the greatest conviction that God had been in this from the beginning. In that moment, he saw how the struggles made for a great journey. What fun is there if everything goes smoothly and easily? As difficult as it was, adversity had become his friend and teacher. And it had driven him to deeper faith.

Arvid hugged Ruth. Hugged Mulli. Smiled at the $50,000 cheque for MCF that was given to Mulli at the finish line for beating the record. Rejoiced at the $30,000 that would be given because of how much he beat the record by, in addition to the hundreds of thousands that poured in during the race from people of all walks of life.

And felt the peace that came with having been used by God to accomplish something he would not have been able to do on his own.

It was the following morning when Arvid sat in a coffee shop with Ruth, Mulli and some of the other crew as they were reflecting on what had just happened. Arvid looked tired, yet strangely not exhausted. Someone asked him about what motivated him to take on this challenge.

"God convicted me about five years ago that the ability to make a difference actually is within our reach. I have come across too many people who are simply saying that the problem is so big and that their little contribution doesn't matter. Mully Children's Family has taught me that the ability to make change is real. It comes down to a question of attitude and our ability to respond. This is why I am so passionate about MCF.

"I also think you need to lead by example. I can't ask someone to support this if I'm not willing to put in a hundred percent effort. I don't have the money to write big cheques, but I have the ability to inspire, motivate and challenge people to see that there is a whole lot more that we can do than what we're doing today. I think children who have been abandoned by society, who have been abandoned by everybody but God, need us to respond to them. And that's what kept me going at two o'clock in the morning."

He took a drink of his coffee. It was surprising that he wasn't flat out in bed. How does a guy go 22 hours a day for 13 days and not absolutely crash at the end of it? He thought back to the time at Mattawa when it all looked so hopeless. As if everything he had worked for had fallen down around him. But he didn't quit. He took his much needed break and got up 17 hours later. It didn't come down to the kind of bike he had or how good a cyclist he was. It came down to a gut-wrenching choice to push through every wall in front of him, to get back on the bike and to keep pedalling.

And God honoured his courage.

He blinked before he continued. "We think that this all comes down to money. And the money is important. No doubt. But saving a child's life has nothing to do with what is in your bank," Arvid said. "It has to do with what is in your heart. When your heart is changed, you are motivated to give. And God will bless that in ways we cannot comprehend."

During the entire race—from the moment he left Vancouver to the moment he ended in Halifax—not one time, not for one second, did Arvid feel any pain from the osteoarthritis in his hip.

CHAPTER 42

The trouble began with a whisper.

Nothing was spoken out loud. Not at first anyway. It was a comment. A question, really. A doubt that one of the teachers at MCF, of all people, placed inside Mara's mind. She had been doing well at MCF. From her beginning when her mother stole her away from her father, offered her as a prostitute, burned her with scalding water and hacked her nearly to death with a machete, Mara had grown into a talkative teenager with a flair for singing.

"Is MCF really everything you expected it to be?" Kamau asked.

That was it. That's how it started. There wasn't anything directly wrong with the words in and of themselves. But his words only carried a fraction of what he intended to communicate. The rest came in the tone he asked it in. And the way in which he said it cast the first seed of doubt in Mara's mind.

"What do you mean?" she asked.

"Do you think you have it as good here as you could have elsewhere?"

He was taller than her and wore a long-sleeved shirt despite the heat. He stood closer to her and spoke quieter than what would be considered normal. School had ended for the day. The other students had left. They were alone.

"I like it here."

"Sure. But it could be better for you."

"I don't understand."

"What if you could study in another place? Maybe pick a university of your choice."

"Why would I do that? Daddy Mulli will provide for me."

"Will he? You do not need his help. This is no place for a girl like you."

A quiet voice inside her mind that told her he was wrong. It was like a lie detector going off inside her heart. But in that instant, she hesitated, and instead of running, she listened.

"There are good things and bad things here. Like anywhere else," she said.

"What kind of bad things?"

None. But her mind was doing strange things to her.

Many bad things, Mara. You know.

What kind of bad things? I get food, clothing, school, friends, love. I have everything.

Not everything.

Yes, everything.

Do you have freedom?

Yes.

Really? You can go right now and leave?

Why would I want to?

But if you wanted to, you couldn't.

Why would I want to leave?

To have a life. To go where you want. To buy alcohol.

Alcohol? I don't want alcohol.

Sure you do.

My mother had alcohol and look what it did to her.

Look what it does to anyone who drinks too much. But you wouldn't drink too much. You would be able to control it. It would only be one drink.

"I don't have much freedom here."

"That is true," he replied. " Tell me, would you like some money?"

"Of course."

Kamau saw one of the other teachers approaching the classroom beside him. He stepped back. Smiled in a way to make it seem the conversation was about something different than what it was.

"We will talk again soon."

The next morning she got up with everyone else and had breakfast. But instead of going to class, she went down by the river and spent the day alone. She even skipped choir practice.

The following day Esther found Mara and asked her to come and speak with her and Mulli. They met under a tree to protect them from the blistering sun.

"We have been missing you," Mulli said. "Your teachers say you have not been in school. Is everything all right?"

She shifted in her chair. "I don't feel comfortable here."

"Please, tell me what is wrong," Mulli asked.

"I need some things."

"What kind of things do you need? Do you need shoes or some clothes?" Esther asked.

"I need alcohol."

"Why do you need alcohol?" Mulli asked.

"I just do."

"Is there something hurting you that you would like to talk about?"

"It would only be one drink. I would not overdo it."

"I do not understand this, Mara," Esther asked. "In your heart, you are not this kind of girl who likes alcohol. We are your parents. Please tell us what is wrong."

"I have no freedom here. I want to leave and go to Thika and Nairobi. I want to live my own life."

"Could you tell me where you would live and where you would get the money? Do you have a job? And is that the kind of job that you want to have? Will that help you in reaching your goals?"

"I don't know."

She vaguely recalled the person she used to be. She would smile and hug Mulli and Esther whenever she saw them. But in such a short time she had changed into someone who neither Mulli nor Esther recognized.

And the strange thing was that Mara was having a tough time recognizing who she had become, too. It was like there was two of her. Her real self. And an evil twin. She felt herself slipping into the other one. Like she was being pulled by a magnet with part of her wanting to resist, and the other part of her agreeing to go.

"Mara, you are our daughter and we love you. We will pray for you. You don't need alcohol. It is not the wise way to go. Everything you need is right here."

She thanked them for the conversation and smiled.

But inside, she remained unconvinced.

That evening Kamau met her as she left her evening study class.

"How are your studies going?" Kamau asked.

"I don't like them."

"I don't blame you."

He checked behind him to see if anyone was watching. Or listening. He looked nervous, like the way people do when they have crossed a line and are in new territory.

"Tomorrow I will take you to Thika," he said.

Mara's heart leapt for all the wrong reasons. "What will I do there?"

"You will meet someone there who will help you. You will have freedom. You will go to university. And you will have the life you have always wanted."

She smiled. He did too. But it wasn't a genuine smile. And had Mara looked closer, she would have recognized it for the sham that it was.

"Thank you," she said, excited. "I can't wait."

Kamau checked behind him again. His eyes shifted left and right just to make sure they were truly alone. He spoke quieter. Mara had to strain to hear him.

"Would you be willing to do something in exchange for this?"

The catch. Here it was. If he had came right out the other day and told it to her then, she would have sensed the wrongness of it and reported him. But he was cunning and she had taken the first bait. Now she was in. Besides, why not help out the man who was going to give her what she had always wanted?

"What do you need?" she asked.

He swallowed. Then he smiled to shake off the nervousness. It was a disgusting smile, really. Skin deep. The look in the eyes and the smile are supposed to match up. But even though he showed his stained yellow teeth and grinned to give the impression he was on the level, his eyes deceived him. It was plain for Mara to see.

If she had been looking for it.

But the promise of apparent freedom can be tempting, and so she only saw what she wanted to see.

"Nothing much," he lied. "We would just need you to tell people certain things about this place."

"What kind of things?" she asked.

His smile faded. He was all business now. Those uneasy eyes of his pierced into her. "That MCF is not a good place."

She thought a moment. She felt uneasy. The future was all laid out. Saying a few questionable things about MCF seemed a fair trade-off for receiving the life she always wanted. She tried to convince herself that no place on earth was perfect. But that MCF was not a good place? She had a hard time with that. And she should have walked away. But the lure of the life she craved won out, so she agreed to do it. Besides, it wasn't any problem to say a few words against the people who had rescued her. It was a small price to pay for a good stiff drink.

"When do we leave?"

Mara went to bed that evening without saying goodnight to anyone. That in and of itself was way out of the ordinary. She pulled the blanket over herself and laid her head against the pillow. She closed her eyes and felt the joy of the adventure that lay ahead.

Finally, her ship had come in.

She waited at the end of the MCF Ndalani driveway where it met with the road. She was looking for any sign of one of the other teachers or workers when she saw Kamau.

"Ready to go?" he asked.

"All set."

They waited for the next matatu. It was risky. At any time they could be seen by someone and their plan would be crushed. She knew they wouldn't have much time. Matatus didn't come around that often. She knew she had to have an excuse ready in case she was caught. And she knew that this was just one hurdle she had to get over before her life of independence would be hers.

But what she didn't know was that Kamau had been secretly plotting with others outside of MCF to bring Mulli down. An insidious group had conspired together and laid out a plan to spread lies about Mulli and the MCF organization. Their motivation was beyond logic. Their only goal was to attempt to destroy what God was doing through Mulli's faithfulness. Somehow, someway, they had allowed a thought into their minds. And they dwelt on that thought. And that thought became a desire. And the desire turned into a detailed approach about how they would go about trying to destroy MCF.

And luring Mara into their scheme was the first step in that mission.

A matatu picked them up, he paid her fare, and off they went to live the dream.

The ride to Thika was uneventful. At least upon looking back she would be able to say that part of her evening was boring. When they arrived they got off and stood on the sidewalk. Mara looked around. Buildings. Cars. Crowds of people. Thika is a market town. Everyone is trying to sell everything. It's home to the gorgeous Fourteen Falls, too. Not that it mattered. They weren't there for the tourism.

Come to think of it, Mara wasn't a hundred percent sure what she was there for. She was supposed to tell people something and in exchange she would go to university and get alcohol and…Was that it? Did she understand that right? It all felt a bit hazy at the moment. But she shook those thoughts from her mind. She was in Thika. She had arrived.

"Wait here," he said. "We will come back for you."

That should have been a bit of a hint. He said *we* and not *I*. Exactly who was *we* anyway? The inconsistent details were lost on her in light of the overload the city was having on her senses. He gave her no money. Gave her no food. But he did give her a brief wave on his way back onto a matatu. Then he disappeared out of sight.

She waited. Being in a city without any money to spend isn't as fun. She had time to think. What was this all again? The plan was that Mara would get her freedom and a university education in exchange for speaking out against the terrible "atrocities" happening at MCF. What were those atrocities again? Atrocities like all the love and food and clothing and education and opportunities that MCF was giving abandoned street children? Children like Mara, who before they met Mulli were looking at a bright future in a dingy juvenile slum.

They didn't set a time as to when Kamau would return for her. She wondered who all was part of the group he loosely referred to as *we*. She waited for an hour. Then two. No problem. Small price to pay for freedom. But then three and four hours rolled around and she had the first uneasy feeling in her stomach that something might not be working the way she had thought.

Her hopes for adventure sank with the setting sun. And the approaching darkness concerned her. Thika is all right by day. But Thika by night is no good. Especially when a person is alone.

Especially for a single girl.

She looked down the road at every passing matatu, hoping to see Kamau's eager face. But all she saw were headlights. She turned the other way, and what she saw sent a jolt of adrenaline through her system.

Two strong members of *Mungiki*—a violent gang with activities in Nairobi, Thika and other parts of Kenya—approached. Late twenties, fuzzy look in their eyes from all the drugs they had done, and the long hair that characterized their gang.

"What are you doing here?" the taller one asked.

"Waiting for someone."

"We can help you get a place for the night," the other said.

Again, the warning bells should have gone off. But instead, their invitation brought a note of relief to Mara.

She agreed. So they got into a matatu. They paid, gentlemen that they were, and rode through town. She wondered how long this would be and hoped they would get off soon. But they stayed on and took her outside of Thika.

The city lights disappeared behind them as they headed out into the darkness. That wasn't any good. Part of her wanted to rewind everything. Only a few short hours ago she was at MCF. Now she was…well, that was part of the problem. She wasn't exactly sure where she was, and she wasn't exactly sure who these guys were that had offered to pay her fare on the matatu.

That uneasy feeling in her stomach only grew in intensity. This was all going from worse to horrific. Everything felt so murky in her mind. Who was in control here anyway? And where were they taking her again? A place to sleep, right? So why was it so far out of town? And where was Kamau and…

She felt the walls of the matatu begin to close in on her. She suddenly became claustrophobic. This all started to feel like the really bad idea that it was. And the only certainty she had was the doubt about what was coming next.

They got off at a stop in what was surely the middle of nowhere. Other passengers got off, too, so how bad could it be? But those other passengers walked in one direction.

And she and her two new friends walked in the other direction.

They headed down an unlit dirt pathway. They passed small, rusted sheet metal houses that faded away in the distance. Every step felt heavier. They came to the end of the path, and she saw a dingy mud-wall house with a sagging metal roof and a wooden door with a heavy lock on the outside.

Mara's pulse quickened. What to do? Turn and run and risk having them think she was trying to escape? Or play along and hope this would all work out? She swallowed in an ineffective attempt to calm herself down. The tall one took a key out of his pocket, unlocked the door and led her inside.

When she saw the inside of the room she felt like throwing up. The walls were made of sticks and mud. No beds. Thin, dirty mattresses on the mud floor. No chairs. No table. No food. The hairs on the back of her neck stood up.

They pulled out some marijuana and offered it to her. This wasn't exactly what she had in mind. Nothing was. She shook her head.

And it was when she heard the lock in the inside closing that the error of her choices finally gripped her.

She turned to face them but looked down at the ground. She didn't have the courage to make eye contact. "I want to go back to Mully Children's Family," she said in a voice that was so frail and fragile that she wondered if they had heard. Tears started forming in her eyes. This hadn't quite worked out the way she planned. In retrospect, her dream had been derailed from the moment it seemed to start. But she was going to have other things to worry about in a few short seconds from now. "I want to go back and—"

"Shut up!" the taller one screamed at her. He pulled out a knife. It shocked her how fast he was able to get that blade of steel out from wherever he had been hiding it and point it at her face. He stepped closer. His eyes drilled into her. It was odd how similar they looked to Kamau's, who was strangely absent in her most desperate time. "You scream and you're dead."

He said that with such a calculated and cold tone that it convinced her he had carried out that threat with others who dared challenge him.

Having a knife in her face was scary enough. Still, she shifted her eyes to see if there was any reason for hope. But there were no windows. No other means of escape.

"I don't want to be here," she said.

But that option wasn't on the table anymore.

It was the shorter one who hit her first. It was such a crushing blow to her face that it knocked her clean off her feet. She crashed to the ground, her head spinning, and tried to get up to defend herself. As she did the taller one smashed his fist so hard into her forehead that she nearly fell unconscious.

She hit the ground again. She wasn't able to get back up. A piercing migraine pounded in her brain. She'd been here before with her mother. Somehow it all started to come back to her.

The two gang members rolled her over onto her back. Then they continued with what they had brought her here for.

How long it went on, she couldn't tell. Time stands still during unspeakable agony. When they were finally done she lay there on the ground in physical, mental and emotional torment.

And she wondered if this would be the end of her.

CHAPTER 43

"She's not in her room either," Esther said.

Mulli, Esther and the team leaders had searched the property for Mara and came up empty. They talked to the students and to the teachers to see if anyone had information about her. Even Kamau.

"I have not seen her," he lied. "I hope she is all right."

Mulli had a day filled with appointments ahead of him, as usual. But he left everything behind to go after one missing child, as usual. He got into his vehicle and took off down the road to find her, wondering how far she had gotten.

She would have needed a matatu to get out of Ndalani. It's possible that she could have chosen instead to walk all the way to the nearby town of Matuu, but that would have been a long journey and someone would likely have seen her. If she wanted something more exciting than Matuu she would have gone to Thika. And if she got caught up in the Thika underworld there was no telling where she could end up.

Like on the cold floor of a gang's hideout.

Mara touched her face and felt the swelling around her eyes. Her jaw ached. Was it broken? The pounding in her head felt like her skull was about to explode. She sat up and saw the thin line of light coming through the bottom of the door.

She got up. A rush of pain pulsed through the back of her head and down her neck. She struggled to the door, desperate for a way to get out of this mess.

But her hope was crushed when she tried to turn the handle and was met with the resistance of a lock on the outside. She sat back down again, slowly, hoping the pain would subside. *How could I have been this stupid?* She moved her jaw. It hurt. Everything did. *How could I have been this stupid?*

She began to cry, yet she was tough and tried to push herself to not feel sorry for her situation.

Focus on getting out. And pray. Why don't you pray?

Because this was my choice and God won't help me now.

Of course he will. God will help.

She closed her eyes, not that she needed to—it was dark enough—and pleaded with God to get her out. She may have stayed there for a few minutes, maybe a few hours. It was hard to tell. Without some outside means of orientation she lost the ability to perceive how fast or slow time was progressing.

And with the unavoidable return of the gang members to look forward to, she wasn't sure which option she preferred: have them come back now and get it over with or drag out the inevitable?

At some point she heard the lock on the door opening. A jolt ripped through her system. Her mind already relayed to her body the impact the blows were going to have on her. It was like she could feel the pain before it arrived.

The door opened and the shorter one came in. A flood of sunshine filled the room, illuminating the bruises on her face. The rays of light glistened off the scars on her arms and forehead that were given to her courtesy of her mother's machete all those years ago. She swallowed and hoped this would be quick.

But the shorter one sat down beside her and opened a brown bag. Inside were bread and a bottle of juice. He offered it to her. She didn't know if it was a trick. Poison, perhaps. He assured her it was for her and laid it down beside her. She took the bread, broke off a piece and began to eat.

"I will be back soon," he said.

Was that good or bad? As he got up to leave, Mara took the opportunity to scan the room to see if she could find something sharp.

He left, and she heard the lock on the door clang shut. There was nothing worthwhile in this hovel. Just the mattresses, her and a whole lot of despair.

She finished the bread. Drank the juice. And entertained herself for the rest of the day by thinking how much better it would have been if only she had listened to Mulli and Esther a few short days ago.

The shorter one came back in the evening. He seemed energetic. He greeted her like she was his long lost friend. The immorality of what he done to her last night completely escaped him. Another package in his hand. This time in a plastic bag.

"I have something for you," he said.

He pulled out marijuana joints and lit one for her.

Don't take it. Tell him no.

Are you crazy? Look what happened last night. You don't say no to these guys.

You take this, there's no telling what will happen next.

It's one joint. One lousy joint. What's the problem?

You think it's bad now? Don't go down this path.

But it will feel so good. All my troubles will disappear. I just want some freedom.

Freedom? How are drugs going to make you free? They're going to put you in bondage.

You know the lock on the door?

Yes.

I'm not getting out.

Don't say that.

This is the most freedom I'm going to have.

Don't give up. Don't make a bad situation worse.

I just need a break from all of this.

She took the joint and inhaled. She suddenly felt lightheaded. Another stiff drag and the room began to tilt. This wasn't just marijuana. She'd had it before. It hadn't done this to her. There was something else in there. Something more powerful.

She looked at the walls. That was strange. Why was everything leaning over so much? Didn't the person who built this house understand that the walls were supposed to go straight up and down?

She wasn't entirely sure where she was anymore. And that was fine with her. Because anyplace was better than here. She leaned her head back, felt a tingling on the skin of her forearms, and for the moment, nothing hurt.

The search through Matuu and Thika brought Mulli no closer to finding his daughter. He asked people if they had seen her. Talked with shop owners. Drove through the streets looking for any sign of her. She was one child in a country with a never-ending number of orphans. Finding one was going to be difficult. But still he searched.

He returned to Ndalani. It made no sense to him. None of it. He didn't understand. Didn't understand how someone who had been offered everything she needed at MCF would turn her back on it and head out into the street.

He prayed for her safety. For her health. For her entire being to know she was loved.

And that she could come back home.

Which was exactly what Mara wanted, too.

The effects of the drugs wore off. That left her with having to face her old nemesis of reality. No matter. It was only a question of time before he would return with another package of marijuana and cocaine. If she could not get away physically, then at least she would be able to leave mentally.

She became sick that evening. Her head hurt. Her stomach heaved and she threw up constantly. It left a disgusting smell in the dungeon the gang members called home. She pleaded with the shorter one to let her go to the hospital. But he refused. Prisoners only get certain privileges. His kindness only extended as far as he was able to benefit from it.

She didn't know what was making her so unwell. She had never been this sick before. It was worse than malaria. Maybe it was bad drugs. Maybe it was dehydration. Maybe a combination of things.

After a couple of days she began to feel better. The shorter one brought her water and food. The taller one didn't come around as much. Not that she cared. She watched the shorter one leave for the day as she studied the structure of the house. The cracks in the doorway let in enough light to see where part of the mud wall wasn't as secure as the other places. She debated whether she would have enough time to dig her way out before he returned.

That made her pulse quicken for two reasons. First, the thought of getting out and having her normal life back brought incredible relief. But second, she worried that if this didn't work and she got caught this could all end very badly for her.

Do it. Do it now. Find a way to escape.

But I might die. I'm better off waiting.

Waiting for what? Who is going to come get you?

Daddy Mulli.

How would he find you in this place? Who would ever think to look here? You have to get out and you have to get out now.

She considered that voice and was about to start digging with her hands into the mud walls when another voice spoke to her.

You don't really want to leave, do you?

I can't stay here anymore.

Where would you get drugs? If you return to MCF you will not get them there.

As obvious as the choice should have been, her drugged-up mind had a difficult time discerning the difference between a life of freedom and a life trapped in addiction.

Mara scraped away at the mud wall. It was caked together well and the tough material felt almost like concrete. She worked at it the entire day and wondered if she would finish in time. She felt the anxiety of how she would have to explain a half-finished hole to the shorter one when he returned.

She punched through the wall and stretched her hand out to freedom. She looked out and saw the path leading up to the road. She tried to gauge by the amount of sunlight how much time she had left. She dug faster and would have gotten it done had she not heard the door unlocking.

Her body shot out a painful burst of adrenaline that made her fingers feel like they were being electrocuted. She grabbed her blanket. She pushed herself against the wall and pretended to be asleep. The door opened.

She heard nothing. But she felt eyes looking at her. She wasn't going to open hers. No way. She stayed there, faking being asleep. Though if the person at the door looked any closer he might have seen the pulse in her neck doing overtime.

Whatever the person at the door wanted, he left as quickly as he came. When she heard the door shut again she slowly opened one eye to confirm that the person wasn't still inside. Seeing the room empty she hurried to the door and peeked through a crack and saw the shorter one leaving. She hurried back and threw the blanket away to finish Operation Escape. She scraped away with her hands. She managed to make the hole big enough for her to squeeze through and crawl outside.

She stood up and squinted in the bright sunshine. She hurried to the path, her legs adjusting to what it meant to walk again after a month of captivity.

She tried to remember which way she was supposed to turn. The last time she was here it was dark, and with all the time that had passed she doubted if she could remember. No worry. Just pick a direction and keep going. It sounded good and it probably would have worked had she not run right into the shorter gang member standing right there.

He was just as surprised as she was. Mara couldn't believe her misfortune. What were the odds? She studied his expression. She wasn't sure if he was ready to kill her or give her more marijuana. A strange bond had formed between them with drugs being the common denominator. And when she saw his expression beginning to change from surprise to anger, her mind raced to find a solution.

And the one she came up with was brilliant.

"When are you going to take me to the market?" she asked.

He was caught off guard. Inside she was shaking with such fear that she felt anyone could see right through her eyes and spot it. But she stood her ground. She had made poor choices. But she was tough and she put all her confidence in this last-ditch effort.

"To the market?"

"Yes. We have been friends for this long, and I want you to go and buy me something. Are we going?"

He was so taken aback, so surprised by her apparent friendship, that all he could do was nod his head in agreement.

He took her to the market. They walked through the outdoor stores with rows and rows of merchandise laid out. He made conversation with her. She answered as best she could. She wasn't concentrating on what he said. She was focused on other things. Her eyes scanned everything. She tried to find the road. A policeman. Anything.

She felt the comfort of seeing other people again. Being in a crowd gave her a sense of protection. Up ahead they found a table where they sat down. She asked him for something to drink. His mother ran a store nearby and he told her he would be right back.

The moment he left Mara started looking for help. She edged to the front of her chair and watched as he blended in with the crowd. If he turned back now and caught her talking to someone it might end any chance she would have of coming back to the market. She waited until he was out of sight and then hurried to people on the sidewalk.

She found a young couple walking towards her. She might have done better if she wouldn't have looked so terrified. But desperation is hard to control and her cries for help scared them.

"Please help me. Help me. I am in trouble. I have been kidnapped."

The facts were right but the couple pushed away from her, thinking her to be a drug addict looking for money, which was really only half true. She glanced over her shoulder to see if he was on his way back yet.

She was in such a controlled panic that she didn't even realize that she was holding her breath. When her mind sent out the warning that the oxygen content in her body was dropping dangerously low she responded by taking in a gulp of air. She pushed through to the next person she saw. A girl about her age. Wearing a crisp school uniform. Standing on the sidewalk. Waiting for a ride.

"I need help. Do you have a cellphone?"

The girl was caught off guard. She saw Mara's condition and was ready to presume she was a street child high on glue, but something in her eyes convinced her otherwise.

"Do you have a cellphone?!" Mara repeated. She glanced behind. The anxiety in her tone conveyed the desperate feeling that she wondered if her game was almost up.

"I'm sorry. I'm so sorry, I don't."

Mara's eyes went wild with worry. She turned and bumped into a rack of shirts. She stumbled right into a man wearing a dark blue suit. She looked up at him. Late thirties. Bald head that he had shaved to make it look that way. He instinctively reached out to help her.

"May I borrow your cellphone?" She looked behind her. And what she saw caused her so much fear that she thought for sure she would die right there of anxiety. The short gang member was making his way through the crowd back to the table. The empty table. The one she was supposed to be at when he got there. Or else. She wasn't sure what to do. Forget this and go back to the table so as to avoid being caught by him and maybe give away her last chance of escape? Or try her chances with the man in the blue suit and risk being found out and killed right here in the street?

She stood there, paralyzed with fear. But then the gang member stopped, as if remembering something, and went back.

"Please. Please, I beg you."

"Yes, of course."

He handed it to her and she took it in her shaking hands.

Her memory froze. What was Mulli's number again? What was it? She tried to settle her frantic mind. She knew it. She knew the number. It was as ingrained into her as much as her last name. How could something so obvious vanish so quickly?

Think. Think. Think.

Everything went blank. Why would her brain do that when she needed it the most? She dialled what she thought were the first few numbers and then realized that it was wrong. She looked back. *Is that creep coming? Is he going to see me here? What is the number?!*

"Please, how can I help you?"

She didn't respond. Her brain was in overdrive. She remembered being at MCF Ndalani. Remembered what it was like to be with everyone. Remembered Mulli's face.

And that's when she recalled the number. She dialled and put the phone to her ear and waited for it to connect.

Nothing.

She alternated between looking at the number to confirm it was correct and clutching it to her ear to see if it was ringing. Why is this taking so long? She read the number. Yes it was right. She looked out.

"Hello?" said a familiar voice.

"Daddy? Daddy, is that you? It is Mara."

Mulli had since gone to Germany. He was helping with the preparations for his daughter Mueni's wedding that was taking place tomorrow.

"Yes, Mara. Are you all right?"

"I was kidnapped by Mungiki and I can't get away."

"Where are you?"

"I am in the Thika open market. I was tricked by Kamau and now I am here."

"I will organize John and Muasa to come pick you up."

"Thank you. I am so sorry."

"Everything will be all right. I love you and I will see you soon."

She hung up and gave the phone back to the stranger, thanking him for his kindness.

She returned back to the table. She tried to calm herself down. She would need to keep the shorter one here long enough to allow John and Muasa to arrive. She tried to think of things to ask him to keep the dull conversation going, but her mind drifted towards Mulli's last line.

I love you and I will see you soon.

That sounded familiar. She had heard that before. And not just from Mulli.

"Ready to go?"

Startled, she looked up and saw the shorter one standing in front of her. How did he get here without her noticing?

"That is not very nice," she said, putting on all charm she could manage given the circumstances. "You did not bring me my drink. Did you forget?"

"We're going back. Now."

"Did you buy the jacket you were looking at? I think it would look good on you."

"Get up. Let's go."

Whatever friendship she thought she might be able to fake was clearly overruled by his ultimate purpose in having her as his property. Friendship was fine with him, provided she did what he told her to do.

And resistance was something that neither he nor the knife he was carrying would tolerate.

She got up and walked with him out of the market, trying to find reasons to slow down, looking in all directions for any hint of her rescue. She did the mental math as best she could of how long it would take for her rescuers to drive from MCF Ndalani to Thika to get her. She looked at store windows, made small talk that irked him, and asked him to buy her something. They walked into the path covered by trees and disappeared.

Which was unfortunate. Because had they stayed in the open a moment longer they would have seen John and Muasa approaching.

Mara didn't sleep that night. All she wanted was for the sun to rise so she could convince him to go back to market. But time seemed to stop. She waited in the darkness, wondering if her ordeal would soon be over or if she would be moved to another location and sink further into the abyss of the underworld. Replaying Mulli's voice over again in her mind brought her comfort. No matter how many times she had tried to leave, she always came crawling back to MCF.

I love you and I will see you soon.

And it amazed her that Mulli would still welcome her.

The sun rose. Finally. After a second prompting, the shorter one agreed to take her to the market. They walked down the path, through the merchandise, and to the table they sat at the day before. He bought her a drink. She wasn't sure what it was. She didn't care. She talked with him. It was tough to carry on a conversation with a drug-dealing, murdering gang member at the best of times, let alone when she was having to concentrate on both the conversation and her real objective of keeping an eye out for her rescuers.

If they were even coming.

Would they come two days in a row? Would they come now or later? Had they already been there and they'd come back again when she was in her cell? How long would they keep coming back if they kept missing each other?

She scanned the area so often that she wasn't seeing anything new anymore. It made her wonder if she had become so accustomed to seeing nothing of value that it would make her miss them when they arrived.

But then she did see them. Muasa was easiest to spot. He was tall and stood out in a crowd. They spoke with one of the store managers, who shook his head.

Look over here! Look over here!

She could shout out now. Scream to them where she was sitting. But it was tricky. The long-haired thug in front of her had bragged to her about the number of throats he had slit in his lifetime. If a maniac like him got spooked, there was no telling what he would do. Even in broad daylight.

John and Muasa looked through the merchandise area. From their vantage point they were too far away to pick her out in the crowd of people. They crossed the street to speak with another merchant, and then, instead of coming towards them, they turned and walked in the other direction.

No. No! This way. Turn this way!

Knife or no knife, she was ready to risk it. But before she did, she had one last idea.

"I need to go to the bathroom," she said.

It wasn't a request. She wasn't asking. She got up and walked at a slower pace than normal towards the bathroom, which was in the general direction of where she had seen John and Muasa last. She didn't turn around. That would be a dead giveaway. She angled her direction slightly to aim more at where she thought John and Muasa might be.

She passed through the crowd and quickened her pace. With every footstep she wondered if she would finally reach the end of this disaster. She half expected to feel the gang member's hand on her shoulder. Or his knife in her back. But this was it. This was the last stand. She was not going back. It was do or die.

Up ahead she saw the kind, familiar face of Muasa high above everyone else. She bolted. As fast as she could, she raced through the crowd, knocking into people. It caused enough commotion to make some people think she was stealing.

The Mungiki thug didn't notice. Had he turned he would have seen her making a break for it. But instead he looked straight ahead in the opposite direction.

"John! Muasa!" Mara shouted out to them in a voice loud enough to cause them to turn around.

She glanced behind her and saw that the thug was still at the table.

"Are you all right?" John said as he ran with her, leading her in the direction of the car.

"I am okay," she said.

They reached the car and got in. They drove off, and Mara looked back, half expecting her kidnapper to smash through the window of the car with his knife in hand to finish her off once and for all.

As they turned onto the highway Mara began to cry with relief.

Muasa dialled Mulli's number. As he was waiting for it to connect he prayed out loud. "Father, we thank you that Mara is now safe. You have rescued her, and we thank you for this."

"Hello?" Mulli answered.

"Mister Mulli. This is Muasa. We have found her."

Mulli's heart pounded. He wanted to be sure what he heard. "Can you repeat this?"

"We have found her."

"Praise God," Mulli said. "Excellent. Excellent work. Thank you. May I speak with her?"

Muasa handed Mara the phone. She cried so hard that it was difficult for her to say the words. But Mulli had plenty of practice speaking with crying children. He could make out everything she was saying.

"I am so sorry for what has happened, Daddy. Please forgive me."

"I love you, Mara. I have forgiven you even before you asked for it," Mulli said. "Without any conditions."

Her bottom lip quivered. Her eyes welled with tears. "Thank you," she whispered.

"You are most welcome. I am looking forward to seeing you again."

"I am looking forward to seeing you, too."

She handed the phone back to Muasa. She glanced out the window at the passing Kenyan countryside. She had seen it on the way going out to Thika.

It felt good to be heading in the other direction.

When Mulli came back from Germany he met with Kamau first. He invited him to sit across from him. Mulli asked him if the accusations were correct.

Kamau was tough. And at first he pretended that it was not his idea, that he was just complicit in part of a larger conspiracy against MCF.

"So you agree that you incited one of my children against me?"

"No, No, that is not right."

"But it is right," Mulli said in a tone that was so stern, so convincing, that all of Kamau's facade of toughness melted. Kamau realized he was going up against a side of Mulli that few people ever had to face. So he decided it was time to change tactics.

Kamau consented to his role in the plot against Mulli. He changed his demeanour. Acted sad. Sorrowful. A victim of other people who made him do it.

But Mulli didn't bite. He saw what was going on. This wasn't really repentance. It wasn't really asking forgiveness. It was just a deceiver's attempt to try to assuage Mulli to prevent him from doing what Kamau knew was coming next.

"You are fired," Mulli said.

That spelled disaster. People who left MCF depended on getting a letter of recommendation to help them get their next position. Being terminated meant his chances of finding employment were seriously damaged.

"All right," Kamau said.

But Mulli wasn't done. He saw what Kamau was doing. Kamau wasn't really accepting being fired. He was still playing games. Trying to find a way to keep Mulli from doing the right thing. But Mulli wouldn't back down. Kamau was poison. Through and through. And he was going to get what was coming to him. Mulli leaned forward.

"And you will have your chance to speak about what you did with the police."

The fallout from the planned attack against Mulli was wide and devastating. The coordinated efforts of people bent on committing evil took their toll. Still, Mulli held fast to not retaliating. He decided instead to live out himself what he had preached to all the people in the IDP camps—that God is a just judge and it is his job alone to take revenge. Mulli encouraged everyone in the MCF team to pray for the attackers. To treat them well.

It was deathly grim for a period. But God gave Mulli the assurance that he would come out the victor. And when MCF was delivered from everything, Mulli felt the satisfaction that comes with waiting on God's timing and providence.

And God did go after those who attacked Mulli. The divine judgment that wrecked havoc in the lives of those who sought to destroy Mulli was so destructive that some even pleaded with Mulli to intervene on their behalf with God.

Which, of course, he did.

It was late in the evening when Mulli arrived in Ndalani. He found Mara sitting in the devotion area waiting for him. He hugged her, and she felt the relief that came with being in his presence. Somehow he was able set the world right.

She cried as a flood of emotion came over her. It felt good to be touched in a healthy way. It was as if the memories of the past weeks were being eroded and replaced with the love of a man who had given everything to help her. He sat down with her, reassured her of his love for her, and talked with her about the ordeal.

There was a healing that happened in sharing about the past. As difficult as it was, it was better to process and forgive than to ignore and harbour bitterness. She confirmed she had received medical attention and was ready to come back to school. They talked about her favourite classes and what she wanted to be when she finished school. She told him she wanted to be a hairdresser.

As they parted ways for the evening, Mulli hugged her again. "I love you and I will see you soon," he said.

"I love you, too."

As Mara went back to her dormitory she let those words wash over her. *I love you and I will see you soon.* She had heard those words before. It had been years ago. But they felt as good now as they had back then. She smiled and recalled how her father had said those same words to her when she was just a child.

I love you and I will see you soon.

CHAPTER 44

The Horn of Africa looked like a nuclear bomb had gone off. The region had lacked rain for so long that in places you could look as far as possible and not see anything but dry, cracked ground. It was as lifeless as the surface of the moon. A place completely incapable of supporting the hundreds of thousands of dying souls who called this place of disaster home.

The vast wasteland of destruction went on for what seemed like forever. One of the areas severely affected by the drought was the Turkana region of northwest Kenya. The suffering of the people weighed heavy on Mulli's spirit, soul and body. Hearing the reports and seeing the updates on television gripped him to such an extent that just thinking about the rank hopelessness of that many people not only caused him to feel sympathy for their situation but compelled him to act in such a way as to make a difference.

It was impossible from a human perspective. An organization as big as MCF had an ever-growing number of children to support. To extend themselves still further would seem to jeopardize the operation. But the decision to commit resources to Turkana was born not out of a logical review of the MCF finances, but out of a conviction in Mulli's spirit to follow what God was calling him to do in spite of the apparent hopelessness of the situation. Mulli followed the divine revelation and packed his bags and headed out with his son Isaac.

Mulli's main objective was to partner with organizations that were already working in the area doing an incredible job to assist those staring death in the eye. They boarded a plane and flew to Turkana on a mission to determine how MCF could best help.

It was apparent from the air. The desperation was visible from miles up. Mulli looked through the window and saw the shift in landscape from green to grey. Living down there was a life sentence—a guilty verdict passed on people whose only crime was being born in that area. It made Mulli think that he had done nothing to grow up in his family or to have his position at MCF. It could have just as easily been him down there. The people there were characterized by suffering from morning to evening as they existed without the prospect of believing that it could be different for anyone who would come after them.

The plane touched down. When the door opened Mulli was greeted with such a blast of heat that it dried out his throat and reached down into his lungs. He stepped out onto the pavement and met a driver, who took him and Isaac to the town of Lodwar.

The drive there was enough to cause Mulli's mouth to open in disbelief. It wasn't what he saw that created the sorrow but what he *didn't* see. It was empty. Where were all the people? Where was anything? It was deserted. Like a plague had come through to wipe people out.

They arrived at an IDP camp that was established after the post-election violence. If the Eldoret IDP camp where MCF had helped thousands of people was a difficult situation, this IDP camp in Turkana was the complete epitome of the most desperate form of life on the planet.

Children didn't run. They barely walked. Their emaciated bodies made them look as if they were the walking dead. Their eyes were sunken in, hollow sockets that seemed to exhaust all their energy just to switch direction of focus. They couldn't smile. Not anymore. The muscles in their faces had long forgotten what it meant to respond to the inner workings of joy.

Mulli entered one of the tents. He saw a woman sitting on the ground. He guessed that she was in her forties. It was hard to tell with her being reduced to skin and bones. Her face was so thin that it didn't even look human anymore. He sat down on the mud beside her. Her husband lay on the ground sleeping with their seven children sitting around him. The children each had a torn pair of shorts.

She introduced herself as Akites. Her husband had an illness. No one was sure what it was. Knowing what was killing you was reserved for those precious few in the world who could afford to see a doctor. They hadn't had anything to eat in a number of days. How long it had been was anybody's guess. They were starving, and they had lost the desire to keep track. They stopped counting after three. Mulli asked if he could pray for them; she agreed, and he closed his eyes.

This was as desperate a situation as Mulli had ever seen. This was not a prayer for a house, for a job, or for school fees. It was a prayer for survival, for

God to provide enough food for them to survive through this. He laid hands on the husband and believed for him to be healed.

Mulli went from hut to hut, seeing the devastation in each person's life. Beside the camp was a church that was made up of only benches and a few posts. No roof. No walls. It would have been impossible to know it was a church unless someone had told him. He met with two of the pastors and prayed with them for God to intervene.

Mulli stayed awake most of the night. The images of the suffering masses burned into his mind, making it impossible for him to think about anything else.

What can I do? What can I do to help?

Help? Nothing, Mulli. They are dying. Can't you see? You think this is devastation? This is my playground. This is where I am happiest. Suffering, hopelessness and fear. My trademarks. Nothing is as rewarding as this.

God will help. I must help.

If God loved these people he would have prevented this from happening in the first place.

I am not here to understand why; I am here to determine how.

You are wasting your resources. Is this what God wants? Taking food and giving it to people who will die anyway? There are too many people on this planet as it is. Let natural selection take its course.

You are liar from the beginning. And who are you to talk of suffering, hopelessness and fear? That's where you are going.

There is no hell.

There is. And you're spending eternity there. And one day I'll be rid of you. Until then, I will fight you every step of the way as I serve God to help anyone I can.

Mulli got up the next morning and drove out with Isaac and the guide to various villages some 65 kilometres southeast of Lodwar. The view was depressing. Small settlements made up of ripped tents dotted the bleak landscape. Dust and sand driven by the wind clouded the area. The occasional dying acacia tree or shrub marked the only sign that life would continue if humans did not.

Up ahead in the far distance Mulli saw a group of young boys. At the sound of the vehicle the boys ran away.

"What is the problem?" Mulli asked.

"They don't know what to expect," the guide said. "They are afraid that you might want to harm them."

"Stop the car."

The guide stopped in the middle of the road and Mulli got out. He spoke Swahili to them, but the boys either did not understand or did not trust him enough. It took five minutes for one of the boys to gather the courage to come closer. His face was worn from the dehydration and blowing sand. He motioned for water, and Mulli gave it to him. That drew in the other boys. Mulli expected them to guzzle the water. But they didn't. Curiously, they sipped it. Slowly.

"If they drink it quickly, they will vomit," the guide said. "They have not had water in at least two days. This was their last chance."

"Can you speak to them?" Mulli asked. "Can you tell them that Jesus loves them?"

The guide translated Mulli's words. When they drove off the boys waved with excitement, though their eyes conveyed the reality that their struggle was far from over.

Off to the side they saw withered cows decaying in the blistering sun. Farther on they came to a settlement. They stopped and visited a tent that was so dilapidated that Mulli had to crawl to get into it. They met an 85-year-old woman who was so frail and thin Mulli thought she might collapse and die right in front of him. Mulli was about to talk to her when 22 children came in after him. The woman indicated that these were her grandchildren. She pointed repeatedly to her stomach, indicating how desperate she was for something to eat.

"There is no more hope in Turkana," she said. "I have been here my whole life, and there has never been anything as bad as what has been here the last three years. Not one drop of rain." She stared ahead; her eyes were unable to focus on Mulli any longer. She had been struggling for years against the drought. Man versus nature. But she had lost the ability to hang on to optimism. And it troubled her to think that the food that was keeping her going might be better spent on giving one of the 22 a better chance.

"It is time for death to take me," she said.

Mulli looked at the children. They did not know happiness. Most were too young to have ever experienced the peace that comes with being able to eat until you're full. He saw their exhausted expressions. They didn't belong on children's faces. They looked old. He was so overcome by the situation that he struggled to offer them any courage. And finally he closed his eyes and felt the onslaught of emotion.

The grandmother, however, was past that. She had cried in the past. But that was months ago. Tears had helped her come to terms with what she was experiencing. But now, all she had was reality. There wasn't any lower that she could go.

"The people who are supposed to give food to us don't do it," she said. "They sell it off and only give small portions to us. Even when we are dying, it is still not enough for their compassion. We starve, and people make money off of us."

Mulli returned to Ndalani. He sent out appeals for finances to support the rescue work in Turkana, and people responded generously. Mulli organized a team from MCF to travel with him and Esther to Turkana. They purchased food and water and set up a distribution area. Word spread and people came from far distances to line up for hours in the expectation of receiving food.

Mulli prayed for the meal and then began to hand out food to adults and over 550 children. They also brought relief packages for 40 families who were on the brink of extinction. They continued to feed some 750 people every day with resources that seemed to be just enough to accomplish what they needed.

Mulli looked out and saw a young boy who clutched his orange drink and his two pieces of bread. The boy, who was perhaps two, looked for a place to sit down and began to eat his bread. He twisted off the cap of the drink and put the bottle between his feet. He bit into the bread and began to chew. He swallowed his first bite and sank his teeth into a larger bite.

The boy glanced up and saw Mulli. He would have smiled, but he was too busy eating.

Mulli understood.

Mulli and Esther organized the team to continue on with the work while they returned home. That evening as Mulli walked from the school area to his small, unassuming home, Dalila, one of the girls who had been rescued from the IDP camp, asked him how his trip had gone.

"Very good," he said with a smile. He asked her about her day. She told him.

"I am glad to have you home, Daddy," she said.

"And I am very glad to be home."

"Could I ask you a question?"

"Of course," Mulli said. He stood with her under the dazzling night sky. The stars flooded the heavens above them.

"There are so many children that are helped here at MCF. But there are many, many more that are still in the streets. There are people in Turkana who are starving." She broke off, trying to make sense of the concern she had. She thought she had this question worked out before she came to see Mulli. But now that she was here she felt confused. She gathered her thoughts as best she could and continued.

"If the need is so great, and only a few people like me are helped, what does that mean for all the others who don't get help?"

Mulli nodded. He understood her heart. How was it that she was picked and many others were not?

"I am accountable for what I can do, and you are accountable for what you can do. People can look at what we are doing and say 'the need is so great, how can you solve it?' But what we do matters to each child that we rescue. You have been rescued. It matters to you.

"What I can do is give my life to be obedient to what God has called me to do. The greatest challenge in life is when we switch from being people who want to receive to becoming people who want to give. We who have given our lives to Jesus Christ have everlasting life. We have said goodbye to the old life. We are not looking to make a name for ourselves or to secure our position in this world or to make our life comfortable. We have Jesus. What more do we need? Nothing. We need nothing more.

"If we think, *Oh, I need this. God must give it to me.* No. That is not correct. We have Jesus. We need to understand that we have everything in him. And when we do, we will understand the purpose of life. We are born to serve. This is our purpose. We are born to serve God and to serve others. It's just that not all of us recognize this."

She thought about his answer and wondered what it would mean for her.

"Then I am curious to know what I will be able to do," she said.

"Sleep well," Mulli said.

"You too, Daddy Mulli."

Mulli walked back under the peaceful Kenyan night sky. As he went to bed he thought about everything that had happened since he got up that morning. It was a full day. As usual. He had been presented with a massive challenge of feeding people, and instead of retreating he pushed forward. It forced him to look beyond anything humanly possible. It was a privilege, really. By abandoning himself he not only saw the joy of serving others, but he saw God as well.

It had involved looking at the impossible and watching God part the waters to make it possible. He had encouraged children who were once on the street and who were now leading productive lives. He had faced financial pressures, operational issues and spiritual attacks—and the Lord had delivered him out of them all. He had seen the joy of a starving child eating, the compassion a person receives when they hear for the first time that Jesus loves them, and the motivation a young girl feels when she sees that her life will make a difference. It inspired him to think of what was coming next.

And as he drifted off to sleep he thought about how the events of the last 24 hours were as unpredictable and as fulfilling as he could ever have imagined.

It was a day like any other.

CASTLE QUAY BOOKS

OTHER CASTLE QUAY TITLES INCLUDE:

Bent Hope (Tim Huff)
The Beautiful Disappointment (Colin McCartney)
The Cardboard Shack Beneath the Bridge (Tim Huff)
Certainty (Grant Richison)
The Chicago Healer (Paul Boge)
The Cities of Fortune (Paul Boge)
Dancing with Dynamite (Tim Huff)
Deciding to Know God in a Deeper Way (Sam Tita)
The Defilers (Deborah Gyapong)
I Sat Where They Sat (Arnold Bowler)
Jesus and Caesar (Brian Stiller)
Keep On Standing (Darlene Polachic)
The Leadership Edge (Elaine Stewart-Rhude)
Leaving a Legacy (David C. Bentall)
Making Your Dreams Your Destiny (Judy Rushfeldt)
Mentoring Wisdom (Dr. Carson Pue)
Mere Christian (Michael Coren)
One Smooth Stone (Marcia Lee Laycock)
Red Letter Revolution (Colin McCartney)
Reflections (Cal Bombay)
Seven Angels for Seven Days (Angelina Fast-Vlaar)
Stop Preaching and Start Communicating (Tony Gentilucci)
Through Fire & Sea (Marilyn Meyers)
To My Family (Diane Roblin-Lee)
Vision that Works (David Collins)
Walking Towards Hope (Paul Beckingham)
The Way They Should Go (Kirsten Femson)
You Never Know What You Have Till You Give It Away (Brian Stiller)

BAYRIDGE BOOKS TITLES:

Counterfeit Code: Answering The Da Vinci Code Heresies (Jim Beverley)
More Faithful Than We Think (Lloyd Mackey)
Save My Children (Emily Wierenga)
Wars Are Never Enough: The Joao Matwawana Story (John F. Keith)
What the Preacher Forgot to Tell Me (Faith Linton)

For more information and to explore the rest of our titles visit
www.castlequaybooks.com